REVIEWS OF UNITED KINGDOM
STATISTICAL SOURCES

VOLUME XI

COAL, GAS

AND

ELECTRICITY

REVIEWS OF UNITED KINGDOM STATISTICAL SOURCES
Editor: W. F. Maunder

Volume I
1. *Personal Social Services*, B. P. Davies
2. *Voluntary Organizations in the Personal Social Service Field*, G. J. Murray

Volume II
3. *Central Government Routine Health Statistics*, Michael Alderson
4. *Social Security Statistics*, Frank Whitehead

Volume III
5. *Housing in Great Britain*, Stuart Farthing
6. *Housing in Northern Ireland*, Michael Fleming

Volume IV
7. *Leisure*, F. M. M. Lewes and S. R. Parker
8. *Tourism*, L. J. Lickorish

Volume V
9. *General Sources of Statistics*, G. F. Lock

Volume VI
10. *Wealth*, A. B. Atkinson and A. J. Harrison
11. *Personal Incomes*, T. Stark

Volume VII
12. *Road Passenger Transport*, D. L. Munby
13. *Road Goods Transport*, A. H. Watson

Volume VIII
14. *Land Use*, J. T. Coppock
15. *Town and Country Planning*, L. F. Gebbett

Volume IX
16. *Health Surveys and Related Studies*, M. R. Alderson and R. Dowie

Volume X
17. *Ports and Inland Waterways*, R. E. Baxter
18. *Civil Aviation*, C. Phillips

REVIEWS OF UNITED KINGDOM STATISTICAL SOURCES
Edited by W. F. Maunder
Professor of Economic and Social Statistics
University of Exeter
VOLUME XI

COAL

by

D. J. HARRIS
Lecturer in Management, University of Bath

GAS

by

H. NABB
Marketing Services Manager, South West Gas

ELECTRICITY

by

D. NUTTALL
Formerly of Yorkshire Electricity Board

Published for
The Royal Statistical Society and
the Social Science Research Council

PERGAMON PRESS
OXFORD · NEW YORK · TORONTO · SYDNEY · PARIS · FRANKFURT

U.K.	Pergamon Press Ltd., Headington Hill Hall, Oxford OX3 0BW, England
U.S.A.	Pergamon Press Inc., Maxwell House, Fairview Park, Elmsford, New York 10523, U.S.A.
CANADA	Pergamon of Canada Ltd., 75 The East Mall, Toronto, Ontario, Canada
AUSTRALIA	Pergamon Press (Aust.) Pty. Ltd., 19a Boundary Street, Rushcutters Bay, N.S.W. 2011, Australia
FRANCE	Pergamon Press SARL, 24 rue des Ecoles, 75240 Paris, Cedex 05, France
FEDERAL REPUBLIC OF GERMANY	Pergamon Press GmbH, 6242 Kronberg-Taunus, Pferdstrasse 1, Federal Republic of Germany

Copyright © 1980 Royal Statistical Society and Social Science Research Council.

All Rights Reserved. No part of this publication may be reproduced, stored in a retrieval system or transmitted in any form or by any means: electronic, electrostatic, magnetic tape, mechanical, photocopying, recording or otherwise, without permission in writing from the copyright holders

First edition 1980

British Library Cataloguing in Publication Data.
Reviews of United Kingdom statistical sources.
Vol.11: Coal; Gas; and Electricity
1. Great Britain—Statistical services
I. Maunder, Wynne Frederick II. Harris, D. J. III. Nabb, H.
IV. Nuttall, D. V. Royal Statistical Society VI. Social Science
Research Council (Great Britain)
314.1 HA37.G7 79–40222

ISBN 0-08-022461-X

For Bibliographic purposes this volume should be cited as: Harris D. J., Nabb H., and Nuttall, D., *Coal, Gas and Electricity* Pergamon Press Limited on behalf of the Royal Statistical Society and the Social Science Research Council, 1979

Printed and bound in Great Britain by William Clowes (Beccles) Limited, Beccles and London

VOLUME CONTENTS

Foreword	vii
Introduction	ix
Energy—a Prologue	1
Review No. 19: Coal	19
Subject Index to Coal	95
Review No. 20: Gas	99
Subject Index to Gas	189
Review No. 21: Electricity	195
Subject Index to Electricity	293

FOREWORD

The Sources and Nature of the Statistics of the United Kingdom produced under the auspices of the Royal Statistical Society and edited by Maurice Kendall filled a notable gap on the library shelves when it made its appearance in the early post-war years. Through a series of critical reviews by many of the foremost national experts, it constituted a valuable contemporary guide to statisticians working in many fields as well as a benchmark to which historians of the development of Statistics in this country are likely to return again and again. The Social Science Research Council and the Society were both delighted when Professor Maunder came forward with the proposal that a revised version should be produced, indicating as well his willingness to take on the onerous task of editor. The two bodies were more than happy to act as co-sponsors of the project and to help in its planning through a joint steering committee. The result, we are confident, will be adjudged a worthy successor to the previous volumes by the very much larger 'statistics public' that has come into being in the intervening years.

Dr C. S. SMITH

Secretary
Social Science Research Council

October 1978

R. F. A. HOPES

Honorary Secretary
Royal Statistical Society

October 1978

MEMBERSHIP OF THE JOINT STEERING COMMITTEE
(October 1978)

Chairman: Miss S. V. Cunliffe

Representing the Royal Statistical Society:
Mr M. C. Fessey
Prof H. Goldstein
Dr S. Rosenbaum

Representing the Social Science Research Council:
Mr A. S. Noble
Mrs J. Peretz
Dr W. Taylor

Secretary: Mr D. E. Allen

INTRODUCTION

The inclusion in the series of reviews of sources of statistics in the field of energy scarcely requires either explanation or justification. What, however, may call for comment is the partial coverage of the present volume in that it deals with coal, gas and electricity but neglects oil. This state of affairs is frankly fortuitous in that, although its ultimate natural affinity may at least be arguable, it is scheduling factors alone which are responsible for dictating the treatment of petroleum statistics in the planned chemicals volume instead of here. However, as some degree of amelioration to the situation, it may be noted that the preliminary section by D. J. Harris on the total energy sector does cover oil as well as the other fuels.

The primary aim of this series is to act as a work of reference to the sources of statistical material of all kinds, both official and unofficial. It seeks to enable the user to discover what data are available on the subject in which he is interested, from where they may be obtained, and what the limitations are to their use. Data are regarded as available not only if published in the normal printed format but also if they are likely to be released to a *bona fide* enquirer in any other form, such as duplicated documents, computer print-out or even magnetic tape. On the other hand, no reference is made to material which, even if it is known to exist, is not accessible to the general run of potential users. The distinction, of course, is not clear-cut and mention of a source is not to be regarded as a guarantee that data will be released; in particular cases it may very well be a matter for negotiation. The latter caution applies with particular force to the question of obtaining computer print-outs of custom specified tabulations. Where original records are held on magnetic tape it might appear that there should be no insuperable problem, apart from confidentiality, in obtaining any feasible analysis at a cost; in practice, it may well turn out that there are capacity restraints which override any simple cost calculation. Thus, what is requested might make demands on computer and programming resources to the extent that the routine work of the agency concerned would be intolerably affected.

The intention is that the sources for each topic should be reviewed in detail, and the brief supplied to authors has called for comprehensive coverage at the level of 'national interest'. This term does not denote any necessary restriction to statistics collected on a national basis (still less, of course, to national aggregates) but it means that sources of a purely local character, without wider interest in either content or methodology, are excluded. Indeed, the mere task of identifying all material of this latter kind is an impossibility. The interpretation of the brief has obviously involved discretion and it is up to the users of these reviews to say what unreasonable gaps become apparent to them. They are cordially invited to do so by communicating with me.

To facilitate the use of the series as a work of reference, certain features have been incorporated which are worth a word or two of explanation.

First, the text of each review is designed, in so far as varying subject matter permits, to follow a standard form of arrangement so that users may expect a similar pattern to be followed throughout the series. The starting point is a brief summary of the activity concerned and its organisation, in order to give a clear background understanding of how data are collected, what is being measured, the stage at which measurements are made, what the reporting units are, the channels through which returns are routed and where they are processed. As a further part of this introductory material, there is a discussion of the specific problems of definition and measurement to which the topic gives rise. The core sections on available sources which follow are arranged at the author's discretion—by origin, by subject subdivision, or by type of data; there is too much heterogeneity between topics to permit any imposition of complete uniformity on all authors. The final section is devoted to a discussion of general shortcomings and possibly desirable improvements. In case a contrary expectation should be aroused, it should be said that authors have not been asked to produce a comprehensive plan for the reform of statistical reporting in the whole of their field. However, a review of existing sources is a natural opportunity to make some suggestions for future policy on the collection and publication of statistics within the scope concerned.

Secondly, detailed factual information about statistical series and other data is given in a Quick Reference List (QRL). The exact nature of the entries is best seen by glancing at the list and accordingly they are not described here. Again, the ordering is not prescribed except that entries are not classified by publication source since it is presumed that it is this which is unknown to the reader. In general, the routine type of information which is given in the QRL is not repeated verbally in the text; the former, however, serves as a search route to the latter in that a reference (by section number) is shown against a QRL entry when there is a related discussion in the text.

Third, a subject index to each review acts as a more or less conventional line of enquiry on textual references; however, it is a computerised system and, for an individual review, the only peculiarity which it introduces is the possibility of easily permuting entries. Thus an entry in the index may appear as

Conversion appliances for natural gas

and also be shown as:

Appliances for natural gas, conversion of

as well as:

Natural gas, conversion of appliances for

INTRODUCTION

The object at this level is merely to facilitate search by giving as many variants as possible. In addition, individual review subject indexes are merged into a cumulative index which is held on magnetic tape and may possibly be used to produce a printed version from time to time if that seems desirable. Computer print-outs of the cumulative index to date are available on application to me at the Department of Economics, University of Exeter. In addition, selective searches of this index may be made by the input of key-words; the result is a print-out of all entries in which the key-word appears in the initial position in the subject index of any review. Like the cumulative index itself, this is a facility which may be of increasing help as the number of reviews in print grows.

It should be noted that the prologue on energy in this volume does not have its own index; what has been done is to include entries from it in each of the three main subject indexes, where they are noted as '*see* Energy Review'.

Fourth, each review contains two listings of publications. The QRL Key gives full details of the publications shown as sources and text references to them are made in the form [QRL serial number]; this list is confined essentially to data publications. The other listing is a general bibliography of works discussing wider aspects; text references in this case are made in the form [B serial number].

Finally, an attempt is made to reproduce the more important returns or forms used in data collection so that it may be seen what tabulations it is possible to make as well as helping to clarify the basis of those actually available. Unfortunately, there are severe practical limitations on the number of such forms that it is possible to append to a review and authors perforce have to be highly selective. In the present instance the authors of both the Coal and Gas reviews were unable to obtain from the industries any forms which they felt were suitable for reproduction.

If all or any of these features succeed in their intention of increasing the value of the series in its basic function as a work of reference it will be gratifying; the extent to which the purpose is achieved, however, will be difficult to assess without 'feedback' from the readership. Users, therefore, will be rendering an essential service if they will send me a note of specific instances where, in consulting a review, they have failed to find the information sought.

As editor, I must express my very grateful thanks to all the members of the Joint Steering Committee of the Royal Statistical Society and the Social Science Research Council. It would be unfair to saddle them with any responsibility for shortcomings in execution but they have directed the overall strategy with as admirable a mixture of guidance and forbearance as any editor of such a series could desire. Especial thanks are due to the Secretary of the Committee who is an unfailing source of help even when sorely pressed by the more urgent demands of his other offices.

The authors join me in thanking all those who gave up their time to attend the seminars held to discuss the first drafts of their reviews and which contributed materially to improving the final versions. We are most grateful to Mr Thomas Dalby of Pergamon Press Ltd. for all his help, particularly during the vital production stages. The subject entries for the three reviews in this volume were compiled by Mrs Juliet Horwood who has also been responsible for many other aspects of the work. Our thanks go also to Mrs Gill Skinner, of the Social Studies Data

Processing Unit at the University of Exeter, who has written the computer programs for the production of the subject indexes.

University of Exeter W. F. MAUNDER
November
  1978

ENERGY—A Prologue

by

D. J. HARRIS

TABLE OF CONTENTS

1.	**Introduction**	5
1.1.	*The Purpose of Energy Statistics*	5
2.	**Energy Planning**	7
2.1.	*Government Attempts*	7
2.2.	*Energy Modelling*	7
2.3.	*Other UK Studies*	8
2.4.	*Wider Energy Models*	8
3.	**Comparability of Fuels**	9
4.	**Published Energy Statistics**	12
5.	**Energy Consumption**	14
	Quick Reference List	15
	Key to Publications	17
Bibliography		18

CHAPTER 1

INTRODUCTION

The reviews that follow will examine in detail the statistical data available for three fuel industries, namely the coal industry, electricity, and gas. Each of these reviews concentrates on the industry under discussion and whilst there will be some cross referencing their approach will be based on the industry and not on the energy sector as a whole.

This particular review concentrates entirely on the energy sector and the statistical data associated with it. It should be noted that the energy sector is more than the sum of the three industries mentioned above. One important addition in the energy sector would be data relating to the contribution of petroleum. In other words the energy sector is made up of a number of energy inputs only some of which are described in detail in the sections set aside for the separate industries.

When examining statistical tables where the word energy appears there are generally three categories of such tables. The first includes tables where each fuel is presented in terms of its natural and original units. That is coal data would appear as tons of coal, oil as tonnes of oil, gas as therms, and electricity as gigawatt or terrawatt hours. Clearly these are disparate units which are difficult to aggregate or compare one with another. The two other categories transform such disparate data to common scales. One such transformation would be to either tons of coal equivalent, or alternatively million tonnes of oil equivalent. Another transformation is one where the original units are converted to a scale that in some way measures the heat supplied by the various fuels; there are sub-categories within this scale depending on whether the measurement is for primary fuel input, heat supplied, or useful energy and these are discussed more fully below in section 3.

It should also be noted that fuels are classified as either primary or secondary. The former includes coal, crude petroleum, natural gas, and electricity produced from nuclear or hydro power. Secondary fuels include all other electricity plus energy derived from coke and breeze, manufactured fuel, creosote and pitch mixtures, non crude petroleum, and town, coke oven or blast furnace gas.

1.1. The Purpose of Energy Statistics

It should perhaps be emphasised that the collection and collation of energy data is different from data collection for individual fuels in two important respects. First there is no 'energy industry' required to collect data for presentation in 'Annual Reports and Accounts'. This leads to the second but related point: energy data are usually not primary data; they are derived from the individual industries and may be transformed from the original measuring units of those industries.

Energy statistics are produced and published for a number of different reasons and these often determine the way the data are published. One reason for their production is to provide figures for the total production and consumption of energy. These may be achieved in a number of ways. They could be published in terms of the production and consumption of the separate fuels and in this case disparate scales could be used. Alternatively, total production and consumption figures could be published in forms that transform the original units to a common scale. This allows aggregation between fuels. In principle it does not matter which common scale is used although, in practice, some scales present more problems in transformation than others.

Another reason for collecting energy statistics may be to identify the consumption of energy in sectors of the economy. This is often published for final consumers and/or the main industrial groups. When such analyses are conducted the data are presented either in the original units of the primary fuels or on a heat supplied basis.

The production of energy balances is another important reason why energy data are collected. These are growing in importance elsewhere in the world and are thus needed for the reasons of international comparisons. There are other reasons however for the establishment and development of energy balances. As Roberts and Hawkins [B 3] point out, one of the requirements of economic analyses is to trace, for any fuel, its use in various forms. These energy balances may be in partial form, that is, they do not go beyond the primary fuels or trace through from supply to final use. If the energy balances are complete, data for the conversion from one fuel into another are provided and the fuel's use is traced through from source to final use.

A fourth reason for the production of energy data may be for planning purposes, such as the production of forecasts based on the statistical relationship between energy consumption and gross domestic product. A broader reason may be connected with the attempt to plan the energy industries on a sectoral basis rather than on the basis of individual industries. The next section will briefly review some of these.

CHAPTER 2

ENERGY PLANNING

2.1. Government Attempts

The government has produced two White Papers on Fuel Policy [B 9] [B 10]. These were written and published in the mid-nineteen sixties and were concerned largely with ways in which the coal industry could be protected, so as to avoid the social costs of running down too quickly. Other considerations in the determination of fuel policy were at that time concerned with the balance of payments, security, and the possible shortage of oil. The Department of Energy has produced a number of *Energy Papers* that consider possible energy problems, and discuss a number of alternative ways by which these may be overcome. A first step in this process was the establishment of the Advisory Council of Research and Development for Fuel and Power (ACORD). This is to be concerned with the formulation of a national energy research and development strategy.

2.2. Energy Modelling

The Department of Energy has taken initiatives with respect to co-ordination between the fuel industries. These have manifested themselves, largely in relation to energy models. Since 1967 a 'total sum approach' has been encouraged in relation to planning for the future. This approach was encouraged and undertaken by the Energy Model Group, which was formed in 1967 by the Ministry of Power, but now incorporated in the Economic and Statistics Division of the Department of Energy. The long-term aim of the Model Group is to produce a computable model of the UK energy economy that balances supply and demand by fuel in each market at a time. One of the objectives of having a computable model is to achieve, as far as possible, the co-ordination of fuel policy. Another is the reconciliation of the investment proposals of the fuel industries, attempting to make sure that the sum of the parts does not exceed the anticipated total investment in energy and determining where any adjustment is needed. See Hutber [B 2] for further details on this approach.

The early manifestations of the attempts of the Department of Energy were on the production of forecasts rather than with developing a framework by which the forecasts could be achieved. This emphasis may change with the Department's involvement in discussions with the industries of forecasts in relation to the industries' corporate plans. There are two points of note in this development. The first is that the industries have a means by which they may reconcile their individual needs and aspirations to those of the nation. This is provided through the Advisory Council and the Energy Debates and Energy Papers. Secondly—since the exercise is a participative and collaborative—each industry is aware not only of its own strategy but of that of the other fuel industries.

2.3. Other UK Studies

A number of people and institutions have published surveys and/or articles in relation to energy supply and fuel policy. The interested reader should refer to Beckerman *et al.* [B 1] and Political and Economic Planning [B 11] for analysis made by those who claim to be disinterested parties. Robinson has published a number of papers that are relevant background reading to a discussion of fuel policy [B 4] [B 5]. Also the 1974 National Economic Development Office Report [B 7] concerns itself with energy conservation in the United Kingdom, including future options.

2.4. Wider Energy Models

On a geographically wider scale, there has been a major international publication in the energy field and this is provided by the Workshop on Alternative Energy Strategies (WAES) [B 8], which concerns itself with energy demand and supply studies for the major energy consuming countries of the world. The study provides a number of scenarios, making different assumptions regarding the inputs into the models, including, for the UK, assumptions about the degree of government intervention.

CHAPTER 3

COMPARABILITY OF FUELS

It has already been noted that fuels are classified in terms of a primary/secondary classification and within each of the fuels the quality of the product is variable. This classification and variability raises problems in relation to comparing one fuel against another. For example, what is the worth of one ton of oil against one ton of coal? Clearly to start answering that question one would have to ask which ton of oil and which ton of coal? But, more than that, one would have to ask which ton of oil for which purpose, and which ton of coal for which purpose? In other words, the use to which the fuel is put will affect the measure of its worth.

Roberts and Hawkins have summarised the arguments in *Statistical News* [B 3]. They point out that while one ton of petroleum products contains about the same amount of potential energy as 1.7 tons of coal, one ton of motor spirit or diesel oil cannot be replaced directly by 1.7 tons of coal. Fuels are not substitutable one for the other in terms of final usage. When replacement is considered the use to which a fuel is put must be taken into account. The major uses are for heat, light or motive power.

Comparability is complicated by other factors. One is that the different efficiencies with which the individual fuels are converted depend on the sophistication of the equipment used for conversion. Second, in the conversion process the fuels can produce by-products, and it is difficult to measure their contribution to measuring the original fuels efficiency.

As Roberts and Hawkins point out, one could attempt to compare by using the prices of fuels and this is done in some input/output tables. However, it is generally recognised that there are too many factors, other than the efficiencies of the fuels, that can affect price and thus it is regarded as being an unstable indicator of the efficiencies of the individual fuels. Further details of adding fuels together by value may be seen in Turvey and Nobay [B 6].

Fuels are however compared, and this usually takes place in one of three ways, although there are additional ways in which this measurement could take place. The first assesses *primary fuel* input before allowing for conversion and distribution losses. The second measures the *heat supplied* to final users, either directly as primary fuel or after conversion into electricity. The third is *useful energy*, that is, the amount of energy available to the consumer after all losses are taken into account. The latter losses depend on the quality and type of appliances and equipment in which the fuel is used as well as the fuel itself. Although a good concept, statistics on useful energy are not felt to be sufficiently reliable to be included in published data.

Thus it is clear that certain conversion factors exist for the comparison of fuels. The table below summarises some of the internationally used conversion factors used in the WAES Study of Energy Demand Studies [QRL 13] for the United Kingdom. It should be noted that the thermal content of United Kingdom coal is somewhat lower than the conventional figure of 28.8 GJ per tonne that is often used internationally.

WAES Conversion Factors for UK Energy Demand Studies

Energy 10^{18} joules $= 10^9$ GJ
$= 947 \times 10^6$ Btu
$= 278$ TWh
$= 22.7$ million tonnes of oil equivalent
$= 39.2$ million tonnes of coal equivalent
$= 25.0$ thousand million metres cubed of natural gas

Power 10^{18} joules/year $= 32$ GW $= 32 \times 10^9$ watts
$= 0.45$ million barrels per day oil equivalent

Calorific Values 1 tonne oil equivalent $= 44.0$ GJ
1 tonne coal equivalent $= 25.5$ GJ
10^3 standard m³ natural gas (at 0°C 760 mm dry)
$= 37.9 \times 10^3$ standard ft³
(at 60°F 30 in. wet)
$= 40.0$ GJ
10^6 b/d oil equivalent $= 2.2 \times 10^9$ GJ per annum
$= 2.2 \times 10^{18}$ J per annum

Electricity A 1000 MW ($= 1$ GW) power station at 60 per cent load factor and at 35 per cent conversion efficiency (assumed for 1985) requires annually a primary energy input of 54×10^{15} joules, or 1.23 million tonnes of oil equivalent, or 2.12 million tonnes of coal equivalent. At 37.5 per cent efficiency (for year 2000) an input of 50.5×10^{15} joules is assumed to be required for a 1 GWh nuclear station.

For internal purposes in the UK and the EEC the conversion factors are summarised below.

Primary Fuel Conversion
1 tonne of petroleum products $= 1.67$ tons of coal
255 therms of natural gas and colliery methane $= 1$ ton of coal

Calorific Value
1 tonne of oil equivalent $= 10$ gigacalories
This approach is adopted in *Energy Trends* [QRL 6]. The table of conversion factors based on this are admitted by this publication to be 'rough and ready' and are published at the end of *Energy Trends*. Also the *Digest of United Kingdom Energy*

Statistics [QRL 4] provides details of average gross calorific values from which thermal contents can be derived.

Calorific Value EEC
1 tonne coal equivalent (tce) is defined as having 7000 calories per gram, that is, 1 tce = 7 gigacalories.

Whilst such conversions may be justifiably used for broad comparisons, when detailed analysis of final users is needed the conversion factors overlook some difficulties. In summary they overlook the fact that fuels are not homogeneous in quality, that they need equipment of different efficiencies for conversion into final use (which will affect the amount of useful energy forthcoming) and more important, fuels are not always substitutable in terms of final use.

CHAPTER 4

PUBLISHED ENERGY STATISTICS

It is likely that this section will duplicate sections in the reviews of the individual industries, since they also highlight the major sources of statistics. This section will concentrate on Government statistics since these are, in the main, the ones that provide data over industries.

The Government Statistical Service publishes a booklet each year that gives a brief guide to Government sources [B 12]. This may be obtained, free of charge, from the Central Statistical Office. A much more detailed guide to energy data may be found in *Guide to Official Statistics* [B 13].

As far as statistics relating to energy comparisons between industries are concerned, one of the most important sources is the *Digest of United Kingdom Energy Statistics* [QRL 4], which contains information in relation to United Kingdom energy production and consumption. The next section will discuss in more detail the data produced in relation to energy consumption, but it is important to note that the *Digest* shows the relationship between energy and gross domestic product, the growth of energy consumption, and expenditure on fuel and energy. It also provides data on commodity analysis of purchases in the energy sector. Also published is the energy coefficient, which is defined as the average rate of increase in primary energy consumption compared with the average rate of increase in gross domestic product at factor cost and constant prices.

Energy Trends [QRL 6] is also an important source of data and contains monthly and quarterly tables of production and consumption of fuels and aggregated energy consumption, together with some commentary on the figures. It includes unadjusted and seasonally adjusted energy consumption figures on a primary fuel input basis for the total energy sector and the primary fuels in that sector. Monthly data are for the latest three months and for the corresponding months of the previous year. Quarterly figures are published on a rolling basis, that is the figures are advanced 1 month in each year in the subsequent issues of *Energy Trends*. The quarterly figures provide data on a heat supplied basis.

The *Monthly Digest of Statistics* [QRL 7] provides a collection of the main series from all Government departments. The *Annual Abstract of Statistics* [QRL 1] provides a longer run of years. It provides data on a heat supplied basis for the latest ten years. This source publishes figures relating to the contribution of each primary fuel to total energy produced, use of fuel and losses in conversion, and distribution by fuel producers and final energy consumption analysed by fuel and classes of consumers.

Other sources of data on energy usually provide data on an annual basis like the *Digest* but do not provide as much detail as the *Digest of United Kingdom Energy Statistics* [QRL 4]. One of these is *United Kingdom Mineral Statistics* [QRL 12], which contains data on energy consumption for the latest 22 years in total and by primary fuel consumed. The figures are published on a primary fuel input basis but in terms of a tonne of coal. *Annual Statistics* [QRL 2] (produced by the Iron and Steel Institute) publishes energy consumption by industry figures for the latest two years. These are further disaggregated into fuel types. the figures are on a heat supplied basis and expressed in thousands of terajoules. This source also publishes data in the original units of the fuels but measured in metric terms.

Regional data are published in two publications. *Regional Statistics* [QRL 8] publishes data on a heat supplied basis and original units on energy consumption for each standard region and country of the United Kingdom. Energy consumption is disaggregated into industry, domestic and all other classes of final consumers. *The Scottish Abstract of Statistics* [QRL 9] publishes data for energy consumption in Scotland on a primary fuel input basis and in terms of original units.

For European data on energy the OECD *Statistics of Energy* [QRL 10], the *Bulletin of Energy Statistics for Europe* [QRL 3] and *Energy Statistics* [QRL 5] are important sources of data. All three give energy statistics in the form of balance sheets expressed in tonnes of coal equivalent.

The methodology for energy statistics employed in the United Kingdom is now much closer than hitherto to that used by the Statistical Office of the European Communities. Some important differences, however, remain. These relate to conversion factors used to arrive at the common units of measurement and in the definitions of some of the sectors.

The expression of energy production and consumption in the Community is in metric units of tonnes of coal equivalent (tce) having a net calorific value of 7,000 calories per gram, i.e. 1 tce = 7 gigacalories.

The *Digest* [QRL 4] gives a brief indication of the more important conventions adopted by the Community, but a fuller discussion is given in the Community's *Energy Statistics* [QRL 5].

CHAPTER 5

ENERGY CONSUMPTION

Statistics of fuel consumption are derived mainly from returns rendered by consumers to the Department of Energy, or from the records of the individual producers. Some of the sources of energy consumption data have been referred to in the previous section. This section will concentrate on two of these, namely the *Digest* [QRL 4] and the *Monthly Digest* [QRL 7].

The *Digest of UK Energy Statistics* [QRL 4] is one of the main sources of statistics on energy consumption. It provides data on total energy consumption and also on the availability and consumption of primary fuels and their equivalents. The units used are varied and include coal equivalent, oil equivalent, therms and petajoules. The *Digest* publishes data on energy consumption by final consumers in original units as well as on a heat supplied basis. Energy balances are available in terms of therms and petajoules. The introductory notes of the *Digest* give full details on the methods by which these are done. The *Digest* also shows the relationship between energy and gross domestic product, the growth of energy consumption and the expenditure on fuel and energy.

The *Monthly Digest of Statistics* [QRL 7] provides data of energy consumption on the basis of both primary fuel input, and final users. The former is calculated on the basis of 'millions of tons of coal equivalent'. Monthly and annual figures are provided for total energy. Unadjusted and seasonally adjusted figures are given for monthly tables. Details of this and 'corrections' made for temperature may be found in the *Monthly Digest* [QRL 7].

Information on energy consumption by final users is also provided in the *Monthly Digest*. Final users include iron and steel, other industries, domestic transport and other final consumers. Figures are kept annually for four years, but there are also quarterly figures provided. The unit of comparison for this data is on a heat supplied basis, and is measured in millions of therms.

Another source of data on fuel use was published in 1974 entitled *A Statistical Survey of Industrial Fuel and Energy Use* [QRL 11]. As the title suggests the survey was concerned with industrial fuel stocks, and the relationship of energy consumption in industry to the cost of goods sold.

QUICK REFERENCE LIST—TABLE OF CONTENTS

General	16
Production	16
Consumption	16
Stocks	17

QUICK REFERENCE LIST

Type of data	Breakdown/details of analysis	Area	Frequency	Publication (see QRL key)	Text and remarks
General					
Conversion factors	Conversion factors in energy, power, calorific value units	GB	Occasional	[QRL 13]	2.4 and 3
UK conversion factors	Primary fuel and calorific value	GB	(i) Annual (ii) Monthly	(i) [QRL 4] (ii) [QRL 6]	3
EEC conversion factors	Calorific value	EEC	Annual	[QRL 5]	3
Production					
Energy production	Total production	GB	Annual	[QRL 4]	4
Energy production	Total production	GB	Monthly	[QRL 6]	4
Energy production	Contribution of each primary fuel	GB	Annual	[QRL 1]	4
Energy production	Losses in conversion	GB	Annual	[QRL 1]	4
Energy production	By fuel	GB	Annual	[QRL 1]	4
Consumption					
Energy consumption	Relationship with gross domestic product	UK	Annual	[QRL 4]	4
Energy coefficient	Average rate of increase in primary energy consumption and average rate of increase in gross product	UK	Annual	[QRL 4]	4 At factor cost and constant prices
Energy consumption	Unadjusted and seasonally adjusted consumption on a heat supplied basis	UK	Monthly	[QRL 6]	4
Energy consumption	On a primary fuel input basis	UK	Annual	[QRL 12]	4
Energy consumption	By fuel input	UK	Monthly	[QRL 7]	5
Energy consumption	By industry	UK	Annual	[QRL 2]	4
Energy consumption by regions	On a heat supplied and original units basis	UK	Annual	[QRL 8]	4
Energy consumption in Scotland	Measured on a primary fuel basis and original units	Scotland	Annual	[QRL 9]	4

ENERGY CONSUMPTION

Energy consumption in Europe	Energy statistics in balance sheet form	OECD	Annual	[QRL 10]	4
Energy consumption in Europe	Energy statistics in balance sheet form	ECE	Annual	[QRL 3]	4
Energy consumption in Europe	Energy statistics in balance sheet form	ECE	Annual	[QRL 5]	4
By final consumer	Original fuel units and on a heat supplied basis	UK	Annual	[QRL 4]	5
By final user	Primary fuel input	UK	Monthly	[QRL 7]	5
Energy balances	In therms and petajoules	GB	Annual	[QRL 4]	5
Stocks					
Fuel stocks	Industrial fuel stocks	GB	Occasionally	[QRL 11]	5 Survey by CBI

Quick Reference List Key to Publications

Reference number	Organisation responsible	Title	Publisher	Frequency	Remarks
[QRL 1]	Central Statistical Office	*Annual Abstract of Statistics*	HMSO	Annual	
[QRL 2]	Iron and Steel Institute	*Annual Statistics*	HMSO	Annual	
[QRL 3]	Statistical Office of the European Communities	*Bulletin of Energy Statistics for Europe*	ECE	Annual	
[QRL 4]	Department of Energy	*Digest of United Kingdom Energy Statistics*	HMSO	Annual	
[QRL 5]	Statistical Office of the European Communities	*Energy Statistics*	ECE	Annual	
[QRL 6]	Department of Energy	*Energy Trends*	HMSO	Monthly	
[QRL 7]	Central Statistical Office	*Monthly Digest of Statistics*	HMSO	Monthly	
[QRL 8]	Central Statistical Office	*Regional Statistics*	HMSO	Annual	
[QRL 9]	Scottish Office	*The Scottish Abstract of Statistics*	HMSO	Annual	
[QRL 10]	OECD	*Statistics of Energy*	OECD	Annual	
[QRL 11]	Confederation of British Industry/Department of Energy	*A Statistical Survey of Industrial Fuel and Energy Use*	HMSO	Occasional	Reports on surveys for July to December period 1974
[QRL 12]	Business Statistics Office	*United Kingdom Mineral Statistics*	HMSO	Annual	
[QRL 13]	Workshop on Alternative Energy Strategies	*Occasional Papers*		Occasional	

BIBLIOGRAPHY

[B 1]   W. Beckerman et al. *The British Economy, 1975*. NIESR, 1965.
[B 2]   F. W. Hutber. 'Modelling of Energy Supply and Demand'. *Energy Modelling*, 1973
[B 3]   W. N. T. Roberts and W. A. Hawkins. 'Energy Balances—some recent developments. *Statistical News*, November 1976.
[B 4]   C. Robinson. 'A Policy for Fuel'. *Institute of Economic Affairs*, Occasional Paper 31, 1969.
[B 5]   C. Robinson. 'What Kind of Fuel Policy for Britain?'. *Journal of the Institute of Fuel*, 1972.
[B 6]   R. Turvey and A. R. Nobay. 'On Measuring Energy Consumption'. *Economic Journal*, 1965.
[B 7]   National Economic Development Office. *Energy Conservation in the United Kingdom, Achievements, Aims and Options.* HMSO, 1974
[B 8]   Workshop on Alternative Energy Strategies (WAES). *Energy Demand Studies: Major consuming countries.* MIT Press, 1976.
[B 9]   Department of Fuel and Power. *Fuel Policy*, Cmnd 2798. HMSO, 1965.
[B 10] Department of Fuel and Power. *Fuel Policy*, Cmnd 3438. HMSO, 1967.
[B 11] Political and Economic Planning. *A Fuel Policy for Britain*. 1966.
[B 12] Government Statistical Service. *Government Statistics: A brief guide to sources.* HMSO, Annual.
[B 13] Government Statistical Service. *Guide to Official Statistics.* HMSO, 1976.

19: COAL

D. J. Harris

REFERENCE DATE OF SOURCES REVIEWED

This review is believed to represent the position, broadly speaking, as it obtained in March 1977. Later revisions have been inserted up to the proof reading stage, May 1979, taking account as far as possible of any major changes in the situation.

INDEX TO INITIALS USED IN THE TEXT

BCURA	British Coal Utilisation Research Association
CEPCEO	Association of Coal Producers of the European Community
ECSC	European Coal and Steel Community
EEC	European Economic Community
EFTA	European Free Trade Association
IEA	International Energy Agency
MRDE	Mining Research and Development Establishment
NCB	National Coal Board
NUM	National Union of Mineworkers
OECD	Organization for Economic Co-operation and Development
OMS	Output per Manshift
RMPS	Redundant Mineworkers (Payment Scheme)
SMRE	Safety in Mines Research Establishment
tce	tonnes of coal equivalent

CONTENTS OF REVIEW 19

1.	**Introduction**	27
1.1.	*General Review of the Industry*	27
2.	**Before Nationalisation**	30
3.	**Nationalisation**	33
3.1	*General Introduction*	33
3.2	*Coal Sources*	33
	3.2.1. Deep-Mined Coal	34
	3.2.2. Open-Cast Coal	34
	3.2.3. Manufactured Fuels and Coke	34
3.3	*NCB Organisation*	34
	3.3.1. Deep Mining	34
	3.3.2. Open-Cast Mining	35
	3.3.3. Ancillaries	35
	3.3.4. Marketing	35
3.4.	*Deep-Mine Coal Production*	35
4.	**Statistics in the Modern Coal Industry**	37
4.1	*General*	37
4.2.	*National Coal Board*	37
4.3.	*Government Sources*	39
4.4.	*Other Sources of Data*	40
4.5.	*International Statistics*	41
4.6.	*The Statistical Calendar*	41
4.7.	*Geographical Coverage*	41
5.	**Statistics on Output**	42
5.1.	*General Definitions*	42
	5.1.1. Organisations	42
	5.1.2. Saleable Output	42
	5.1.3. Output per Manshift	43
	5.1.4. Mechanised Output	44
	5.1.5. Tonnage Lost, Disputes	44
5.2.	*Statistical Tables*	44
	5.2.1. General Output	44
	5.2.2. Output by Areas	45
	5.2.3. Undistributed Stocks and Exports	45

5.3.	*NCB Annual Reports and Accounts*	45
5.4.	*Digest of United Kingdom Energy Statistics*	46
	5.4.1. General Output	46
	5.4.2. Output by Areas	47
5.5.	*Energy Trends*	47
5.6.	*Monthly Digest of Statistics*	47
5.7.	*Business Monitors*	48
5.8.	*United Kingdom Mineral Statistics*	48
5.9.	*Regional Data*	48
5.10.	*Eurostat*	49
6.	**Coal Sales and Consumption**	50
6.1	*General*	50
	6.1.1. Public Power Stations	50
	6.1.2. Coke Ovens	51
	6.1.3. Industry	51
	6.1.4. Domestic	51
	6.1.5. Other Inland Markets	52
	6.1.6. Stocks	52
	6.1.7. Imports and Exports	52
6.2.	*NCB Statistical Tables*	52
	6.2.1. General Consumption	52
6.3.	*NCB Annual Reports and Accounts*	53
6.4.	*Digest of United Kingdom Energy Statistics*	53
	6.4.1. General Consumption	54
	6.4.2. Consumption by Countries	54
	6.4.3. Imports and Exports of Coal	54
6.5.	*Energy Trends*	55
6.6.	*Monthly Digest of Statistics*	55
	6.6.1. General Consumption	55
	6.6.2. Coal Consumption by Market	56
6.7.	*United Kingdom Mineral Statistics*	56
7.	**Manpower**	57
7.1.	*General Definitions*	57
	7.1.1. Wage-Earners on Colliery Books	57
	7.1.2. Recruitment	57
	7.1.3. Wastage	58
	7.1.4. Absence	58
	7.1.5. Average Daily Manshifts	58
	7.1.6. Earnings	58
	7.1.7. Earnings per Manshift	59
	7.1.8. Average Weekly Earnings	59
7.2.	*NCB Statistical Tables*	59
	7.2.1. General Manpower	59
	7.2.2. Manpower by Areas	59
	7.2.3. Age Distribution	59

	7.2.4. Recruitment and Wastage	60
	7.2.5. Manshifts by Place of Work	60
	7.2.6. Total Numbers	60
	7.2.7. Earnings	60
7.3.	*NCB Annual Reports and Accounts*	60
7.4.	*Digest of United Kingdom Energy Statistics*	61
	7.4.1. Manpower General	61
	7.4.2. Manpower Employed	61
	7.4.3. Recruitment and Wastage	61
	7.4.4. Area Data	62
7.5.	*Monthly Digest of Statistics*	62
7.6.	*Department of Employment Gazette*	62
7.7.	*British Labour Statistics Yearbooks*	63
7.8.	*The NUM National Executive Committee Reports*	63
	7.8.1. Redundant Mineworkers (Payment Scheme)	63
	7.8.2. Lump Sum Payments	63
7.9.	*Business Monitors*	63
8.	**Financial Statistics**	64
8.1.	*General*	64
8.2.	*NCB (Coal Products) Ltd*	65
8.3.	*NCB Ancillaries Ltd*	65
8.4.	*NCB and Subsidiaries*	66
8.5.	*Capital*	66
	8.5.1. Annual Reports and Accounts	66
	8.5.1.1. Stocks of Products	67
	8.5.1.2. Key Operating Statistics	67
	8.5.1.3. Consolidated Balance Sheet	67
	8.5.1.4. Notes to the Accounts	68
	8.5.1.5. Schedules	68
	8.5.1.6. Summary of Results	68
	8.5.2. Report on the Census of Production	69
	8.5.3. Business Monitors	70
	8.5.4. The European Coal and Steel Community	70
8.6.	*Revenue, Expenditure and Costs*	70
	8.6.1. Annual Reports and Accounts	70
	8.6.1.1. Operating Profit (Loss)	70
	8.6.1.2. Turnover	71
	8.6.1.3. Consolidated Profit and Loss Account	71
	8.6.1.4. Schedules	72
	8.6.2. NCB Digest of United Kingdom Energy Statistics	73
9.	**Statistics and the EEC**	75
9.1.	*Background*	75
9.2.	*European Economic Community*	75
	9.2.1. Reconciliation of Statistics	75

10.	**Safety and Health in Mines**	78
10.1.	*NCB Statistical Tables*	78
10.2.	*Safety in Mines Research Establishment*	79
10.3.	*Other Sources*	79
11.	**Research and Development**	80
11.1.	*Statistics and Information on R and D*	80
12.	**Improvements and Future Developments**	81

Quick Reference List
    Key to Publications   91

Bibliography   93

Subject Index   95

CHAPTER 1

INTRODUCTION

This review is concerned with statistical sources for the coal industry; it covers topic areas that include coal output, sales and consumption, manpower, capital, revenue expenditure, and costs, safety and research activities within the industry.

The coal industry is unusually well documented with statistics, both in volume of information and in length of historical series. Section 2 deals with pre-nationalisation statistical sources. Section 3 covers the organisation of the industry since nationalisation. Section 4 surveys the main sources of data in more detail. Researchers wanting a quick guide to sources of statistics for coal should first refer to Section 4.

Statistics for the coal industry are kept by the industry and published by Government and other agencies and these will be reviewed below. It is important to stress that in addition to these, the *bone fide* researcher would be well advised to get in touch directly with the industry and also the Department of Energy. In case of the industry, the Statistics Department is normally helpful. This author would like to acknowledge the guidance given by Mr K. G. Wood and in particular by Mr S. M. Rizvi of the NCB in this respect. My thanks for their help are also extended to Messrs W. N. T. Roberts, W. A. Hawkins, D. Davies and F. W. Hutber of the Department of Energy. I would also like to thank Mr C. I. K. Forster of the NCB's Central Planning Unit for comments that he made on an earlier draft of this review.

1.1. General Review of the Industry

The coal industry in the United Kingdom has, during its life, displayed many characteristics. During its early history it contributed in a major way to the Industrial Revolution by providing almost all of the energy required. While other fuels were used towards the end of the nineteenth century, gas and electricity were secondary fuels derived from coal. In this period the coal industry's market control was dominant. With the advent of the 1920's the demand for coal began to decline with immediate and far reaching results. In particular, profitability declined, there was an increasing lack of willingness of the mine owners to invest, and there was a considerable amount of industry unrest. The Second World War changed the situation once more, with the demand for coal and coal miners increasing. The glut of coal that was available at the beginning of the war was soon to be diminished and thereafter there was a constant fear that the shortage of coal would hamper the war effort.

After the war the industry was nationalised, and this changed its entire structure and outlook. The National Coal Board (NCB) was established in January 1947, becoming the biggest employer in the Western world, and taking over some 900 previously independent mines, with a turnover of around £360 million per annum. These undertakings charged no less than 8000 different prices for coal. As Schumacher [B 24] noted, the newly instituted National Coal Board's problems were formidable:

"Colliery reconstruction, the building up of qualified staffs, the development of a coherent price structure and of a meaningful wage structure were some of the industry's major tasks from day one to the end of the fifties. In every case it was a matter of bringing order out of something not far short of chaos."

For ten years following nationalisation increased output was the prime concern of the Coal Board. Costs if not forgotten were neglected, while long-term planning and re-organisation were, to some extent, over-shadowed by the need to deal with continuing difficulties. This was also the period when energy requirements were rising at about 4.5 million tons of coal equivalent per annum, and the industry was unable to meet these demands. Consequently, coal remained subject to statutory control until 1958. In this period the NCB produced two plans. The first was in 1949 and called *Plan for Coal* [B 47], the second *Investing in Coal* [B 45] which was published in 1956. This was also the period when the Fleck Committee [B 52] reported on the organisation of the industry whilst the Hartley Committee [B 39] reported on Europe's growing energy needs. On the production side the main method of obtaining coal had not significantly changed from the seventeenth century. The 'Longwall' method was still used in which all the coal in the pit was extracted. This meant that a team of hewers would cut coal together at the coal face, erecting timber supports as they advanced. As the face advanced the space left behind would be filled with waste except for a small number of roadways through the waste. But this relied on the physical strength and ingenuity of a team of hewers and their support staff. Because of this, mechanisation of the coal face was a concern during the whole of the decade and a significant breakthrough was achieved by the invention of the Anderton Shearer. After it was developed it is claimed that it contributed to the rapid rise in productivity, which began in 1958. The reader requiring fuller details of this period is referred to Roberts [B 21].

In spite of these productivity increases coal began to be in short supply because of the excessive demands; major users of coal were encouraged to seek new sources of primary fuel. Thus, the railway and electricity supply industries were encouraged to use oil, and the Government decided to launch a programme for generating electricity by atomic power. The NCB recognised these changes in its *Revised Plan for Coal* published in 1959 [B 57], but the switch to use of other fuels went too far, and instead of just easing the existing problems of the coal industry, a new set of problems was substituted.

In the early 1960's the demand for the coal began to decline and the industry's problems became those associated with excess capacity rather than excess demand. Between 1958 and 1965, 259 pits were shut. These had an output of $32\frac{1}{2}$ million tons and a labour force of about 159,000 people. In 1964 the NCB still had about 150 grossly unprofitable pits where working expenses exceeded revenue by over

1.1. INTRODUCTION

50p per ton and these pits had a labour force of 118,000 and an output of approximately 33 million tons which at that time represented about one-fifth of the Board's deep mined output and about one-quarter of its employment [B 20].

Left to the market mechanism the decline of the coal industry might have been even more substantial in the sixties. However, the industry was protected to the extent of there being a tax on fuel and heating oil, a preference given to coal in electricity generation, and a ban on overseas coal and Soviet oil at times when they were cheap enough to be marketed in Britain [B 22].

But the steady decline of the industry lasted into the 1970's and between 1969 and 1973 the number of colliery wage-earners fell from 336,000 to 268,000. In 1973 there was another dramatic turn in the fortunes of the industry, this time not entirely unrelated to the oil crisis. There was no longer a surplus but a shortage of coal; the central question of general concern was to attempt to stop the contraction of the coal industry which had by that time been going on for at least fifteen years. In addition the coal industry in the early 1970's was involved in two major industrial disputes which further aggravated the shortage of coal. These disputes were in 1972 and 1974 respectively. The effects of coal shortage were particularly dramatically highlighted in 1974. This resulted in electricity cuts and also a three day working week for most firms. Clearly these would need to be taken into account when interpreting data relating to 1974 generally and also specifically for the coal industry. Later the Department of Energy published the findings of an examination of the coal industry and emphasised that in spite of oil discoveries in the North Sea, the coal industry was likely to expand in the future, reversing the decline which had lasted nearly 20 years [B 30] [B 44] [B 48] [B 49]. Geological exploration work has established that the UK has large reserves of coal. The new Selby project illustrates that the NCB has to establish not only the existence of coal, that it can be mined, but that it has to be mined without disturbing the environment to a substantial extent.

The coal industry, like many other industries has been subjected to different market and environmental constraints. The industry has naturally found it difficult to respond to these changes quickly, mainly because a coal mine can take between ten and twelve years to become fully productive. Similarly, when the industry was in decline it either had not wished, or was not allowed, to make rapid adaptations with regard to the labour force for social reasons although we have seen that over time these adaptations have been major.

As with the industry there have been radical changes in the output and standardisation of statistics. Most of these have taken place since nationalisation in 1947 and consequently the emphasis in this review will be from 1947 onwards.

CHAPTER 2

BEFORE NATIONALISATION

The history of the industry goes back beyond the Middle Ages and statistical sources are difficult to trace back that far. But those who are interested should refer to books by J. U. Nef [B 19] and two works by Robert L. Galloway [B 10] [B 11]. The first is made up of two volumes and is regarded as a classic among mining histories and covers the period 1550–1700. It is particularly interesting in so far as it has many references to original sources of information. Galloway's first series first published in 1898 covers the period pre-1066 to 1835, while the second series published in 1904 brings the account up to 1850.

For histories that cover the eighteenth century and later, the interested reader should refer to books by the following authors. Ashton and Sykes [B 5] deal with the coal industry in the eighteenth century, concentrating on economic aspects of the industry's performance. There is a useful eight-page bibliography. Lewis [B 16] included a collection of extracts from original documents in his study of coal-mining in the eighteenth and nineteenth centuries.

For nineteenth and twentieth century histories a number of books could be referred to, among which are those by H. F. Bulman [B 6] and W. Stanley Jevons [B 14], W. W. Haynes [B 13] and H. Wilson [B 25] which provide general accounts of the histories of the industry. More specialist histories are given by J. W. Rowe [B 23] who concentrates on wages in the coal industry, and R. Arnot Page [B 2] [B 3] [B 4] who deals with the history of the Miners Federation. Also, not to be forgotten is the *Children's Employment Commission, First Report* published in 1842 [B 28], which is a landmark in social history and resulted, as far as the coal industry is concerned, with the prohibition of employment of women and children underground.

In the twentieth century the industry has been the subject of a number of investigations and legislation. These began with the 'Sanker' Commission, The *Coal Industry Commission* of 1919 [B 29], which investigated almost every aspect of the industry and discussed the possibility of nationalisation. This was followed in 1925 by a *Royal Commission* [B 58] which was known as the 'Samuel' Commission. This Commission enquired into and reported upon the economic position of the coal industry and made recommendations for its improvement. In 1942 the *Greene Commission* [B 50] was appointed to consider wage issues, the methods and machinery of determining wages and conditions of employment in the coal mining industry. This Commission presented four Reports as a result of their investigations. In 1945–1946 the Ministry of Fuel and Power made a regional survey of the coalfields [B 51]. This survey was made up of a number of reports that described a particular coalfield and its coal, what measures should be taken to enable the optimum use of resources and what welfare services would be needed for mining communities. Finally there was the 'Reid' Report in 1945 which laid the foundation for subsequent nationalisation of the coal mining industry [B 35].

As far as legislation is concerned four Acts are important. The first is the *Coal Mines Act* of 1911 [B 32] which consolidated much of the previous legislation and required that all fatal accidents and serious non-fatal accidents had to be reported to the Mines Inspectorate which was then part of the Home Office. The *Coal Mines Act* of 1930 [B 33] established the Coal Mines Reorganisation Commission and the coal selling schemes, which were to regulate the production, supply, and sale of coal. The *Coal Mines Act* of 1938 [B 34] replaced the Coal Mines Reorganisation Commission with a Coal Commission in which was also vested mineral royalties. Fourthly came the *Coal Industry Nationalisation Act* 1946 [B 31] which established the industry under public ownership.

The statistical sources for this period are varied. Collieries were required by statute to make statistical returns over a century ago. These have been published in the *Colliery Year Book* [QRL 10] which did not cease publication until 1964. Thus, the quantity of coal produced has been recorded for over a century as have the numbers of people employed in the industry. Selected records, that the Board inherited, have been deposited in the Public Record Office. These include details of *The District Selling Schemes*, which were set up under the Coal Mines Act 1930 to rationalise the marketing for coal. Records deposited cover the years 1930 to 1946. The same Act also established the *Mines Reorganisation Commission* to stimulate amalgamation schemes of colliery companies for greater efficiency. Records of these schemes for the years 1931 to 1939 have also been deposited in the Public Record Office.

Other records kept in the Public Record Office include those of *The Coal Commission*, *The Mining Association of Great Britain*, and those that relate to *The Coking Industry*. The Coal Commission was created by the Coal Act of 1938 and had two functions which were to bring coal into public ownership and to take over the work previously done by the Mines Reorganisation Commission. The records for the Coal Commission are kept for the years 1938 to 1944. The Mining Association of Great Britain was the association of coal owners, and their records are kept for the years 1936 to 1946. For the Coking Industry the records cover the years 1919 to 1966.

Records of collieries, colliery companies and local owners' organisations before 1947 have been deposited at County Record Offices which have been designated by the Public Record Office to receive public records. Further information on these sources of statistical data may be obtained from the Chief Records Officer at NCB Headquarters.

There are non-regular sources of statistics. The reader, for example, should refer to A. Finlay Gibson's compilation of statistics for coal mining published in 1922 [B 9]. Similarly, the reader should refer to two PEP Reports. The first, published in 1936 [B 53], referred exclusively to the coal mining industry. The second [B 27] was concerned with the fuel and power industries in general, and was published in 1947.

Statistics kept by Government departments have been published in the *Ministry of Labour Gazette* [QRL 11]; the *Ministry of Fuel and Power Statistical Digest* [QRL 13]; the *Annual Abstract of Statistics* [QRL 1]; and the Annual Reports of the Secretary of Mines Inspectorate [QRL 25]. Readers should refer to the issues of the period when investigating the statistics covered and their interpretation.

CHAPTER 3

NATIONALISATION

3.1. General Introduction

The *Coal Industry Nationalisation Act* 1946 [B 31] charged the NCB with getting coal, ensuring the efficient development of the country's coal resources and making coal available at such qualities, quantities and prices as might seem to them best calculated to further the public interest. The Act also set the Board the statutory duty of consulting with unions to establish agreements for conciliation machinery to settle terms and conditions of employment.

It was noted earlier that the NCB inherited a large number of pits. Many of these were old and out of date. They were subject to markedly different geological conditions which, due to the nature of the industry, can and do affect the performance of individual mines and individual areas. Thus the notion of average or national statistics ought to be treated with a considerable caution. Indeed, Sir Hubert Houldsworth, then Chairman of the National Coal Board, said in 1953:

"All generalisations about the coal industry or the miner are dangerous; most of them are simply untrue... in a sense there is no industry: there are statistically only 900 pits."

Geological conditions are not the only form of variation within the industry. Others include the nature of the coal produced, and the linked activities which the NCB have continued and developed from the former colliery owners, because they were directly in support of the industry's main product. These are examined in Section 3.3 and 3.3.3 below.

3.2. Coal Sources

Basically three broad distinctions may be made in relation to coal, and these refer to coal that comes from deep mines, from open-cast operations and manufactured fuels and coke. In addition to these there are other sources that provide smaller amounts of coal. For example some coal is recovered from such things as colliery tips, coal is mined in small private mines and some coal is imported. This section will concentrate on the three main sources.

3.2.1. Deep-Mined Coal

Most of the United Kingdom coal comes from deep mines, that is from mines in which a shaft or inclined drift is sunk from the surface. From the shaft or drift a number of radiating underground tunnels are constructed to mine the coal.

Bituminous coal and anthracite are the most important types of coal in terms of usefulness. Anthracite is a smokeless fuel and is important in the domestic market for this reason, mainly for use for direct or indirect heating purposes, that is, open fires or in central heating boilers. Bituminous coal tends to be used in power stations for steam raising purposes, in obtaining coal by-products or in the production of manufactured fuels and coke.

3.2.2. Open-Cast Coal

Open-cast coal mining is undertaken by stripping away top layers of soil and strata with earth moving equipment so as to expose shallow seams of coal. The open-cast sites are worked by contractors. These provide the same types of coal as deep mines.

3.2.3. Manufactured Fuels and Coke

Largely as a result of Clean Air Act of 1956 the NCB has developed a comprehensive range of manufactured fuels to supplement the smokeless fuels that existed before this time. These were anthracite and dry steam coal, which are naturally smokeless but are not available in large quantities, and coke. The latter is produced by heating coal to a high temperature in the absence of air. Since the middle nineteen fifties other manufactured fuels have been developed that may be used either in open fires and/or central heating appliances. These products include Homefire, Coalite, Rexco, Sunbrite and Phurnacite, but only some of these are manufactured by the NCB.

3.3. NCB Organisation

The NCB owns collieries, open-cast sites, houses and other property. It has also set up two holding companies concerned with the ancillary businesses organised around the NCB, which are described in a little more detail in Section 3.3.3, but more particularly in 8.2, 8.3 and 8.4.

3.3.1. Deep Mining

For deep mining there are three levels of management—the Board, Areas and Collieries. There are 12 Areas each headed by an Area Director who is directly accountable to the Board. At Area Headquarters, the main Headquarter Departments are represented. Each Area has its own Statistics Department directly responsible to the Area Director, but also having a functional responsibility to the Statistics Department at Hobart House, the headquarters of the National Coal Board.

The NCB Areas do not conform in coverage to more usually used definitions. For example, the Kent coalfield is now included in the NCB Area known as South Midlands. The Establishing Acts did not impose a particular structure on the NCB. It has chosen its Areas on the basis of convenient administrative regions to cover. These have changed from time to time as the distribution of coal production has changed.

3.3.2. *Open-Cast Mining*

The Open-cast Executive has three levels of management—Headquarters, Region and Site. Although it has some functional departments, the Executive is responsible to the NCB and uses some of the services provided by the NCB Headquarters and NCB Areas. The Executive is represented on the Board of the NCB.

3.3.3. *Ancillaries*

Whilst the major concern of the NCB is in the production of coal there are a number of ancillary businesses in which the NCB is involved. This involvement is largely organised through the Board's Coal Products Division and NCB (Ancillaries) Limited.

These are described in more detail in Sections 8.2, 8.3, and 8.4.

3.3.4. *Marketing*

The Board's organisation for sales is based on seven Sales Regions. Each Region is divided into Sales Districts.

Apart from responsibilities with regard to the marketing of coal, this department is also concerned with the collection of a tremendous volume of statistics with respect to sales. The collation of statistics is done both at Headquarters and at Regional level, but is not usually easily available to the outside researcher.

3.4. Deep-Mine Coal Production

When the industry was nationalised in 1947 the most common method of mining was to break coal in the seam with explosives, then load it on to conveyors with shovels. The need to modernise the industry was recognised by the Reid Committee [B 35]. Progress has been achieved with respect to haulage of coal, pit electrification but most of all with mechanisation at the coal face.

The modernisation of haulage systems has been a major engineering achievement. Before 1947 it was usual for ponies to haul coal and stores underground in tubs. Only 80 or so locomotives were used underground at that time for these purposes. This figure has now risen to over 1000. Locomotives are used to haul mine cars, and in many pits these are sometimes coupled with belt conveyors that carry coal and stores to the shaft bottom and elsewhere underground.

Electrification of lift winding systems was in hand before nationalisation, but progress increased after 1947 and many winding systems are now capable of being a fully automated operation.

The greatest change has been achieved at the coal face where almost all coal is now cut by power loading machines. These cut and load the coal on to conveyors in one operation. Moreover the traditional methods of supporting the roof with hand-set pit props and bars have been superseded by power-operated supports. These supports are self-advancing and operate hydraulically, either singly or in batches.

CHAPTER 4

STATISTICS IN THE MODERN COAL INDUSTRY

4.1. General

Since nationalisation nearly all information relating to the coal industry has been collected and collated by the NCB. Data have been collected and collated in standard form from the lower formations and operating units with the form, nature and frequency of information collection being primarily determined by operational considerations within the industry. Moreover, statistics published by other sources are, with the exception of coal consumption and distribution coal stocks, almost entirely collected and collated in the first place by the NCB.

In the NCB the collieries collect data that are then collated by the Area boards. As was mentioned in 3.3.1 the Statistics Departments have a functional relationship with the Statistics Department at Hobart House, but are also directly responsible to the Area Director.

There have been two earlier reviews of statistical sources for the coal mining industry. The first is by R. F. George and may be found in the books edited by M. G. Kendall that formed the original set of reviews which are now being up-dated [B 15]. The second may be found in *British Economic Statistics* by Carter and Roy [B 7]. Both of these were published in the nineteen fifties but the reader should refer to these, particularly for information in relation to data for the early years of nationalisation.

4.2. National Coal Board

There is a variety of sources of statistical data on the coal industry. Clearly one of the major sources is that which is published by the NCB itself. Most of this is collected by the Statistics Department either at Area level or by the Statistics Department at Headquarters. Additionally, data with respect to Sales come through the Marketing Department including its regional organisation.

Those interested in regional aspects of the coal mining industry would be well advised to get in touch with the NCB Areas Statistics Departments and appropriate Sales Regions.

The most important sources of primary data from these are given by the NCB *Annual Reports and Accounts* [QRL 3] and the NCB *Statistical Tables* [QRL 28].

Statistics for the coal industry in the UK up to 26th March 1978 were not metric and thus output figures were in terms of tons until this time.

The above NCB publications are on general release, but there are internal publications which are sometimes made available to the researcher, and a particularly useful summary to refer to in this respect was the Register of Routine Statistical Statements, produced by the Statistical Department at Hobart House. The July 1971 Register, for example, had as main headings: cross reference between basic returns received and statements issued, statistical return forms in current use, and such key figures as related to output and manpower production, marketing, safety, health and welfare, ancillaries and other miscellaneous data.

The Register described the content of the forms, the level for which they were kept (i.e. whether national, area, or some other geographical unit), the frequency with which they were collected and collated, and also their sources. This is obviously an important source of primary data. The Statistics Department also publishes periodically statistical studies that are produced as Information Papers.

In addition, other publications produced by the NCB provide some statistical data but are more usually valuable as providing general background to the data and/or comment relating to the data. Some of these publications are produced by the National Coal Board through its Public Relations Department. Of particular interest is *Books on Coal* [B 26] which is the National Coal Board's bibliography produced for the researcher, the student, and the general reader. Although this is kept up to date, it is more useful for material that relates to the past rather than to the present. The contents include reference to the history of the industry, the industry under private ownership, nationalisation and after, industrial relations, trade unions, geology, mining methods, careers, coal utilisation, literature, autobiographies, accidents, archives and energy. It also suggests where data may be found about the industry and refers to the *Annual Reports and Accounts* [QRL 3] and the *Digest of United Kingdom Energy Statistics* [QRL 13].

Many other papers are produced internally and those that are available through publication are listed by the NCB Library. The list is available on request and unless prices are given, publications are free from the appropriate department. The reader should get in touch directly with the Public Relations Department or the Library at Hobart House for further details of these publications.

A very important source of data is material that is lodged in folders publicly available in the NCB Library at Hobart House. These returns almost invariably come from the NCB Statistics Department, but are usually near to the form in which they are collected from the Areas. There is a substantial amount of data available in this form. It would be impossible to cover their full range and the reader is best advised to get in touch directly with the Library.

On a regular basis the NCB produces a number of publications in an attempt to ensure effective communication within the industry. *Management News* [B 46] gives a background briefing on policy topics. It also summarises press statements that have been handed out and refers to other publications and films when they have a relation to the coal industry. *Inbye* [B 43] reviews topics of interest and is directed towards the industry's management officials. *Coal News* [B 36] is a tabloid newspaper intended for everyone in the industry.

4.3. Government Sources

The Government Statistical Service publishes a booklet each year that gives a brief guide to Government sources [B 41]. This may be obtained, free of charge, from the Central Statistical Office. A more detailed description is given in *Guide to Official Statistics* [B 42] in which a section is devoted to sources of data on energy.

There are a number of Government publications that provide statistical data about coal and coal mining as well as other industries. General economic data may be found in *Trade and Industry* [QRL 32] which contains statistics and commentary from the Departments of Industry, Trade, and Prices and Consumer Protection. The *Department of Employment Gazette* [QRL 11] includes articles, tables and charts on manpower, employment, unemployment, hours worked, wage rates, earnings, labour costs, retail prices, stoppages and other miscellaneous data that relate to employment. The *New Earnings Survey* [QRL 21] refers to earnings from employment by industry, occupation, region, etc. at April of each year. Other publications that may be of interest are *Time Rates of Wages and Hours of Work* [QRL 31], *Changes in Rates of Wages and Hours of Work* [QRL 9], *British Labour Statistics Historical Abstract 1886–1968* [QRL 4] and *British Labour Statistics Yearbooks* [QRL 5].

There are a number of publications that devote sections specifically to coal and coal mining. One of the most important is the *Digest of United Kingdom Energy Statistics* [QRL 13], which contains tables and charts of United Kingdom energy production and consumption. The *Digest* also contains separate sections that deal with the production and consumption of individual fuels, fuel prices and foreign trade in fuels. The *Digest* publishes many of its tables on the basis of both financial and calendar years. The former is done because the *Digest* follows the example of the industry which is required by Statute to keep information on a financial year base. However, most national statistics are kept on the basis of calendar years and such tables as the *Digest* produces on this basis are useful when comparing with other countries.

Energy Trends [QRL 16] is also an important source of data and contains monthly and quarterly tables of production and consumption of fuels and aggregated energy consumption, together with some commentary on the figures. This is produced monthly and is free at least at the time of publication. It is particularly useful in that it produces short term statistics and very rapidly. It provides data on output, and manpower for the latest month, the year to date, and annually for the latest 6 years. The *Monthly Digest of Statistics* [QRL 18] provides a collection of the main series from all Government departments. For coal it has a supply and consumption balance sheet showing the tonnages produced, imported and exported, and consumed by the main sectors and the changes in coal stocks. Most of the information is on an annual financial year basis. A *Supplement of Definitions and Explanatory Notes* is published with the January issue of the *Monthly Digest*. The *Annual Abstract of Statistics* [QRL 1] contains many more series than the *Monthly Digest* and provides a longer run of years. The *United Kingdom Mineral Statistics* [QRL 33] has similar coverage to that of the *Annual Abstract* but covers a longer run of years. For example it provides data from 1873 on the annual total production of coal. An additional series is the annual tonnage of coal produced by deep mines and opencast working subdivided between bituminous and anthracite coal.

Regional statistics are provided in the *Scottish Economic Bulletin* [QRL 27], *Digest of Welsh Statistics* [QRL 14], and *Northern Ireland Digest of Statistics* [QRL 22]. Of more direct importance as far as coal is concerned is *Regional Statistics* [QRL 24] which contains area data on a financial year basis. In particular it provides data with regard to deep-mined coal, open-cast coal and coal consumption by main groups of industry. The *Scottish Abstract of Statistics* [QRL 26] contains detailed data on coal on an annual calendar year basis, data in balance sheet form giving sources of supply, consumption by sectors, employment and productivity in NCB mines in Scotland. Financial data covering capital expenditure, costs and revenue, and salaries and wages are also given. The *Digest of Welsh Statistics* provides detailed regional data on coal in Wales. Data are provided for some topics on a financial year basis and for others on calendar years.

Business Monitors [QRL 7] may also provide useful data. They are in three main series, but the Production Monitors are probably the most useful for coal. *Production Monitors* are produced Quarterly (PQ), Monthly (PM) and Annually (PA). The quarterly series provides data on sales usually in value terms, but sometimes quantity is also shown. PQ 101 provided data on total purchases, sales, stocks, work in progress, capital expenditure, employment, wages and salaries, PQ 101 included analysis of costs and output of establishments by size, of full and part-time employment by sex, net capital expenditure, and net output per region. Some of the data in PQ 101 refers to deep-mined coal only. Additionally, information for some aspects of open-cast operations may be found in PQ 500 which is primarily concerned with construction. The appropriate annual monitor for coal is PA 101, but PA 261 also provides some relevant data since it refers to Coke Ovens and Manufactured Fuel. The *Business Monitors* for coal, quarterly and annually, are based on statistical returns from the NCB.

Irregular, but official, sources are provided by various reports about the industry. Notable among these would be the reports of Select Committees, National Board for Prices and Incomes, the Price Commission and the Pay Board. In particular, the reader may wish to refer to the Select Committee Reports on the Coal Industry in 1969 [B 59], Cmnd 4455 of the National Board for Prices and Incomes [B 37], Report No. 12 of the price Commission [B 55], Cmnd 5567 of the Pay Board [B 60] and Cmnd 4903 of the Department of Employment, better known as the 'Wilberforce Report' [B 54]. Other references are also given in the Bibliography.

The Department of Energy also produces a number of papers and reports. The Department of Energy's *Energy Papers* are of general interest and *Energy Paper No. 11* is of particular interest to the coal industry [B 38]. The Department has also published the interim and final reports of the *Coal Industry Examination*, already referred to [B 30] [B 44].

4.4. Other Sources of Data

The Bibliography includes a list of books and articles which provide useful data on the local industry. One important additional source of information that can be described as neither a Government nor an NCB source is provided by the *Domestic Coal Consumer Council* [QRL 15]. This is a particularly important source of data to the general public or the consumer of coal.

4.5. International Statistics

International statistics are collected and published by a number of organisations. Since becoming a member of the European Economic Community, data published with respect to the Nine are of particular interest. Notable among these sources is *Eurostat Energy Statistics* [QRL 17]. These are published annually and monthly, but there may also be the 'occasional' paper. They are compiled by the Statistical Office of the European Communities and provide energy balance sheets for each member country. The *Bulletin of Energy Statistics for Europe* [QRL 6] provides similar information but on an annual basis only.

Other international bodies which collect data are the United Nations, OECD, the European Coal and Steel Community Commission Papers, and the most significant publications here are: *Statistics of Energy* [QRL 29] and *World Energy Supplies (United nations Series J)*, [QRL 34]. Occasional reports are also produced by CEPCEO which is the Association of Coal Producers of the European Community. Spain is sometimes added to the Community countries, in which case the association is known as the Association of Coal in Europe.

A fuller discussion of the development statistics within Europe is given in Section 9 of this Review.

4.6. The Statistical Calendar

Statistics are kept for either financial or calendar years. As far as coal is concerned, where statistics are kept for financial years this refers to the accounting year which is usually a period of 52 weeks ending on the last Saturday in March. NCB statistics are usually published on this basis since this is a legal requirement arising out of the NCB's Establishment Act.

Calendar year figures also relate to periods of 52 weeks. Figures collected on this basis are useful for international comparisons. There are occasions when there may be 53 weeks (as defined above) in the year, but the tables normally would make this explicit.

4.7. Geographical Coverage

Since little or no coal is produced in any form in Northern Ireland many of the statistical tables produced refer only to Great Britain. One major exception is in the case of coal sales and consumption where geographical coverage is extended to include Northern Ireland and thus is on a United Kingdom basis.

CHAPTER 5

STATISTICS ON OUTPUT

There are a large number of sources of data with regard to output figures. Some care has to be exercised in the interpretation of the figures, due to the different meanings that may be put to the headings included in the tables which would have to be referred to for detailed interpretation. Moreover descriptions and definitions change over time which provides further reason why the notes that accompany statistical tables should always be referred to. However, it would be advantageous to raise some general points that ought to be looked for by the user of the tables.

5.1. General Definitions

5.1.1. *Organisations*

It is necessary for example to distinguish what coverage is included in the tables, that is whether the output figures refer just to National Coal Board Collieries or Open-Cast operations or Licensed Mines or combinations of the three possible producers of coal. NCB collieries produce deep-mined coal as opposed to open-cast sites. Licensed Mines are small mines that are licensed by the NCB but operated by non-NCB employees. In effect they are run privately.

5.1.2. *Saleable Output*

The definitions of what constitutes saleable output of coal may differ from source to source. Again detailed interpretations will be explained usually with tables, but generally speaking the interpretation of saleable output is as defined by National Coal Board. For deep-mined coal this is taken to be the total coal sold, plus free coal or that disposed of at concessionary prices, plus an increase or less a decrease for colliery stocks of saleable coal. Slurry, which is coal and mineral matter recovered from washery effluent, is included if sold or when used in colliery boilers. Also, if coal is recovered from tips and sold, this will be included in output figures. Quantities of coal extracted in work on capital account are excluded from NCB definitions of saleable output but are included for licensed mines and other coal.

For open-cast mines, saleable output is defined as the amount of coal despatched from production sites after deducting screening losses, plus the increase or less the decrease in stocks of saleable coal at sites. Screening losses are incurred when the coal is washed and graded before despatching to customers.

Coal may be mined on a 'capital' or 'revenue' basis. The former arises when pits are being developed for future mining but that development, e.g. in retreat Longwall, involves the incidental production of coal. Revenue account is defined as coal produced after pit developments.

5.1.3. *Output per Manshift*

This is defined normally as the saleable output of coal from revenue account divided by the total number of manshifts worked on that account. Saleable output here does not include coal recovered from colliery tips but would include coal recovered from slurry.

This is regarded as being an important indicator of productivity and hence output per manshift for deep-mined coal is further sub-divided into four categories as below.

Manshifts are defined in (a), (b) and (c) as the normal attendance at a colliery of one man for one working day, which in most cases for underground is taken to be $7\frac{1}{4}$ hours plus one winding time or 8 hours on the surface inclusive of mealtimes.

The number of manshifts worked is measured in terms of the total time worked, that is it includes overtime. Weekend, overtime and part-time shifts worked are counted as a proportion on the length of the worker's normal shift and included in total manshifts worked. Periods or attendance at trainee centres are excluded.

(a) *Face output per manshift*

This is normally defined in the United Kingdom as the total output of saleable revenue coal divided by manshifts worked. The manshifts included in the denominator include those worked by shotfirers and gate-end supervisors working on coal faces up to but excluding the first point of exchange. This is usually defined as the delivery end of the face conveyor on the Longwall faces.

(b) *Output per manshift elsewhere underground*

This numerator is the same as (a) but the denominator will be manshifts worked underground minus those worked at the face.

(c) *Surface output per manshift*

Again the numerator is the same and the denominator becomes: manshifts worked on the surface.

(d) *Output per man year*

This is sometimes used as an indicator of the 'efficiency' of a colliery and is defined as the output of saleable coal from revenue working (as before) divided by the average number of wage earners in colliery books.

In general terms these definitions may be misleading as indicators of efficiency. For example, they do not reflect the amount of the labour productivity gains that may be accounted for by the substitution of capital for labour. This statement holds when these indicators are used by other industries. More specifically, in relation to coal the figures need to be interpreted within a framework set by geological conditions since productivity figures will be fundamentally affected by such things as the state of the seam (its depth, slope, and thickness) as well as the conditions of the roof.

When comparing productivity between pits or between countries, care must also be exercised when interpreting these indices. It is often argued that productivity gains may be achieved by closing down pits where output per man is lowest [B 20] and often it is true that these indices are used when pit closures are considered.

5.1.4. *Mechanised Output*

This is usually expressed as the ratio of saleable output from production faces with power loading machines to total saleable output from revenue working. It is generally accepted that power loading has increased productivity, but generally produces a smaller average size of coal since the coal is often smashed by these processes.

5.1.5. *Tonnage Lost, Disputes*

These figures relate to either holidays or output lost because of industrial disputes. They are clearly estimates of what may have happened if the collieries had been working. Under the heading of holidays would come annual holiday weeks, statutory holidays and the rest days during which the whole colliery is idle in a productive sense.

Disputes relate to stoppages involving all or part of the colliery and also restriction of output because of trade disputes.

5.2. NCB Statistical Tables [QRL 28]

There are a number of sources that give data relating to the above definitions as well as other output indicators. One of these sources is the National Coal Board *Statistical Tables* [QRL 28]. These notes refer to 1975/76 tables produced by the NCB.

5.2.1. *General Output*

As far as output is concerned there is information on output from NCB mines, open-cast mines and licensed and other mines. These figures have been collected from 1947 on an annual basis, but there have been two changes made in the table over this time. The first refers to the change made after 1962 when figures were kept for financial years after this date and not calendar years as had previously been the case. The second change is connected with the period 1962 to 1971/72 during which time figures for open-cast workings included output from licensed mines. Before 1962 and after 1972/73 open-cast figures and those of licensed and other mines were kept separately.

This source also gives data on many of the measures conventionally used, and defined above, including output per manshift on an overall basis as well as for 'face', 'elsewhere underground' and for the surface. These outputs are measured in cwt. Other data relate to the number of producing collieries at the end of the year, the total output from NCB mines, output per man year and mechanised output as a percentage of total output. There is also an estimate of the tonnage lost in the NCB mines due to disputes.

As far as major Longwall faces are concerned the *Tables* provide information on the number of producing faces, daily output per face and output per manshift. The data are based on a sample week's output in September and refer to advancing as well as retreating Longwall faces. The latter, sometimes known as 'retreat' mining, is where system roadways are first driven to the working boundary and faces are then worked backwards to the pit bottom.

It should be noted that it is only for 1972/73 and after that the definition of output given in the introduction is valid. Before then the definition had been changed twice, once in 1953 and once in 1957.

5.2.2. *Output by Areas*

The NCB *Statistical Tables* [QRL 28] also provide output data for each of the NCB areas but it should be noted that these 'areas' as defined by the NCB do not necessarily conform to the same geographical boundaries as one would find in non-NCB sources.

Data are provided for two years (current and previous) on the number of producing collieries at the end of March, their saleable output, an estimate of saleable output lost by disputes, and the overall output per manshift. Output figures from South Wales and Scotland are defined as including coal recovered from tips.

5.2.3. *Undistributed Stocks and Exports*

Other NCB tables from this source that may be useful in relation to output data are those concerned with undistributed stocks and exports. These are dealt with in more detail in the section on Sales and Consumption in this Review because it was felt that the tables were more relevant there.

5.3. NCB Annual Reports and Accounts

Naturally there is some duplication between the *Annual Reports and Accounts* [QRL 3] and the *Statistical Tables* [QRL 28] produced by the NCB. The *Annual Reports and Accounts* are a statutory requirement on the industry, whereas the *Statistical Tables* are published on a voluntary basis. The *Annual Reports and Accounts* tend to give a summary of the data without a great deal of detail. For example, the 1975/76 *Annual Report* gives figures for: deep mines saleable output; open-cast and other saleable output; overall output per manshift; face output per manshift and area outputs, but these figures are in the main given for only two years, viz. the current year and the immediately preceding one. Thus there may appear to be duplication, but in reality these are trivial. The two sources are meant for different audiences. The *Annual Reports and Accounts* are a direct consequence of statutory requirements imposed on the industry to publish results reflecting the activities of the NCB during the financial year. The *Statistical Tables* are produced voluntarily and provide additional data as well as data complementary to the *Annual Reports and Accounts*.

However, the *Annual Reports and Accounts* should be looked at for output figures because they sometimes contain figures not to be found in the *Statistical Tables*. For example, the 1974/75 *Annual Reports and Accounts* had a figure for daily output per face (tons) which was not found in the *Statistical Tables* that year.

Other data on the output provided by the *Annual Reports and Accounts* include NCB saleable output, change in stocks and value of production.

5.4. Digest of United Kingdom Energy Statistics [QRL 13]

This source of data, which will be referred to simply as the *Digest*, provides an important alternative to 5.2 and 5.3 above, and also provides data not otherwise covered by them. Generally speaking the *Digest* data are provided for the latest year and the 10 previous years. Some tables are both for financial and calendar years. The tables vary in geographical coverage and care has to be exercised with respect to this. Some of the tables refer to the United Kingdom, others refer to Great Britain. As far as coal production is concerned Northern Ireland's impact is insignificant. Thus the difference between UK and GB coal production is either negligible or nil. Notes in this Review refer to the 1976 *Digest*.

5.4.1. *General Output*

Data on the basis of calendar and financial years are provided for Great Britain for NCB mines and licensed mines. The *Digest* definitions are sometimes slightly different from those of the NCB. For example, total production for the NCB mines in the *Digest* includes coal produced on capital account. As far as output is concerned data are provided for production of deep-mined coal, open-cast coal, and other production, output per manshift and output per man years, calculated on an annual basis. In addition output per manshift, output per man year, and dispute tonnage lost figures are provided as well as estimates of tonnages lost due to holidays. Other data found in the *Digest* relate to coal production and distributed and undistributed stocks and capital output. Other deep-mined production figures are kept under the heading of licensed mines and other NCB output. Figures that relate to undistributed stocks refer to stocks held at collieries and also at open-cast sites and central stocking grounds.

Data may also be found in the *Digest* relating to the number of pits in operation at the end of the year, the revenue derived from output and the number of workers whose average output falls within certain class intervals—between twenty and seventy hundredweights approximately. Coverage is usually for financial years and the coverage is for NCB mines in Great Britain.

The *Digest* also publishes data relating to the production of coke, manufactured fuels and naturally smokeless fuels such as anthracite and dry steam coal. The smokeless manufactured fuels produced by the NCB include Phurnacite, Multiheat, Homefire and Roomheat. The *Digest* provides data for the production of these as well as the production of other manufactured fuels whether smokeless or not. As far as coke is concerned the *Digest* publishes information on the production in the NCB ovens, iron and steel industry ovens, and independent ovens.

5.4.2. *Output by Areas*

The *Digest* also provides data on the basis of areas, but these until 1977 did not conform to 'areas' as defined by the NCB. The areas covered in the *Digest* were generally smaller than the areas defined by the NCB. The *Digest* published in 1977 has abandoned this practice and the figures produced from then relate to the current NCB areas. Figures are for financial years for a number of years and include output of saleable coal, output per manshift overall and the percentage of output which is power loaded for NCB mines. The geographical coverage is for Great Britain. Unlike the other data in the *Digest* the output figures for areas do not include coal from capital account.

5.5. Energy Trends [QRL 16]

This source published information on deep-mined and open-cast site coal production on an unadjusted and seasonally adjusted basis. For deep-mined coal from NCB mines, *Energy Trends* provides an estimate of the tonnages lost due to recognised holidays and disputes. In addition it provides information on productivity and in particular the figures for output per manshift overall and at the face. These calculations are based on revenue working and exclude tip coal. Figures are provided on an annual basis for 6 years and a comparison is also made between this and last year's figures for the current month. *Energy Trends* also publish figures on the basis of 'rolling' quarters.

5.6. Monthly Digest of Statistics [QRL 18]

This source provides data on the annual and monthly figures (in weekly averages) for the supply of coal. As far as the annual figures are concerned the supply figures are given for total production which is sub-divided into deep-mined, open-cast and imported coal. These figures are provided for the last 6 years. Also provided in the annual figures is the average overall output per manshift worked in NCB mines both overall and at the face. These latter output figures do not include coal recovered from tips or coal worked on capital account.

The *Monthly Digest* publishes data also on distributed and undistributed stocks of coal. Distributed stocks exclude the tonnage of coal held in merchants' yards or in the industrial sector.

5.7. Business Monitors [QRL 7]

PQ 101 provides quarterly statistics on coal mining in Great Britain including productivity at NCB mines, coal supply, and undistributed stocks of coal. The coverage of the quarterly monitor is for Great Britain.

PA 101 in 1971/72 has reported on the Census of Production for Coal Mining. The results therein were based on the 1968 Census of Production. These quinquennial censuses have now been superseded by a system of quarterly and annual statistics. These are reported in the Monitors and have included figures of output with analysis of net output from NCB undertakings for the three years 1970, 1971 and 1972.

More generally, the monitors publish some analyses of the annual census of production taken since 1968.

5.8. United Kingdom Mineral Statistics [QRL 33]

This source published annual total production figures for coal since 1873 and deep-mined coal production since 1942. Anthracite and bituminous deep-mined coal have been published since 1955.

5.9. Regional Data

Sections 5.2.2 and 5.4.2 note that the NCB [QRL 28] and the *Digest* [QRL 13] provided data on production on a regional basis. The *Annual Abstract of Statistics* [QRL 1] publishes information for each NCB region, of the tonnages of coal produced by NCB mines and output per manshift (expressed in cwt). Figures are provided for 11 years on a financial basis. The production information for geographical regions may also be obtained from *Regional Statistics* [QRL 24], the *Scottish Abstract of Statistics* [QRL 26], and the *Digest of Welsh Statistics* [QRL 14]. As was noted in Section 4.3 *Regional Statistics* published data for deep-mined coal on output of saleable coal and output per manshift in each NCB area and in total. The series covers 8 financial years. For open-cast coal *Regional Statistics* publishes information on tonnages produced in each standard region and country in the United Kingdom annually for three years. The *Scottish Abstract of Statistics* contains data on coal production in Scotland as does the *Digest of Welsh Statistics* for Wales. *Annual Abstract* also publishes the tonnage of coal produced by the whole industry.

5.10. Eurostat [QRL 17]

There are a number of tables that are produced by *Eurostat* that may be used as a source for the UK coal industry.

Fairly obviously the sources noted above will provide detailed figures about the National Coal Board and its activities either in the United Kingdom or in Great Britain. But the NCB has taken a leading part in developing definitions that are acceptable in Europe and are regarded as the best that can be done with definitions. For the purposes of comparison with other coal industries in EEC, *Eurostat* is an important source of data.

As far as output is concerned monthly output figures are published relating to the countries of the European 9, European 6 (that is the original Common Market countries) and separately for West Germany, France, the Netherlands, Belgium, Ireland and the United Kingdom.

Eurostat also provides data on coal output by NCB areas, licensed and open-cast mines and United Kingdom coal balance sheet, which duplicates much of the information provided in other sources, but also includes imports, such as imports from European 6, from new member countries and third party countries. Some of the definitions used with respect to output per manshift are different from those usually used by the United Kingdom sources. There are also difficulties associated with coal and energy balance sheets because of the different interpretations made with respect to coal equivalents. This is discussed more fully in Section 9 but it should be noted that there can be a significant difference in the UK figures as published in this source compared with UK sources.

CHAPTER 6

COAL SALES AND CONSUMPTION

6.1. General

Unlike most of the other statistics about coal, the collection and collation of statistics on coal consumption by consumers is done mainly by the Department of Energy. This is because the figures relate not to the activities of the coal industry but to the use made of fuel by consumers. It is also important to distinguish that coal is 'consumed' in two major ways, that is, as coal in final use, and also as an intermediary product to produce another fuel, for example electricity. Because of this there tends to be some duplication of data between statistical sources that deal with 'energy' and 'coal' with respect to coal consumption.

This section will concentrate on the coal as a product in its own right. Even then coal sales and consumption figures are generally categorised in a number of ways. For the inland figures the classification includes: power stations, coke ovens, industry (often sub-divided into iron and steel and other industries), domestic and other inland markets. There is also a category for exports, although the amount exported is small in relation to the total inland sales.

Most often these figures are expressed in physical units. Figures for the main classes of consumers relate to Great Britain and Northern Ireland and also tend to include imported coal as part of their totals since imports are an element that are included in consumption in the coal balances. The exact definition of the consumption figures will obviously vary from source to source, but there is sufficient common ground between them to justify a discussion of the main headings that fall within the category of sales and consumption.

Usually the sources use the term 'disposals' rather than sales or consumption. Disposals are normally defined as that quantity of coal sold commercially or consumed by collieries or supplied to ancillary works or disposed of free or at concessionary prices. The term 'Disposals' is used because of the lack of other source data since 1973 when the Department of Energy ceased to collect data with respect to purchases directly from coal consumers and coal merchants. Thus strictly speaking coal 'sales' are not sales to final consumers.

6.1.1. *Public Power Stations*

Power stations use more than half of the coal produced by the NCB. Often coal goes from collieries to power stations by permanently coupled merry-go-round trains. In most of the sources the consumption figures relate to all coal used—irrespective of purpose—at power stations of the Electricity Supply Industry and public transport undertakings although little or no coal is now used for this latter purpose.

6.1.2. *Coke Ovens*

Coke is an essential ingredient for making pig iron. The 1972 *Report on the Census of Production* [QRL 8] gives a great deal of information on coke ovens and manufactured fuel. Included in this are input/output tables for 1970, 1971 and 1972 as well as analysis of capital expenditure and stocks.

The *Digest of United Kingdom Energy Statistics* [QRL 13] provides the main source of data on coke. Data are provided on the consumption of coke in blast furnaces, iron foundries, by disposals to merchants, railways and other public services. This reflects the use of coke in direct final consumption but there are figures provided for the tonnage of coke used by the fuel conversion industries.

For coke breeze there are normally consumption figures available for consumption at iron and steel plants. A distinction is drawn in the *Digest* between hard coke breeze and gas coke breeze and there are consumption figures for both categories.

The *Annual Abstract of Statistics* [QRL 1] publishes coke data in balance sheet form of annual tonnage covering production and total supply, consumption (analysed by main classes of use), shipments and stock changes.

The NCB *Statistical Tables* [QRL 28] also provide information on coke. The *Monthly Digest of Statistics* [QRL 18] no longer provides current data but past editions would provide information.

6.1.3. *Industry*

Apart from the figures in the *Annual Reports and Accounts* [QRL 3], the tables giving coal consumption for the industry sector are normally sub-divided into smaller industry units. 'Large' industrial users are those that consume 1000 tons of coal a year. 'Other' industrials include small industrial, commercial and non-industrial establishments. A distinction is drawn between those industries that may be described as fuel conversion industries and industries that use coal as a form of direct and final fuel consumption. For the latter the figures are usually expressed in terms of millions of tons, whilst the former may be in these terms or on a heat supplied basis and expressed in millions of therms. The choice of base tends to depend on whether coal statistics appear in their own right or whether they appear as part of energy measurement. This distinction is, for example, clearly taken in the *Digest of United Kingdom Energy Statistics* [QRL 13] where coal data appear twice— once in their own right and once in the All Energy section.

6.1.4. *Domestic*

The normal definition used by the NCB for this is that it includes house coal, anthracite and dry steam coal for sale to domestic consumers, shops, offices, hotels and other premises. That is, in effect it includes any household coal going through coal merchants. It also includes coal supplied free of charge or at reduced prices to miners and NCB officials who are allowed to have coal at discretionary prices. Usually these figures are calculated from colliery disposals although this ought to be checked carefully especially when using data for past years.

In the *Digest* [QRL 13] and *Energy Trends* [QRL 16], for example, it is only since April 1973 that domestic consumption figures have been calculated on the basis of disposals from collieries and open-cast sites. Before then it should be noted that the definitions related to coal sold by merchants and also included in this category was coal sold to smaller industrial consumers. The *Monthly Digest of Statistics* [QRL 18] definition of domestic sales and consumption is similar to that used in the *Digest*.

The *Coal Utilization Council* [QRL 15] provides information with respect to domestic sales and consumption of coal. Its publications are not regular in the sense that the Council tends to produce 'one-off' surveys.

6.1.5. *Other Inland Markets*

This is usually a residual item in the sense that it tends to include the items not covered under the other headings noted above.

6.1.6. *Stocks*

Undistributed stocks of coal are held at collieries, open-cast sites and licensed mines. They may be held on the ground or in wagons but are deemed to be stocks before disposal to consumers and ancillary operations of the Board.

6.1.7. *Imports and Exports*

Figures that refer to exports or imports of coal are either actual shipments notified by the NCB, or correspond to figures given in the tables of *Overseas Trade Statistics of the United Kingdom* [QRL 23]. The latter set of figures are based on notifications to HM Customs and there may be a time lag between shipment and notification.

6.2. NCB Statistical Tables [QRL 28]

6.2.1. *General Consumption*

Data in relation to many of the general headings discussed above are covered in this source. There are data on imports and exports (the latter both to European Economic Community Countries and total exports), as well as giving total consumption figures. There are data on coal disposals by grades of coal, markets and undistributed stocks by grades. The categories are large, unscreened, graded smalls, slurry and anthracite. Large coal refers to coals that have a lower limit of size greater than $1\frac{1}{2}$ to 2 inches round hole and includes large cobbles, cobbles, trebles and large nuts. Unscreened coal contains all size components from small to large. Graded coals are those from which the screen aperture at the washery lies between 3/16 and 2½ inches round hole. They include 'doubles', 'nuts', 'singles', 'beans', and 'grains'. Small coal has no lower limit in size but has a maximum upper limit of 2 inches. Slurry and anthracite have been defined previously in 5.1.2.

The market includes fuel convertors into other forms of energy such as gas, electricity, coke ovens and manufactured fuel plants, as well as large and small industrial users. With the advent of natural gas, coal conversion to gas is now very small. The consumer group category also includes headings relating to bituminous house coal, naturally smokeless coal, as well as other inland and export figures. Some of the tables in this source provide detailed data only for the current year but comparison between the current year and the preceding year is for the total for all grades. Coal export figures are given in this source with a breakdown for EEC countries, separately for Norway, Portugal and Sweden and for 'other' countries. The units are thousands of tons and there is a comparison between the current year and its immediate predecessor.

6.3. NCB Annual Reports and Accounts [QRL 3]

The *Annual Reports and Accounts* provide a breakdown of coal sales and consumption. The breakdown refers to power stations, coke ovens, industry, domestic and other inland markets as well as exports. Information is also provided on the income derived from the sale of coal. No allowance is made for free or concessionary coal, nor is any allowance made for the value of coal consumed at collieries. Data are also given on sales income from other products handled by either NCB or its subsidiaries. Included here are coke, gas benzole, crude tar and tar products; processed fuel, miscellaneous products and services such as wagon repairs.

6.4. Digest of United Kingdom Energy Statistics [QRL 13]

The *Digest* provides an analysis of consumption for the current year and the 9 previous years. As is usually the case with the *Digest* quite a lot of data are provided on the basis of both financial and calendar years.

As was noted in Section 6.1.3 data on coal consumption are published in two versions, namely in natural units and in therms, that is on a heat supplied basis. This reflects the dual use of coal, namely as a product in its own right and as an input to produce other forms of energy. When the latter view is taken coal data appear in two places in the *Digest*. In the Energy section of the *Digest* the figures are expressed on a heat supplied basis. In the Coal section of the *Digest* data on coal in relation to fuel conversion industries are expressed in millions of tons.

This section will concentrate on the information available in the Coal section, although of course the reader is advised to refer to the Energy section of the *Digest* when needing data in relation to fuel conversion. In relation to this the Energy section of the *Digest* includes all coal whether NCB recovered or not as well as arrivals, shipments and stock changes of coke, breeze and other solid fuel.

6.4.1. *General Consumption*

Consumption data are published in two ways that refer to sectors and industries for nine industry groups.

The *Digest* gives a much more detailed breakdown of some figures than do the NCB *Statistical Tables* [QRL 28]. In the *Digest*, for example, the information on power stations is split into three sub-sections giving coal consumption by the Central Electricity Generating Board, Scottish Electricity Boards and others. Also included is coal consumption by fuel conversion industries such as gas works, coke ovens, low temperature carbonisation plants and fuel plants. The definitions used are those conventionally used, most of which have already been given.

There is also information with respect to coal consumption used as direct final consumption. This includes figures relating to agriculture, industry, railways, water transport, domestic, public services and other miscellaneous uses. Agriculture as defined in the *Digest* excludes horticulture which is included under other industries. The figures for agriculture are largely estimated ones, and do not always appear as a separate section but are sometimes included under miscellaneous. Industry includes the iron and steel industry and other industry. As far as the iron and steel industry is concerned the definition is related to the coal used for all purposes—other than coke ovens—in iron and steel works or iron foundries having an annual output of 1000 tons or more of iron casting. Because of the emphasis on iron casting rather than steel making the figures under the headings of iron and steel can sometimes include some engineering establishments or parts thereof.

For water transport the figures relate to colliery and open-cast disposals to coastwise bunkers, and estimates of consumption by dock and harbour undertakings and by inland waterways. Included under public services are colliery disposals to National and Local Authorities. Miscellaneous coal figures relate to colliery and open-cast disposals to commercial and non-commercial establishments that are not contained in any of the other categories mentioned such as shipments to the Channel Islands and distribution losses.

Section 6.1.2 made the point that the *Digest* was one of the most important sources of data with respect to the consumption of coke. This is true also of other smokeless fuels either of the manufactured kind or of naturally smokeless products such as anthracite or dry steam coal. Details of the consumption of these by fuel conversion industries and in direct final consumption are given in the *Digest*. Information is also provided on the net shipments of these fuels in or out of the United Kingdom.

6.4.2. *Consumption by Countries*

Broadly the same categories of separate figures are used for consumption in England, Wales, Scotland and Northern Ireland. This breakdown is for two years only, that is the current year and its immediate predecessor.

6.4.3. *Imports and Exports of Coal*

The *Digest* also contains a separate section on the foreign trade coal balance of the United Kingdom, providing both import and export figures. Statistics on imports are shown on the basis of EEC countries and separately for other important supplying countries. Figures are provided for the latest calendar year and the 4 previous ones. Tonnage figures are given but additionally the total value of coal imports and the average value per ton are also given.

Export figures are usually provided for the latest year and the previous 4 years. Information is given on exports from members of the EEC, members of the European Free Trade Association (EFTA) and for each recipient country. As for imports, the figures are expressed in thousands of tons, and the value of exports in total and the average value per ton are also given.

The *Digest* figures for exports are based on notifications to HM Customs during the period and differ from those for actual arrivals and shipments as reported in other sections of the *Digest*. Thus these figures differ from those provided by the NCB *Statistical Tables* [QRL 28] which refer to actual shipments made during the year. The *Digest* figures correspond to figures that may be found in the *Overseas Trade Statistics of the UK* [QRL 23].

6.5. Energy Trends [QRL 16]

Energy Trends provides data on the consumption of coal and duplicates most of the headings found in the *Digest*. One difference is that this source shows clearly that 'industry', 'house coal' and 'anthracite and dry steam' coal are now calculated on the basis of colliery disposals, since this is incorporated into the headings.

Annual figures for the current year and the 5 previous years are shown and also the percentage changes in consumption for the year, current month in the current year, and 'months so far' in the current year. Figures are also provided on a 'rolling' quarters basis.

6.6. Monthly Digest of Statistics [QRL 18]

6.6.1. *General Consumption*

As far as consumption is concerned the *Monthly Digest of Statistics* generally speaking provides data on a less than annual basis, mostly on a monthly basis, but sometimes on a quarterly basis. Figures given monthly cover the latest 2–3 years and annually, the latest 4–6 years. Direct comparisons may be drawn between the year. The *Digest* figures correspond to figures that may be found in the *Overseas* provide the researcher with as much of a detailed breakdown of the headings as does the *Digest*. The definitions used in the *Monthly Digest* are broadly the same as those used in the *Digest* as far as consumption is concerned. Thus, for example, industry in the *Monthly Digest* includes agriculture, iron and steel, and other industry, as do most of the relevant tables in the *Digest*, but the *Monthly Digest* tends not to separate them out. Similar remarks may be made with respect to transport in the *Monthly Digest* which is defined as coal used for all purposes by railways, dock and harbour undertakings, and inland waterways for coastal bunkers. It is therefore the same as 'railways' plus 'water transport' in the *Digest*.

Like the *Digest of UK Energy Statistics*, the *Monthly Digest* provides information on coal as part of energy and coal as coal. With regard to the former, *Monthly Digest* provides information on energy consumption on a primary fuel basis and the basis of final use.

As mentioned earlier the coal consumption section will concentrate on information that treats coal as a product in its own right.

6.6.2. *Coal Consumption by Market*

In this respect this source provides data on the consumption of coal for the main categories of market for inland consumption as well as overseas shipments and miscellaneous. The data are provided on the basis of weekly averages but published on a monthly basis with summaries provided for six years. March, June, September and December are always taken as 5 weeks. The units are thousands of tons. The definitions are the ones conventionally used, but coal used at power stations includes coal used in other public transport stations in addition to coal used to generate electricity for supplying the public. The table provides data on consumption by fuel producers and final users. The latter category is based on colliery disposals to industry, the domestic sector and other sectors such as miners' coal.

The *Monthly Digest* also publishes data on imports and exports of coal as recorded in the *Overseas Trade Statistics of the United Kingdom* [QRL 23].

6.7. United Kingdom Mineral Statistics [QRL 33]

This source since 1950 has published data relating to imports, exports, changes in stocks, and consumption.

CHAPTER 7

MANPOWER

The coal mining industry is a big industry and is labour intensive. Discussions on the changes within the industry are conducted with unions and take place with Joint Advisory Committee through the Colliery Review Procedure and Consultative Committee.

As far as statistics are concerned, the pattern of previous sections will be repeated. Thus we will discuss general interpretations of headings before going on to discuss sources of statistics in detail. Hence definitions will only be discussed in relation to the tables if and when they differ from those we now give. These are based on NCB definitions.

Readers should also refer to the Dean review on Wages and Earnings in this series [B 8] for explanations of specific points in relation to manpower topics.

7.1. General Definitions

7.1.1. *Wage-Earners on Colliery Books*

This is defined as the number of workers in industrial grades employed at collieries and activities connected with the getting, raising, handling, preparation and transport of coal up to the point of despatch to consumers outside the colliery. These activities include coal preparation plants, colliery generating plants and land sale depots, but exclude central workshops and central power stations.

Industrial grade workers include colliery officials up to the rank of overman, but exclude undermanagers, other administrative staff and clerical workers.

Men absent without good reason are normally excluded from the figures after three consecutive weeks of absence. Men who are absent with reason are retained on the colliery books for up to fifteen months.

7.1.2. *Recruitment*

This is defined as the number of men who signed on at collieries during the period, but men known to have transferred from another colliery, without a break in their service, are excluded.

Direct transfers from other Areas are included in Area recruitment as re-entrants, but are excluded from national totals.

7.1.3. *Wastage*

This is defined as the number of men struck off colliery books during the period, less the number of men excluded from recruitment as transfers from other collieries, that is transfers within Areas and, for Great Britain only, also transfers between Areas.

There is sometimes a distinction drawn in the sources between 'voluntary' and 'involuntary' wastage, but these ought to be treated with some caution because it is felt that some men left the industry 'voluntarily' between 1957 and 1972 because of impending closures and redundancies.

7.1.4. *Absence*

Absenteeism is recognised within the industry as a difficult, complex, and so far intractable problem. There have been many investigations, employing statistical analysis, pit by pit surveys, and the use of outside research and consultants, and for more detail of some of these, readers could refer to Liddell [B 17] and Moos [B 18]. There has also been a special sub-committee of the National Consultative Council looking into it.

There are many indicators used in an attempt to measure the nature and size of the problem. Absence percentage is one of the indicators. This is defined as the ratio of absence (both authorised and unauthorised) to the number of men on the books, multiplied by the number of days in the period, but excluding Saturday and Sunday. Authorised absence mainly arises because of sickness or injury, but also includes men who wish to absent themselves for personal reasons and have obtained authorisation to do so. Examples of personal reasons would be death of a near relative, jury service and so on.

7.1.5. *Average Daily Manshifts*

This is defined as the manshifts worked (see definition in output Section 5.1.3) by wage earners on the colliery books divided by the average number of colliery days worked during the fiscal year. Colliery days worked are all days within the five day week, excluding colliery holidays, rest days, and days lost from total stoppages.

7.1.6. *Earnings*

There has been a gradual change from piecework to daywork rates which has implications for the analysis of average earnings.

The figures for earnings represent average cash earnings, for a given period, for wage earners on colliery books. Cash earnings include wages paid (including overtime), payment for sickness etc., five day week bonus payments, guaranteed wage, and provisions for holidays with pay.

Allowances in kind represent the value to workmen of free and concessionary coal (whether taken as coal or cash in lieu) plus house or rent allowance. Travel allowances are not included.

7.1.7. *Earnings per Manshift*

These are defined as total cash earnings or value allowances in kind, divided by the number of manshifts actually worked, including overtime and weekend shifts.

7.1.8. *Average Weekly Earnings*

This is defined as the total cash earnings or allowances in kind divided by the average number of wage earners who have worked in each week (excluding holiday weeks). Thus men who work no shift, and therefore earn no wage in a week, are excluded from this calculation.

7.2. NCB Statistical Tables [QRL 28]

7.2.1. *General Manpower*

This source provides data on the average manpower, recruitment, wastage and net change for the years 1947 to the present. We have already noted that until 1962 the figures were kept on a calendar basis, but since then they have been kept for financial years.

Also to be found are data on absence figures for this period and average weekly earnings for each of the years from 1947 to the present. This figure is sub-divided into cash earnings and the value of allowances in kind.

7.2.2. *Manpower by Areas*

Manpower data by area, according to NCB latest definitions, is also shown in this source for two years only. The table shows the number of wage earners on colliery books at the end of March, the total recruitment during the year, the total wastage during the year, and the percentage absence during the year.

7.2.3. *Age Distribution*

Age distributions for men on colliery books are constructed for the December of the year under consideration and the same month for the previous year. For the current December the distributions are drawn up for underground and surface workers as well as for the total manpower on colliery books. Percentages are also shown for each class interval. For the previous December, the figures are shown for total manpower and percentage in each class interval.

The class intervals for the age distribution are open-ended with under 16, and 65 and over, being the lower and upper class intervals. The class interval is two years up to the age of 20, and five years thereafter.

Each year a census is taken so as to calculate the average age of the men on colliery books at the time when the census was taken. The results of this are in the *NCB Statistical Tables* [QRL 28].

7.2.4. Recruitment and Wastage

The *Tables* [QRL 28] also show total figures given for financial years for the current and last year, for recruitment and wastage.

Recruitment figures are broken down into two categories, namely re-enrolments and newly employed. This latter category is sub-divided into boys under 18, and also youths and adults. The wastage category is further sub-divided into wastage from deaths, retirements, retirements due to medical reasons, and dismissals and redundancies.

7.2.5. Manshifts by Place of Work

The place of work of colliery employees for the latest and previous year is also given in the *Tables* [QRL 28]. The figures are calculated as overall daily averages.

As with output calculations, place of work is broadly defined as, at the face, elsewhere underground, and surface. The 'elsewhere underground' category included officials, transport workers, roadway development and repair workers, engineering services and workers employed elsewhere underground. The figures for surface workers are categorised under officials, winding and banking workers, coal preparation, maintenance and other surface workers. The figures relating to face workers are sub-divided between those at mechanised production faces and those who are at other faces.

7.2.6. Total Numbers

The total number of people employed by the NCB at the end of September for the current and previous year are given in the *Tables* [QRL 28]. The classification of activities is into non-industrial staff and industrial workers. The latter is further sub-divided into those connected with mining activities, direct labour at open-cast sites and ancillary workers. Mining activities includes those employed at collieries, those associated with collieries, central workshops and other services.

7.2.7. Earnings

There are also tables that show average earnings by Areas per manshift. One has Great Britain as its geographical base and the definitions of Areas are those used by the NCB. It shows average area earnings for the current and previous year for all workers, face, underground and surface workers. These average earnings exclude any value for allowances in kind, although the table shows these figures separately for 'all workers' category. There is a similar table to the one just described but the figures relate to average weekly earnings.

7.3. NCB Annual Reports and Accounts [QRL 3]

As we have said before, there is naturally a great deal of duplication between the *Annual Reports and Accounts* of the NCB and their *Statistical Tables* [QRL 28]. In relation to manpower data this statement is again generally true.

However, the *Annual Reports* provide interpretation of the general data available and also discuss the matters pertaining to industrial relations within the industry. Information is also given of beneficiaries of the Redundant Mineworkers Payment Scheme of which there is more detail in Section 7.8.1. This type of data is not always available in the *Statistical Tables*.

Other interesting statistics that appear in the *Annual Reports and Accounts* but not the *Tables* include the results of periodical X-ray for pneumoconiosis and fibrosis. Also the *Annual Report* contains analysis of the causes of disputes within the industry.

7.4. Digest of United Kingdom Energy Statistics [QRL 13]

7.4.1. *Manpower General*

Some of the data that this source provides are the number of wage earners on colliery books at the beginning and end of the year, the changes during the year, as well as wastage and recruitment during the year. It also gives information in relation to the average number of wage earners in each of the calendar years. The *Digest* provides data on average number of wage earners on colliery books, manshifts worked, the percentage of productive labour to total labour, average number of shifts per week per earner, and absence percentage broken down into the categories of voluntary and involuntary absentees. The definition of absence percentage is exactly the same as that used in the NCB *Statistical Tables* [QRL 28]. Manshifts for the purposes of definition does not usually include training and other non-operational manshifts.

7.4.2. *Manpower Employed*

Data are also provided on numbers of people employed in coal production. The table shows employees engaged in production at the end of the year at open-cast mines, and the total for this and for NCB mines and licensed mines all taken together. For the last two categories the table shows the number of wage earners on colliery books, as defined above. The figures are shown for calendar years and financial years.

Finally the table gives information on the total number of NCB employees in the coal mining industry at the end of each September up to 1972. Thereafter the figures relate to year averages. It also provides figures relating to the number of NCB mines still working at the end of the year, which is given for both the financial and calendar years. Also shown (but tucked away in a footnote) is the number of licensed mines still in operation, which is a piece of information difficult to find in any other source.

7.4.3. *Recruitment and Wastage*

Data on recruitment and wastage for NCB mines in Great Britain are provided for financial and calendar years. The recruitment figures are conventionally sub-divided into juveniles, newly employed, adult new entrants and finally re-entrants.

Wastage figures are given for the categories of death, retirement because of age, compensation and long-term sickness cases removed from colliery books, redundancies, dismissals and other wastage.

There are two other headings for which data are kept for the eleven years shown. These relate to the net intake or outflow into/out of the industry and transfers from other collieries.

The definition of what constitutes 'recruitment' and 'wastage' are slightly different from those used by the NCB. For example, direct transfers from other Areas are included in the NCB definition of recruitment for Areas. This does not apply in the *Digest* [QRL 13]. That is, the definition of recruitment is the one used by the NCB for the compilation of their national totals. The explanation for this would seem to be because the *Digest* only shows these figures on a national basis. This also would explain why the definition of wastage differs slightly from that used by the NCB. The *Digest* definition does not include transfers within Areas and transfers between Areas.

7.4.4. *Area Data*

Average numbers of wage earners on colliery books are given by Areas in the *Digest*. With the exception of South Wales the areas shown were introduced by the NCB on the 26th March, 1967 on the basis of collieries in operation at the time. For the purpose of this classification, collieries which were in production in earlier years, but had closed before this Area organisation was introduced, have been allocated to the Areas appropriate for their situation. East and West Wales, however, were combined to form the South Wales Area in 1973 and subsequently this was reflected in the tables.

7.5. Monthly Digest of Statistics [QRL 18]

The *Monthly Digest* publishes data on wage earners on colliery books, recruitment and wastage and absence percentage. As is usual in the *Monthly Digest* the data are for weekly averages. Absence percentage is subdivided into the categories of voluntary and involuntary.

7.6. Department of Employment Gazette [QRL 11]

This source gives statistics relating to redundancy on a quarterly basis, and occasionally gives the number of redundancies in mining and quarrying.

Statistics on average weekly earnings, average hours worked and average hourly earnings are published in the February *Gazette*. Three half yearly periods are given, and one yearly period.

The information on coal is provided by the NCB and refers to a particular pay week in October of each year. Two sets of figures are recorded, the average weekly earnings and the value of allowances in kind. The figures for average weekly earnings include sickness pay and the value of provisions for holidays with pay and rest days. The NCB figures are on a different basis to other inquiries published in the *Gazette*. Readers requiring fuller details should refer to the Dean review on Wages and Earnings in this series [B 8].

7.7. British Labour Statistics Yearbooks [QRL 5]

These provide data similar to the *Gazette* [QRL 11] for coal mining but give a run of ten years' figures.

7.8. The NUM National Executive Committee Reports [QRL 19]

7.8.1. *Redundant Mineworkers (Payment Scheme)*

In 1968 the *Redundant Mineworkers (Payment Scheme)*, often referred to as RMPS, was introduced whereby redundant mineworkers having to leave the industry at or over the age of 55 would have their income supplemented for a period so that they could adjust themselves in their new circumstances.

The *NUM National Executive Committee Reports* after this began to collect data in relation to the above scheme. Included are the total number of beneficiaries, broken down by age and whether employed or not, and the amount paid in benefit for each year. For some years information is available on the number of beneficiaries leaving the scheme and the cause—such as retirement, exhaustion of benefit, death, return to industry.

7.8.2. *Lump Sum Payments*

Under the Coal Industry Act 1973, some mineworkers were allowed to be paid a lump sum when they had to leave the industry due to redundancy. The NUM National Executive have information on the number of lump sums paid.

7.9. Business Monitors [QRL 7]

Business Monitor PA 101 has analysed the distribution of employment within the NCB. PA 261 has carried out a similar analysis for coke ovens and manufactured fuel.

CHAPTER 8

FINANCIAL STATISTICS

8.1. General

There is a wealth of information available on financial and economic statistics. The main published source of these is the *Annual Reports and Accounts* of the National Coal Board [QRL 3], which are produced to conform with the requirements of the Secretary of State for Energy and best commercial accounting practices.

The guidelines for the NCB were broadly given in the *Coal Industry Nationalisation Act* 1946 [B 31]. This imposed statutory duties with respect to finance and in particular required that the Board should at least break even on revenue account when averaged over a number of years.

These broad guidelines have been modified either by legislation general to all nationalised industries, or legislation specific to the coal industry. In 1961 a White Paper [B 40] was published that imposed financial targets on nationalised industries in general. These were different for different industries, but the specific target set on the coal industry was to break even over five years. The financial target was no longer an open ended commitment, but had to be met over a definite time period.

In 1967 a further White Paper [B 56] reviewed the 1961 White Paper referred to above. The general implication of the 1961 White Paper had been that financial targets had to be met and the industries had to do whatever they thought appropriate in terms of pricing and investment to meet these targets. The 1967 White Paper, however, changed this emphasis. In effect the 1967 Paper put greater weight on the industries achieving a 'correct' pricing and investment policy. The suggested correct pricing policy was that prices ought to reflect the true costs of producing the product. Similarly, in terms of investment, cash flow techniques were to be applied to each investment project. Unlike the financial targets set in the 1961 White Paper, the test rate of discount for investment appraisal was to be the same for each nationalised industry. Although some financial targets were modified in the 1967 White Paper, they were not changed in terms of amount, but much less weight was attached to them *per se*, and much more to pricing and investment policy.

There has also been legislation specific to the NCB with respect to financial matters. These have related mainly to capital reconstructions within the industry and to government aid for specific purposes, for example, the social costs of contraction of the industry and contributions towards the deficiency of the mineworkers' pension scheme. Since the formulation of the 1974 *Plan for Coal* [B 48], the industry has set itself the objective of long term competitiveness while covering costs of production and contributing towards financing the new investment programme. The Government, in recognising the substantial time lag before new investment produces revenue, is ready to consider special problems of financing that may arise.

In the *Annual Reports and Accounts* [QRL 3] the results are sub-divided into three sections. The first refers to the NCB and all its subsidiaries. The second set refers to NCB (Coal Products) Limited and its subsidiaries, and the last refers to NCB (Ancillaries) Limited and its subsidiaries.

8.2. NCB (Coal Products) Ltd

NCB (Coal Products) Limited and subsidiaries commenced trading on 1st April 1973 and was made up of a number of individual companies that included National Smokeless Fuels Limited, Thomas Ness Limited, NCB (Exploration) Limited and LS (Leasing) Limited. National Smokeless Fuels Limited is concerned with manufacture and sale of coke, smokeless fuels and various primary products, notably coke oven gas, crude tar and benzole. Thomas Ness Limited manufacture principally tar products, but the company is also interested in the manufacture of PVC heat shrink artefacts and solvents. NCB (Exploration) Limited, as the name suggests, was concerned with offshore exploration, development and delivery of gas and oil from the North Sea. This company with its subsidiary, LS (Leasing) Ltd, was, under the Petroleum and Sub-Marine Pipeline Act, transferred to the British National Oil Corporation in January 1976. This transfer was undertaken at book value. LS (Leasing) Limited was a company through which earlier assets of NCB (Exploration) were leased. In April 1975 a new wholly owned subsidiary company called NCB (Hydrocarbons) Ltd was registered. As the name suggests, the industry's activities are concerned with hydrocarbons including petrochemicals with the intention of obtaining, in the future, chemicals from coal. The *Annual Report and Account* [QRL 3] provides additional information on these subsidiary companies.

8.3. NCB Ancillaries Ltd

NCB (Ancillaries) Ltd and its subsidiaries represent a group of varying activities. These are non-mining activities, and include solid fuel distribution, builders' merchanting, brickmaking, estate and land management, engineering and computer services. The Group has been trading since April 1973. The group develops new activities from time to time such as a company to process anthracite so as to provide a specialist core analysis service to the oil industry. There are associated companies whose activities cover boiler operational and maintenance services, and the provision of a mining and consultancy service. Further details of these companies may be obtained in the *Annual Reports* [QRL 3].

8.4. NCB and Subsidiaries

The NCB produces a consolidated set of accounts for the Board and all of its subsidiaries with some exceptions. For the financial year 1975/1976 the exceptions were the British Coal Utilisation Research Association [BCURA] and the NCB (IEA Services) Ltd. The former is prohibited by its Articles of Association from distributing any revenue surplus. The NCB (IEA Services) Ltd manages research projects on behalf of the International Energy Agency and members of the agency contribute to the costs of the company.

The reader should refer to the notes provided in the *Annual Reports and Accounts* [QRL 3] for details of how partnership and associated companies are consolidated with those of the National Coal Board.

The rest of this section refers to the consolidated accounts, although the Reports and Accounts of the NCB Ancillaries and the NCB Coal Products Groups when examined separately follow much the same pattern.

8.5. Capital

Most of the data relating to 'capital' may be found in the NCB's *Annual Reports and Accounts* [QRL 3], which we will discuss below. An alternative source of figures are the *Reports on the Census of Production* [QRL 8] referring to coal mining. (See Section 8.5.2.)

8.5.1. *Annual Reports and Accounts* [QRL 3]

The content of the accounts changed in 1974/75, with respect to the recording of coal mining process, and the results, capital employed and assets of collieries and open-cast mining, which had been shown separately in the accounts and schedules in previous years, were treated as one activity under the heading of 'Coal Mining Activity'. The accounting period covers the number of weeks up to the last Saturday in March for the appropriate year.

Fixed assets are stated in the Balance Sheet at cost, less provision for depreciation and amounts written off under capital reconstruction of the Board provided for in the Coal Industry Acts 1965 and 1973. Depreciation of fixed assets is normally provided on a straight line basis and is calculated on historical values after deduction of Investment Grants and Regional Development Grants. The length of depreciation varies depending on the type of asset.

For freehold land there is no depreciation, whilst for buildings, houses and leasehold land the depreciation period is taken to be the estimated life of the asset or activity, whichever is the shorter, but with a minimum of 2 per cent. Mines and surface works depreciation period depends on the estimated life of the activity or the coal reserves, but with a maximum of forty years. Depreciation rates for plant, machinery and equipment vary with rates between 4 and 25 per cent according to the estimated life of the asset.

8.5.1.1. *Stocks of Products*

Certain changes were made in 1975/76 with regard to the valuation of stocks. These were made to bring the definitions used more in line with the *Statement of Standard Accounting Practice No. 9*.

Undistributed stocks are valued at cost or net realisable value whichever is the lowest at the time of putting to stock. Stocks are valued at selling prices less specific provisions for loss of weight, degradation in size and quality, and the cost of lifting and marketing. According to the note on 'Accounting Policies' given by the NCB, 'general provisions are made to cover other contingencies and to eliminate any element of profit'. Provision is also made for the unrealised appreciation in the value of stocks representing the effect of increases in selling prices on stocks built up before prices were increased. Stocks of other products and stock in trade are valued at cost or net realisable value, whichever is the lower.

Stocks of stores are valued at standard prices based on replacement costs prevailing at the time of the last delivery, with appropriate allowance being made for the condition of used or damaged stores. In addition, a general provision is held to cover latent obsolescence and redundant stores.

8.5.1.2. *Key Operating Statistics*

The 'Key Operating Statistics' in the *Annual Reports and Accounts* [QRL 3] provides data for the current and previous financial years on the average capital employed and the return on average capital employed for Mining Activities, and also the non-mining activities of NCB (Coal Products) Ltd and NCB (Ancillaries) Ltd.

The definition of capital employed is the total of net fixed assets, net current assets (other than inter-group indebtedness) and deferred liabilities. Average capital employed refers to the mean of the values as at the end of the previous and current years. The return of average capital employed is the ratio of operating profit to average capital employed.

8.5.1.3. *Consolidated Balance Sheet*

The Consolidated Balance Sheet provides data for two years—the current and previous years—for the assets employed by the NCB and its subsidiaries. The assets employed are sub-divided into four categories and refer to fixed assets, investments in associated companies and partnerships, net current assets less deferred liabilities.

As far as fixed assets are concerned, it should be noted that teh NCB's holdings in property are stated at cost less whatever provisions are deemed appropriate and not a market valuation. The book value of such assets may be less than the market value, but the NCB does not feel that this is of significance in the context of the Board's normal trading operations. Also within fixed assets may be a proportion of Investment Grants and Regional Development Grants. This proportion is usually determined by the amount of the grant that relates to assets charged to capital and may be used to reduce the value of assets to which they relate.

The consolidated Balance Sheet also provides data relating to how the assets employed were financed from loans, reserves including revenue surplus, and minority interests.

The Balance Sheet of the NCB (excluding subsidiaries) is shown as a separate table but takes the same form as the Consolidated Balance Sheet except for the separation of investments in subsidiaries.

8.5.1.4. *Notes to the Accounts*

The notes to the Accounts included with each *Annual Report and Account* [QRL 3], as the name suggests, gives an 'interpretation' and explanation of the figures that appear in the Accounts. They also often give additional information. For example, a breakdown for the net current assets by the NCB with its subsidiaries is given in the notes to the accounts and provides figures for the stocks of produce and stock in trade, stocks in stores, debtors, balance of Government grants, and cash and bank balances reduced by current liabilities. Stocks of products and stock in trade is explained further in the notes, and figures may be obtained on both a tonnage and value basis, for ground stocks of coal held by the NCB, stocks held in NCB wagons, and distributed stocks held by subsidiary companies. Coke and processed fuel figures, and figures relating to other stocks, are also provided in these notes.

The notes define terms more carefully than do the tables, but they also provide information not shown elsewhere. For example note 18 of the 1975/76 *Annual Report and Accounts* [QRL 3] gives information in relation to future capital expenditure under headings of commitments in respect of contracts placed and capital expenditure authorised but not committed. This information is provided for two years for the NCB, and separately for the NCB and its subsidiaries.

8.5.1.5. *Schedules*

Schedules are in a sense the working sheets from which the Accounts are compiled. In general terms they provide valuable information. For example a much more detailed analysis of fixed assets and depreciation of provisions is given in the Schedule 1 of the *Annual Report and Accounts* [QRL 3]. Data are provided in money terms, on gross book value, provision for depreciation, and net book value, both by type of assets and by activity for the current financial year and its predecessor.

As far as analysis by type of asset is concerned, the major categories are for the NCB and its subsidiaries and for the NCB on its own. The main headings in both of these categories refer to freehold property, leasehold property (both long and short lease), mines and surface works, and plant machinery and equipment.

The analysis by activities is also done so as to provide data on gross value, provisions for depreciation and net book value. The activities are categorised under two broad headings, which are mining and non-mining activities. For mining activities, data are given separately for each mining area, for miscellaneous activities undertaken by the Board and its subsidiaries, and also central services undertaken by them. Non-mining activities relate to coal products and other ancillary undertakings.

8.5.1.6. *Summary of Results*

The *Annual Reports and Accounts* [QRL 3] provides a summary of results for the current year as well as the nine previous years. As far as capital is concerned, it provides data in relation to the assets employed by the NCB and its subsidiaries, how those assets are financed, and the returns on average capital employed.

The assets employed figures are given under the usual headings as described above. They refer to fixed assets, investment-associated companies, subsidiary companies—not consolidated, net current assets and deferred liabilities.

The ratio of return to average capital employed is given for mining activities and non-mining activities with the latter sub-divided into coal products and ancillary activities.

8.5.2. *Report on the Census of Production* [QRL 8]

Because of working to the 1968 Standard Industrial Classification, the *Census of Production* [QRL 8] covers deep-mined coal but not open-cast mining. For details of data relating to coal sales from open-cast sites the reader would have to refer to *Business Monitors* [QRL 7] that deal with construction, i.e. PA 500. The last full census was in 1968/1969 and there are reasons to believe that this was unlikely to be representative of the true situation at that time. There have been *Census of Production Reports* [QRL 8] in 1968, 1970, 1971 and 1972.

These provide census data for coal capital expenditure and stocks are given for selected years. The geographic coverage of this table is for all classified undertakings in the industry in Great Britain.

The capital expenditure figures relate to undertakings in production and those in production before the end of the appropriate year. The major categories under the heading of capital expenditure refer to new building work, land and existing buildings, plant and machinery and vehicles. Most of these are further sub-divided providing data both on the acquisition and disposals of such items. There are also figures that relate to total net capital expenditure which is defined as acquisition minus disposals.

Net capital expenditure data include details of new buildings, of plant and machinery and of vehicles. The figures include data that relate to undertakings not yet in production at the reference data of the census.

The figures are for one year only and give net capital expenditure figures both in monetary terms for each region, as well as providing data of each region's net capital expenditure as a percentage of the Great Britain total.

The data on stocks and work in progress at the end of the appropriate year are sub-divided into materials, stores and fuel, work in progress, and goods on hand for sale.

The report also provides data on the capital expenditure for coke and manufactured fuels which may be of marginal interest to the researcher if he is concerned with non-mining activities. The coverage is for United Kingdom establishments classified as being part of the sector of coke and manufactured fuels. The figures of the NCB form only a part of these figures.

The 1968 Census was the last quinquennial Census of Production. These have now been replaced by the current system of quarterly and annual statistics and are usually embodied in the *Business Monitors* [QRL 7].

The *Report on the 1968 Census of Production* [QRL 8] is now out of print but photocopies may be obtained through the Business Statistics Office.

8.5.3. *Business Monitors* [QRL 7]

The annual publication of the Business Monitors gives some of the analysis of annual censuses of Production. PA 101 reports on coal and PA 261 on coke ovens and manufactured fuel. Of particular note would be the figures on capital expenditure, both net and gross, and also stocks.

8.5.4. *The European Coal and Steel Community*

The European Coal and Steel Community provides data on the coal mining industry, but they tend to be aggregated in terms of the European Six countries, or the European Nine.

In September 1974 the Commission published a report on the *1974 Survey of Investment in the Community Coalmining and Iron and Steel Industries* [QRL 30]. Of interest in relation to this section are the data that the survey provides on capital expenditure figures in the coal mining industry and capital expenditure figures for pits respectively. The figures are provided for a number of years. Data are provided for Europe 6 and Europe 9 by sectors including collieries, coking plants mine-owned, coking plants which are independent, and briquetting plants. These are shown separately.

Information is also given about pits, by installation, by which is meant type of work. For example, the headings are shaft and underground workings, mechanical equipment below ground, haulage and winding equipment, screening and washing, and finally other surface installations, including buildings. Figures such as these are usually measured in terms of units of accounts, which is a common monetary scale used for EEC countries; that is each currency is converted into a European Unit of Account. Eurostat information sheets give current conversion rates.

8.6. Revenue, Expenditure and Costs

The NCB's financial objective was to break even after payment of interest charges, the receipt of grants under the Coal Industry Act of 1973 and after taking into account profits or non-profits from non-mining subsidiaries. Recently objectives have been revised to provide for a proportion of fixed assets investment from internal sources.

Most of the data relating to revenue expenditure and costs are found in the NCB *Annual Reports and Accounts* [QRL 3]. For this reason we will not have any general definition as in previous sections, but move directly to an explanation of the sources of data available.

8.6.1. *NCB Annual Reports and Accounts* [QRL 3]

8.6.1.1. *Operating Profit (Loss)*

Figures relating to operating profit (loss) are found for the current year and immediately previous year in the summary of results. This provides data for Mining, NCB (Ancillaries) Limited and NCB (Coal Products) Limited.

These figures are given in summary form and should be related to other tables given in the *Annual Reports and Accounts* if serious examination of the figures is being made. For example, the financial results for mining activities are dealt with separately and in more detail elsewhere in the schedules. A schedule provides data relating to the current financial year and immediately preceding, and gives information for both income and costs. As far as income is concerned, the table shows the value of production and the grants under the Coal Industry Acts for each of the two years. This is provided on a total basis and is also shown on a per ton basis. A similar breakdown is made on the total cost side, figures being given for the costs involved on a total, and per ton basis. The costs are sub-divided into wages and related costs, and 'other costs'. The table also shows operating profit (loss) on a total and per ton basis. Operating profit (loss) is defined as the difference between total income and total costs *after* the grants under the Coal Industry Act have been made. Since these are flexible, that is not fixed from year to year, great care has to be used if operating profit figures are to be used as a measure of the efficiency of the industry. The key operating statistics for the NCB and its subsidiaries only provides the total operating profits (losses) figures for mining activities and non-mining activities. Under mining activities the operating profits (losses) are given for coal mining and for 'houses and miscellaneous', although no explanation is made of what precisely is meant by this, although the schedule listing the subsidiary companies indicates the companies involved. It is clear, however, that part of this item includes rent from houses, but it should be noted that the results for houses are after taking credit for the full rents permitted by the Rent Act. Any shortfall between the actual rent charged to mineworker tenants and the permitted rent is borne by the operating activity concerned.

The non-mining activities are divided into NCB (Coal Products) Ltd and NCB (Ancillaries) Ltd. Both of these are further divided into activities. Thus under NCB (Coal Products) Ltd there are data relating to the holding company's cost of administration, the manufacture of coke and smokeless fuels, chemicals and secondary by-products, offshore gas and oil activities up to 1975/76, and an overall figure for associated companies.

The breakdown for NCB (Ancillaries) Ltd is similar with figures for the cost of administration of the holding company, the distribution of solid fuel, appliances and building supplies, the manufacture of bricks, operating profits of estates and land, engineering, computer services and associated companies and partnerships.

8.6.1.2. *Turnover*

The *Annual Reports and Accounts* [QRL 3] also provides data relating to the turnover of the NCB and its subsidiaries. Margin on turnover is calculated for each of the activities where this is thought to be appropriate, that is holding and associated companies are not included for these calculations.

8.6.1.3. *Consolidated Profit and Loss Account*

The *Annual Reports and Accounts* [QRL 3] also provides the Consolidated Profit and Loss Account for the NCB and its subsidiaries. Like the table for key operating statistics, the Consolidated Profit and Loss Account provides data in relation to two years.

Specifically the table provides data on total turnover, operating profits and losses, profit and loss before interest and taxation, loss before extraordinary items, total surplus (deficit) for the year, and data on Special Government Grants when applicable. There are also references to the notes to the accounts which should be read carefully when attempting to interpret these and other figures relating to the accounts.

It may be seen from the notes that turnover figures comprise sales to third parties, services and other receipts including rents, which are itemised in the accompanying Schedules. Sales are included at invoice prices less delivery expenses payable by the Board, and VAT. Turnover figures shown for individual Areas or activities include sales from one Board activity to another, and this may be seen from the statement of Key Operating Statistics.

The Consolidated Profit and Loss Account provides information in relation to profit before and after interest and taxation are taken into account. Operating profits (losses) are also given for mining activities, non-mining activities and associated companies and partnerships.

The accounts have to be read in conjunction with the notes to the accounts since some information has to be 'found'; it does not stand out. There are two particular notes to which reference should be made. The first relates to mining and non-mining activities, operating profits, and describes how operating profits are calculated after crediting and charging a number of items. On the credit side may be found grants under the Coal Industry Act, grants from the European Coal and Steel Community, and rents receivable after outgoings. Of these the first two are variable. Rents receivable obviously vary but at least the NCB knows that there will be 'rents receivable' each year. Deductions from operating profits (losses) are made in respect of deficiency contributions to the Mineworkers Pension Scheme, provision for deficiency on Principal Superannuation Scheme, pneumonconiosis compensation, social costs of contracting the industry, plant hired or leased, depreciation of fixed assets, European Coal and Steel Community Levy, audit fees, and expenses and charitable donations.

The second note with respect of operating profit (loss) refers to associated companies and partnerships and shows how their operating profit is made up of dividends, interest, share of partnership profits and the Board's share of undistributed profits.

8.6.1.4. *Schedules*

The Schedules provided in the *Annual Reports and Accounts* [QRL 3] provide information in more depth than do the Profit and Loss Accounts and hence provide an important source of information on financial statistics.

There is some duplication of information but the Schedules also provide information not always obtained elsewhere in the Accounts. Certainly the information is given in greater detail.

Total income, for example, is divided into a number of headings that include turnover, variations in stocks of products, and grants under Coal Industry Acts 1973. Turnover and variations in stocks of products are taken together to provide for value of production, and with the grants arrive at total income.

Total costs are all given in total amounts and also on the basis of costs per saleable ton for each of the cost classifications used in these tables. These include: wages including allowances in kind, charges directly related to wages—such as national insurance—materials and repairs, mining and civil engineering contract work, power, heat and light, salaries and related expenses, other operating expenses, overheads and services, and finally depreciation. This last item must be interpreted carefully since from time to time assets have been substantially written down which means depreciation is also reduced. The notes should be carefully read to see when these write-offs occur.

The Schedules also provide data in relation to the mining areas, which include information on turnover, profit and loss, value of production, costs, and grants receivable. Turnover figures are quoted as total figures. Profit/Loss figures are both total figures and £ per ton, whilst value of production, costs and grants receivable are only expressed in £ per ton. The figures are derived on the basis that they do not include regional grants. However, the Schedules do show the value of the total of regional grants but *not* sub-divided into Areas.

Income and Expenditure on Revenue Account Statement for the NCB and its subsidiaries is also given in the Schedules. This income statement includes not only revenue derived from coal, but coke, gas benzole, crude tar and tar products, processed fuel and miscellaneous products. Income derived from such services as wagon repairs is also shown in this Schedule. Other income items include rents, other receipts, variation in stocks, grants under the Coal Industry Acts and investment income and share of profits, less losses of associated companies. The above figures and those for total turnover and total income are for two years.

The expenditure is sub-divided into a number of headings that include: wages, holiday, sick and Supplementary Injuries Scheme pay, pensions and national insurance, mining and civil engineering contract work, materials, repairs, power, heat and light, surface damage, hire of plant including leasing charges, rates, insurance charges and common law damages, other expenses and depreciation.

One of the Schedules usually provides a summary of results for ten years for the NCB and its subsidiaries. As far as this section is concerned the schedules provide data on operating profit/loss per ton for the current financial year, and the nine years preceding this. Turnover figures are provided for the same time span. Both figures are provided for the total business. It also summarises the trading results of the NCB and its subsidiaries. This section is sub-divided into mining activities which include figures by Region (and not Areas), housing and miscellaneous activities, as well as regional grants under the Coal Industry Acts. The non-mining activities relate to NCB (Coal Products) Ltd., NCB (Ancillaries) Ltd. The table also provides data in relation to profit/loss before taxation and extraordinary items.

8.6.2. *Digest of United Kingdom Energy Statistics* [QRL 13]

The *Digest* provides one table that is usefully discussed in this section which is concerned with costs, proceeds and earnings in the NCB. The geographical coverage is Great Britain and the figures relate to NCB mines only. These figures are provided separately in the *Digest* for deep mines and open-cast sites but in the NCB reports there is only one figure covering both.

As far as this section is concerned the table provides data for ten years on total costs and costs per ton. Both total costs and costs per ton are sub-divided into five headings which include wages, wage charges, materials and repairs, power, heat and light, and other costs (including depreciation). By wages charges is meant figures such as holiday and sick pay, national insurance, pensions and other charges directly related to wages. Before 1970/71 the wages charges figures only included those related to holiday and sick pay.

The table also provides data in relation to proceeds and profit/loss before interest charges. These figures are provided on a total basis as well as on the basis of tonnage.

CHAPTER 9

STATISTICS AND THE EEC

9.1. Background

At the end of the Second World War Europe was left with an alarming energy problem. Many mines and surface installations had either been destroyed or severely damaged, which affected coal output and coal stocks were virtually exhausted. The London Coal Committee (that is, part of the war-time Anglo-American Combined Production and Resources Board) suggested to their respective Governments that an organisation be set up to encourage satisfactory trading arrangements. As a consequence of this initiative many countries were invited to preliminary talks, out of which developed in January 1946 the European Coal Organisation. The purpose of the European Coal Organisation was to promote the supply and equitable distribution of coal and scarce items of mining supplies and equipment, as well as other goals, such as making recommendations to Governments in relation to the welfare of the coal industry.

The European Coal and Steel Community (ECSC) was formed in 1951 under the Treaty of Paris. Economically the Treaty was designed to create a single common market for coal within which coal produced anywhere in the Community would be able to circulate freely. This Community was, in the event, the forerunner to the European Economic Community established five years later.

In 1954 Mr. Louis Armand was asked to conduct a survey of all matters relating to energy that affected Community members. His report suggested that fuel shortages were slowly becoming a thing of the past and that era would be replaced by one in which different fuels would compete with one another for their share of the energy market. He also suggested that Europe investigated the potential of atomic energy and this resulted directly in the Hartley Report [B 39].

After emphasising, among other things, that coal would continue to remain the mainstay of the energy economy in Western Europe in the future, the report stated that increased output of coal would depend on long-term investment, on the development of improved methods, on miners' pay terms of employment being adequate, and on giving coal the image of a modern and stable industry.

The report also called for increased co-operation between member countries in many fields including the exchange of information. No action, in fact, followed the Hartley Report.

Other moves that took place in the European scene, in the late fifties, of interest, were the beginnings of energy resources inventory undertaken by the EEC Coal Committee in Geneva, and the establishment of the European and Euratom Commissions in Brussels in 1957.

9.2. European Economic Community

Although Great Britain did not become a formal member of the European Economic Community until 1973 it had been intimately concerned, either formally or informally, with the European fuel market for a long time before this.

Some of the benefits of the Community include assistance for redundant or transferred workers and loans at attractive rates for investment projects capable of employing Community workers.

According to the rules of the Community there ought to be a free trade in coal within the Community. Moreover, producers are requested to publish all prices at selected basing points and also transport charges.

Data for the Community are published by the Statistical Office of the European Communities in *Eurostat* [QRL 17].

9.2.1. *Reconciliation of Statistics*

For the European Coal and Steel Community's first ten years, coal statistics were, as a rule, simply worked out from the series supplied from the member countries more or less as they stood. Various corrections were applied to make these more comparable, but these corrections were fairly rough and conversion into terms of comparable calorific values was left untouched. As a result, the data base was not homogeneous since some member countries (the Federal German Republic and the Netherlands) converted the main items in their coal balance-sheet into terms of standard coal, while the others did not.

In 1965, as a result of the deliberations of a working party composed of Coal experts from the Community countries and representatives of the High Authority and the Statistical Office, an agreed method of conversion was adopted by the Community. This is described briefly below, but full details may be obtained from:—

Supplement to: *Bulletin, Energy Statistics.* No. 4—1967 published by Office Statistique des Communautés Européennes [QRL 6].

It should be noticed that this method is not entirely followed by the UK when it supplies data to the EEC since the UK only applies the method to coal supplied to public electrical power stations. However the methodology is currently being reviewed and may change in the not too distant future for the whole of the Community. A comparison of the normal conventions in use in the UK and those in use in the EEC are made in the *Digest* [QRL 13] published in 1976.

Until recently and to avoid unnecessary complications for the statistical services in the member countries, and to keep the number of different series to a minimum, the Working Party on Coal Statistics decided to adopt a modified version of the German–Dutch 'tons of coal equivalent' method. In this method low-grade coal (described by the Community as slurry, middlings and slack) is converted according to the equation:

$$f = 1.39 - 0.0209(A + 0.88W)$$

where f = conversion factor
A = ash content
W = moisture content

and not based on pure calorific value. It is thought to be a reliable indicator of calorific values for coals with trash contents that are not too high, that is for coal with 40% or less of ash and moisture.

Coal statistics in the Community are expressed in metric tons, that is in tonnes of coal equivalent (tce) after taking account of inert matter in the different coal. This is defined as having a net calorific value of 7,000 calories per gram. All coal tonnages with an inert content of less than 20% are included, tonne for tonne; those between 20 and 67–76%, depending on their relative proportions of ash and moisture, are converted as shown above. Coal with inert contents greater than this are considered to have no calorific value.

It is unlikely that there will be changes under the new system adopted for Community statistics. It has been agreed that conversion factors will not be used under the new system. When the change is implemented Community statistics will be published in tonnes or joules.

CHAPTER 10

SAFETY AND HEALTH IN MINES

The mining industry has one of the largest medical services in Britain and the Chief Medical Officer was appointed in 1947. The same year saw the appointment of a National Safety Officer.

Annual Reports dealing with safety and health in mines have been published annually since 1950 by the Mines Inspectorate [QRL 25], but data were collected by them for many years previous to this. The Department of Trade and Industry, as it then was, produced, in 1972, the *Law relating to Safety and Health in Mines and Quarries*, published by HMSO. Volume 1 contains the text of relevant Acts and Regulations, while Volume 2 covers coal mines in detail. In 1975 the Coal Mines (Respirable Dust) Regulations were introduced.

Clearly these publications provided a wealth of data relating to health and safety, and should be referred to when researching in this area. Summary data are published by the NCB both in its *Annual Reports and Accounts* [QRL 3] and in the NCB *Statistical Tables* [QRL 28]. In both sources the data tend to be the same so that only one of the sources is described here in detail, viz. the tables relevant to this heading found in the *Statistical Tables*. However the *Annual Reports* include the results of periodical X-ray for pneumoconiosis and fibrosis which are not available in the *Statistical Tables*.

Most of the definitions are straightforward, but it should be noted that 'serious reportable injuries' are defined as those resulting from accidents immediately reportable to HM Inspector of Mines which cause fractures of the head or of any limb, or dislocation of any limb or any other serious bodily injury. 'Other injuries' are those not defined as serious, but result in absence for more than three days, excluding the day on which the accident occurred.

For the report which indicates the extent to which disability amongst miners goes largely 'unregistered' the reader should refer to Grainger and Hurst [B 12].

10.1. NCB Statistical Tables [QRL 28]

This source gives a breakdown of accidents by their major cause. The causes are sub-divided into 'falls of ground' (both for the face and for roads), falling objects, by use of haulage and transport, from machinery, by use of tools and appliances, by handling supplies, and by stumbling, falling or slipping. There is also a category shown as 'other causes'. These provide the breakdown of the cause of accidents underground. For the surface only total figures are given for accidents.

There is also information for the current and past year for two categories of accidents, namely the number of accidents involving serious reportable injuries, and those in which deaths were involved.

The table also provides for these three categories the accident rate per 100,000 manshifts, and also gives this rate for all accidents.

10.2. Safety in Mines Research Establishment

This was founded in 1908 under the auspices of the Mining Association of Great Britain and transferred to the Mines Department of the Board of Trade, later the Ministry of Power, and later still the Department of Trade.

This department provides a bibliography of the published work of the staff and other workers for whom these bodies provided funds and/or facilities.

10.3. Other Sources

Other sources of information on safety and health are available in *NCB Medical Service Annual Reports* [QRL 20], *Digest of Pneumoconiosis Statistics* [QRL 12], the *Annual Report* of Department of Health and Social Services [QRL 2] and the Institute of Occupational Medicine. The Institute was established in 1969 by the NCB but major research programmes have been undertaken for other industries apart from coal. Its research interests centre on varied aspects of occupational health and hygiene. Readers wanting more details of these aspects should refer to Volume II in the present series of Reviews [B 1].

CHAPTER 11

RESEARCH AND DEVELOPMENT

Coal R and D is undertaken principally by the NCB at the Mining Research and Development Establishment (MRDE) at Bretby in Staffordshire; at the Coal Research Establishment at Stoke Orchard in Gloucestershire; at its subsidiary BCURA Limited at Leatherhead; and under contract by the Institute of Occupational Medicine. This research is financed directly by the NCB and from the funds from the European Coal and Steel Community.

The United Kingdom has also been nominated by the International Energy Agency to take the lead in coal research and development. In 1975/76 a limited company was established to manage the work to be carried out in the United Kingdom in this field.

Other organisations involved in coal R and D include British Gas, which is the lead organisation for coal gasification; the British Steel Corporation, and the Safety in Mines Research Establishment (SMRE) of the Department of Employment.

The Mining Research and Development organisation is mainly concerned with coal mining and preparation. Research is concentrated on exploiting the full potential of power loaders, armoured flexible conveyors and powered support installations.

The Institute of Occupational Medicine, as was noted in the previous section, is the base for almost the whole of the substantial body of medical research for the NCB. The Safety in Mines Research Establishment covers the research aspects of accident studies.

R and D relating to the manufacture of metallurgical coke is undertaken by the NCB as a producer of coal. The main focus of the NCB programme is obtaining better control of size, strength and quality of coke and widening the range of coals that could be used for its manufacture.

The NCB Coal Research Establishment is concerned with researching hydrocarbon liquids. BCURA Limited is conducting research into fluidised combustion technology.

11.1. Statistics and Information on R and D

The NCB *Annual Reports and Accounts* [QRL 3] provide data and commentary on R and D effort in the NCB and its subsidiaries.

An important source is also provided in the Energy Papers of the Department of Energy and *Energy Research and Development in the United Kingdom* [B 38] is of particular relevance here.

CHAPTER 12

IMPROVEMENTS AND FUTURE DEVELOPMENTS

In all walks of life it is extremely easy to be critical of people and the way that they go about things. The criticisms often concentrate on what is thought to be 'wrong' without emphasising that which is deemed to be 'right' and sometimes what is designated as incorrect makes up only a small part of the total.

The present reviewer would like to acknowledge that he has received a great deal of help from organisations and people in the compilation of this Review. It is clear that considerable effort and thought is put into the collection, collation and publication of statistics regarding coal and the coal industry. Moreover it must be stated explicitly that it is generally accepted that the NCB is particularly well served by its statistics.

Bearing these comments in mind however it is also clear that some improvements could be made. Statistics are collected for many purposes, and a definition that may suit one source is not quite so appropriate for others. The NCB is not unlike other organisations in this respect. It collects data for its day to day and longer term management needs, for legal reasons associated with such things as the *Annual Reports and Accounts* [QRL 3] and for other reasons such as research requirements from outside bodies. It is sometimes difficult to reconcile the different requirements of these needs since data, like most things, cannot mean all things to all men. Thus there are some points of detail that the user of coal data has to be aware of. As an example of this one could refer to definitions with respect to coal output.

In some of the sources this includes only coal worked on revenue account and in others it includes coal worked on capital account. Is there a need to distinguish between the two as far as output is concerned? In addition coal output includes coal recovered from tips in some areas (e.g. in South Wales and Scotland) but not others. Why should this be the case? Other examples that come to mind relate to consumption figures where it would now seem appropriate to use the term 'disposals' in all the relevant tables.

But these points and others have been raised with many of the people concerned with the compilation and publication of data and it is likely that they will be dealt with. They are small points that relate to published data and although of concern, can be clarified fairly easily when the appropriate departments or people are contacted.

What gives rise to more concern is what is available in terms of statistics that are not formally published. Because of the exercise of discretion there is some variation in what is made available to enquirers, and this seems especially true when collecting data with respect to different areas in the NCB. There would appear to be no guidelines as to what type of information a colliery, area or Headquarters Department can or cannot give an outside enquirer who cannot get the data he requires from published sources. It should not be a matter of chance as to what response an enquirer is likely to receive. A clear statement of the type of data that are collected, their level, frequency and availability, would be much appreciated. In this respect the Register of Routine Statistical Statements might have an important role to play.

QUICK REFERENCE LIST—TABLE OF CONTENTS

Output	84
Consumption	86
Manpower	87
General Data expressed mainly in Financial Terms	89
Data Reconciliation	90
Injuries	90

QUICK REFERENCE LIST

Type of Data	Breakdown Detail of Analysis	Area	Frequency	Publication (see QRL Key)	Text Reference and Remarks
Output					
Total output	Total production. Anthracite and bituminous	GB	Annual	[QRL 33]	5.8
Total output	Total production	GB	Annual	[QRL 1]	5.9
Total output	Coal output	GB	Monthly/Annual	[QRL 17]	5.10
Total output	NCB mines	GB	Annual	[QRL 28]	5.2.1. 1962 changed from calendar to financial year. Two changes in definition of output in 1953 and 1957 respectively
Total output	NCB mines	GB	Monthly/Annual	[QRL 18]	5.6
Coal mined	NCB mines	GB	Quarterly	[QRL 7]	5.7
Total output	Open cast sites	GB	Annual	[QRL 28]	5.2.1. Open cast figures and those of licensed mines aggregated 1962–1972/73
Total output	Open cast sites	GB	Annual	[QRL 3]	5.3
Total output	Open cast sites	GB	Annual	[QRL 13]	5.4.1
Total output	Open cast sites	GB	Monthly/Annual	[QRL 18]	5.6
Total tonnage	Open cast sites	GB	Annual	[QRL 17]	5.10
Deep mined and open case production	Unadjusted and seasonally adjusted	GB	Annual	[QRL 16]	5.5
Total output	Licensed mines	GB	Annual	[QRL 28]	5.2.1 (see above)
Total output	Licensed mines	GB	Annual	[QRL 17]	5.10
Total output	Licensed mines	GB	Annual	[QRL 13]	5.4.1
Output indices NCB mines	Output per manshift (OMS), face OMS, elsewhere underground surface OMS, output per man year, mechanical output as a percentage of total output and tonnage lost due to dispute	GB	Annual	[QRL 28]	5.2.1

QUICK REFERENCE LIST

Item	Description	Region	Frequency	Ref	Section/Notes
Output indices NCB mines	Saleable output, OMS, face OMS, daily output per face	GB	Annual	[QRL 3]	5.3
Output indices NCB mines	OMS, output per man year, dispute tonnage lost, holiday tonnage lost	GB	Annual	[QRL 13]	5.4.1. Output includes imported coal and coal produced on capital account
Output indices NCB mines	Average output per manshift	GB	Monthly/Annual	[QRL 18]	5.6
Output indices NCB mines	OMS, face OMS	GB	Monthly	[QRL 16]	5.5. Figures based on revenue working and excludes tip coal
Open cast mining output indices	OME, output per man year	GB	Annual	[QRL 28]	5.2.1
Output indices licensed mines	OMS, output per man year	GB	Annual	[QRL 28]	5.2.1
Longwall face production	Number of faces, daily output for face, and OMS	GB	Annual	[QRL 28]	5.2.1. Data on sample weeks output
Coal productivity	Productivity at NCB mines	GB	Quarterly	[QRL 7]	5.7
Output by areas	Number of producing collieries, saleable output, estimate of output lost by disputes, and OMS	GB	Annual	[QRL 28]	5.2.2. Output figures for South Wales and Scotland include coal recovered from tips
Output by areas	Total output per region	GB	Annual	[QRL 3]	5.3
Output by areas	Total output	GB	Monthly/Annual	[QRL 17]	5.10
Output by areas	Output of saleable coal, OMS, percentage of coal power loaded	GB	Annual	[QRL 13]	5.4.2. Areas did not conform to NCB areas until 1977. Output figures for areas do not include coal from capital account
Open cast tonnage	Tonnage produced in each standard region and each country	GB	Annual	[QRL 24]	5.9
Output coke and manufactured fuels	Output from NCB ovens, iron and steel industry ovens and independent ovens	GB	Annual	[QRL 13]	5.4.1
Output of manufactured and naturally smokeless products	Production by product	GB	Annual	[QRL 13]	5.4.1
Undistributed stocks	NCB mines	GB	Annual	[QRL 28]	5.2.3
Stocks	Distributed and undistributed at NCB mines	GB	Monthly	[QRL 18]	5.6
Stocks	Distributed and undistributed stocks	GB	Annual	[QRL 13]	5.4.1

COAL

Type of Data	Breakdown/Detail of Analysis	Area	Frequency	Publication (see QRL Key)	Text Reference and Remarks
Output (*contd.*)					
Stocks	Undistributed stocks at NCB mines	GB	Quarterly	[QRL 7]	5.7
Number of pits in operation	NCB mines	GB	Annual	[QRL 13]	5.4.1
Revenue from output	NCB mines	GB	Annual	[QRL 13]	5.4.1
Consumption					
Coke and manufactured fuel	Input/output tables. Analysis of capital expenditure and stocks	GB	Annual	[QRL 7]	6.1.2. Some information on census basis
Coke	Consumption, sales production	GB	Annual	[QRL 13]	6.1.2
Coke	Balance sheet of total supply and total demand. Consumption analysed by main classes of use, shipments and stock changes	GB	Annual	[QRL 1]	6.1.2
Coke	Consumption by fuel conversion industries and in final direct use	GB	Annual	[QRL 13]	6.4.1
Coal consumption	Total consumption and changes in stock	UK	Annual	[QRL 33]	6.7
Coal consumption	General and coal disposals by grades and markets and undistributed stocks by grades	(i) GB	Annual	[QRL 28]	6.2.1
	Above plus use of coal to produce other fuels	(ii) GB/UK	Annual	[QRL 13]	6.4.1. Much more detailed breakdown than QRL 3 and data in natural units and also therms
	Above plus energy used by final consumers	(iii) GB/UK	Monthly	[QRL 18]	6.6
Coal sales consumption	By industry, data on power stations, coke ovens, industry and domestic market	GB	Annual	[QRL 3]	6.3. Includes data on sales income from NCB subsidiaries
Coal consumption	By market	GB/UK	Monthly/Annual	[QRL 18]	6.6.2

QUICK REFERENCE LIST

Coal consumption	By country, in United Kingdom	UK	Annual	[QRL 13]	6.4.2
Manufactured fuels and smokeless fuels	Consumption by fuel conversion industries and in direct final use	GB/UK	Annual	[QRL 13]	6.4.1
Imports/exports	Imports from EEC and important supplying countries. Exports to EEC and EFTA	GB/UK	Annual	[QRL 13]	6.4.3. Exports are based on notifications from HM Customs and are not actual shipments
Imports/exports	Total figures	GB/UK	Monthly	[QRL 18]	6.6
Exports	Total figures	GB	Annual	[QRL 28]	5.2.3
Imports/exports	Total figures	GB	Annual	[QRL 33]	6.7
Manpower					
Manpower	Total wage earners on colliery books, wage earners. Percentage productive labour to total labour	GB	Annual	[QRL 13]	7.4.1
Manpower by areas	On colliery books at the end of March, total wastage and percentage absence in the year	GB	Annual	[QRL 28]	7.2.2
Wage earners on colliery books	Total and underground	GB	Monthly	[QRL 18]	7.5
Manpower by areas	Average number of wage earners	GB	Annual	[QRL 13]	7.4.4. Areas defined differently from NCB areas until 1977
Manpower	Average earnings	GB	Annual	[QRL 28]	7.2.7
Manpower	Age distribution in class intervals for total manpower, underground and surface workers	GB	Annual	[QRL 28]	7.2.3
Recruitment and wastage	Re-enrolments and newly employed recruits. Involuntary and voluntary wastage	GB	Annual	[QRL 28]	7.2.4
Recruitment and wastage	Recruitment from juveniles, newly employed, adult new entrants and re-entrants	GB	Annual	[QRL 13]	7.4.3. *Digest* only shows national figures
Recruitment and wastage	NCB mines	GB	Monthly	[QRL 18]	7.5

Type of Data	Breakdown/Detail of Analysis	Area	Frequency	Publication (see QRL Key)	Text Reference and Remarks
Manpower (contd.)					
Redundancy	Quarterly figures for redundancy	GB	Quarterly/Monthly	[QRL 11]	7.6
Redundancy	Redundant Miners Payment Scheme (RMPS). Total number of beneficiaries and amount paid classified by age	GB	Annual	[QRL 19]	7.8.1
Redundancy	Number of lump sums paid	GB	Annual	[QRL 19]	7.8.2
Redundancy	Total number of beneficiaries of RMPS	GB	Annual	[QRL 3]	7.3
Manshifts	Place of work. Overall daily averages	GB	Annual	[QRL 28]	7.2.5
Manshifts	Average number of shifts per worker	GB	Annual	[QRL 13]	7.4.1
Manshifts	Average hours worked	GB	Quarterly/Monthly	[QRL 11]	7.6. Figures for a particular week in October of each year
Employment	Distribution of employment within NCB	GB	Annual	[QRL 7]	7.9. PA 101
Manpower	Total employment by categories of staff including those employed at open cast sites, central workshops and other services	GB	Annual	[QRL 28]	7.2.6. Figures are for the end of September
Manpower	Absence	GB	Annual	[QRL 28]	7.2.1
Absence	Voluntary/involuntary	GB	Monthly	[QRL 18]	7.5
Manpower	Absence with breakdown into voluntary and involuntary absences	GB	Annual	[QRL 13]	7.4.1
Earnings	Average cash earnings for a given period, for NCB areas by category of work	GB	Annual	[QRL 28]	7.2.7
Earnings	Deep mines and open cast	GB	Annual	[QRL 13]	8.6.2
Weekly pay	Average weekly pay and value of allowances in kind	GB	Quarterly/Monthly	[QRL 11]	7.6. Figures for a particular week

… QUICK REFERENCE LIST …   89

General data expressed mainly in financial terms

Item	Description	Region	Frequency	Source	Reference
NCB (Coal Products) Ltd.	Companies and products	UK	Annual	[QRL 3]	8.2
NCB (Ancillaries) Ltd.	Companies and products	UK	Annual	[QRL 3]	8.3
Depreciation	By type of asset	GB	Annual	[QRL 3]	8.5.1
Stocks	Value of stock	GB	Annual	[QRL 3]	8.5.1.1
Stocks	Type of stock, value, and tonnage	GB	Annual	[QRL 3]	8.5.1.4
Production	Value of production at NCB mines	GB	Annual	[QRL 3]	8.6.1.1
Proceeds	Deep mine and open cast sites	GB	Annual	[QRL 13]	8.6.2. Separate figures for deep mine and open cast operations
Operating profits (losses)	Mining activities	GB	Annual	[QRL 3]	8.6.1.1
Operating profits (losses)	Total and per ton	GB	Annual	[QRL 3]	8.6.1.1
Operating profits (losses)	NCB and ancillaries	GB	Annual	[QRL 3]	8.6.1.1
Profits (losses)	Before and after interest and depreciation	GB	Annual	[QRL 3]	8.6.1.3
Consolidated profit and loss	NCB and ancillaries	GB	Annual	[QRL 3]	8.6.1.3
Turnover	Margin on each activity	GB	Annual	[QRL 3]	8.6.1.2
Sales	One Board activity to another	GB	Annual	[QRL 3]	8.6.1.3
Average capital employed	(i) for mining activities	GB	Annual	[QRL 3]	8.5.1.2
	(ii) NCB (Coal Products) Ltd. and NCB (Ancillaries) Ltd.	GB	Annual	[QRL 3]	8.5.1.6
Fixed assets	Valuation	GB	Annual	[QRL 3]	8.5.1.3
Fixed assets	Analysis	GB	Annual	[QRL 3]	8.5.1.5
Capital expenditure	Census data for selected years	GB	(i) Occasional (ii) Monthly/Quarterly/Annual	[QRL 8] [QRL 7]	8.5.2 and 8.5.3
Capital expenditure	European figures for industries and pits	Europe	Occasional	[QRL 30]	8.5.4
Work in progress	Census data for selected years	GB	(i) Occasional (ii) Monthly/Quarterly/Annual	(i) [QRL 8] (ii) [QRL 7]	8.5.2 and 8.5.3
Costs	Wage costs and other costs	GB	Annual	[QRL 3]	8.6.1.4
Costs	Deep mines and open cast	GB	Annual	[QRL 3]	8.6.1.3
Costs	Deep mines and open cast	GB	Annual	[QRL 13]	8.6.2. Separate figures for deep mines and open cast

Type of data	Breakdown/Detail of Analysis	Area	Frequency	Publication (see QRL Key)	Text Reference and Remarks
General data expressed mainly in financial terms (*Contd.*)					
Grants	From European Coal and Steel Community	GB	Annual	[QRL 3]	8.6.1.3
Rents	From NCB property	GB	Annual	[QRL 3]	8.6.1.3
Mineworkers pension scheme	Deductions from operating profits (losses) in respect of deficiencies	GB	Annual	[QRL 3]	8.6.1.3
Levy	European Coal and Steel Community	GB	Annual	[QRL 3]	8.6.1.3
Data reconciliation					
Coal data in Europe	Tons of coal equivalent and joules	Europe	Quarterly/ Annual/ Occasional	[QRL 17]	9.2.1
Injuries					
Injuries and accidents	Serious and other injuries	GB	Annual	[QRL 3]	10
Injuries/accidents	Causes	GB	Annual	[QRL 28]	10.1

Quick Reference List Key to Publications

Reference Number	Organisation Responsible	Title	Publisher	Frequency or Date of Publication	Remarks
[QRL 1]	Central Statistical Office	*Annual Abstract of Statistics*	HMSO, London	Annual	
[QRL 2]	Department of Health and Social Services	*Annual Report*	HMSO, London	Annual	
[QRL 3]	NCB	*Annual Reports and Accounts*	NCB	Annual	
[QRL 4]	Department of Employment	*British Labour Statistics Historical Abstract 1886–1968*	HMSO, London	1971	
[QRL 5]	Department of Employment	*British Labour Statistics Yearbooks*	HMSO, London	Annual	
[QRL 6]	EEC	*Bulletin of Energy Statistics for Europe*	Statistical Office of the European Communities (Luxembourg)	Annual	
[QRL 7]	Department of Industry Business Statistics Office	*Business Monitors (PA, PQ, PM)*	HMSO, London	Monthly, Quarterly, Annual, Occasional	
[QRL 8]	Department of Industry	*1968 Census of Production Reports*	Department of Industry	Various dates	Now out of print but photocopies may be obtained from the Business Statistics Office
[QRL 9]	Department of Employment	*Changes in Rates of Wages and Hours of Work*	HMSO, London	Monthly	
[QRL 10]	NCB	*Colliery Year Book*	NCB	Annual	Ceased in 1964
[QRL 11]	Department of Employment	*Department of Employment Gazette*	HMSO, London	Monthly	*Ministry of Labour Gazette*—one of its predecessors
[QRL 12]	Department of Trade and Industry	*Digest of Pneumoconiosis Statistics*	HMSO, London	Annual	
[QRL 13]	Department of Energy	*Digest of United Kingdom Energy Statistics*	HMSO, London	Annual	Formerly, the *Ministry of Fuel and Power Statistical Digest*
[QRL 14]	Welsh Office	*Digest of Welsh Statistics*	HMSO, Cardiff	Annual	
[QRL 15]	Department of Prices and Consumer Affairs	*Domestic Coal Consumer Council*	HMSO, London	Annual/Occasional	
[QRL 16]	Department of Energy	*Energy Trends*	HMSO, London	Monthly	

Reference number	Organisation responsible	Title	Publisher	Frequency or date of publication	Remarks
[QRL 17]	EEC	*Eurostat Energy Statistics*	Statistical Office of the European Communities (Luxembourg)	Annual, Quarterly and Occasional	
[QRL 18]	Central Statistical Office	*Monthly Digest of Statistics*	HMSO, London	Monthly	
[QRL 19]	National Union of Miners	*National Union of Miners National Executive Committee Reports*	NUM	Annual	
[QRL 20]	NCB	*NCB Medical Service Annual Reports*	NCB	Annual	
[QRL 21]	Department of Employment	*New Earnings Survey*	HMSO, London	Six parts between October and April	
[QRL 22]	Northern Ireland Department	*Northern Ireland Digest of Statistics*	HMSO, Belfast	6 Monthly	
[QRL 23]	Department of Trade	*Overseas Trade Statistics of UK*	HMSO, London	Monthly/Annual	
[QRL 24]	Central Statistical Office	*Regional Statistics*	HMSO, London	Annual	
[QRL 25]	Mines Inspectorate	*Report of HM Chief Inspector of Mines and Quarries*	HMSO, London	Annual	
[QRL 26]	Scottish Office	*Scottish Abstract of Statistics*	HMSO, Edinburgh	Annual	
[QRL 27]	Scottish Office	*Scottish Economic Bulletin*	HMSO, Edinburgh	6 Monthly	
[QRL 28]	NCB	*Statistical Tables*	NCB	Annual	
[QRL 29]	OECD	*Statistics of Energy*	OECD	Annual	
[QRL 30]	European Coal and Steel Community	*Survey of Investment in the Community Coalmining and Iron and Steel Industries*	ECSC	Occasional	
[QRL 31]	Department of Employment	*Time Rates of Wages and Hours of Work*	HMSO, London	Annual	
[QRL 32]	Department of Industry	*Trade and Industry*	HMSO, London	Weekly	
[QRL 33]	Business Statistics Office	*United Kingdom Mineral Statistics*	HMSO, London	Annual	
[QRL 34]	United Nations	*World Energy Supplies (United Nations Series J)*	UN	Annual	

BIBLIOGRAPHY

[B 1] Alderson, M. R., 'Central Government Routine Health Statistics' in *Reviews of United Kingdom Statistical Sources*, Volume II, edited by W. F. Maunder, Heinemann, 1973.
[B 2] R. Arnot Page, *The Miners: A History of the Miners' Federation of Great Britain, 1889–1910*, Allen and Unwin, 1949.
[B 3] R. Arnot Page, *The Miners: Years of Struggle: A History of the Miners' Federation (from 1910 onwards)*, Allen and Unwin, 1953.
[B 4] R. Arnot Page, *The Miners in Crisis and War: A History of the Miners' Federation of Great Britain (from 1930 onwards)*, Allen and Unwin, 1961.
[B 5] T. S. Ashton and J. Sykes, *Coal Industry of the Eighteenth Century*, Manchester University Press, 1964.
[B 6] H. F. Bulman, *Coalmining and the Coal Miner*, Methuen, 1920.
[B 7] C. F. Carter and A. D. Roy, *British Economic Statistics: A Report*, Cambridge University Press, 1954.
[B 8] Dean, A., 'Wages and Earnings' in *Reviews of United Kingdom Statistical Sources*, Volume XIII, edited by W. F. Maunder, Pergamon Press, to be published.
[B 9] A. Finlay Gibson, *A Compilation of Statistics (Technological, Commercial and General) of the Coal Mining Industry of the United Kingdom*, Western Mail, 1922.
[B 10] R. L. Galloway, *Annuals of Coal Mining and the Coal Trade*, (i) First Series 1898, (ii) Second Series 1904, Colliery Guardian.
[B 11] R. L. Galloway, *A History of Coal Mining in Great Britain*, David and Charles, 1969.
[B 12] R. W. Grainger and J. Hurst, *A Report on the Incidence of Disability among Miners*, University of Durham, Department of Economics, 1969.
[B 13] W. W. Haynes, *Nationalisation in Practice: The British Coal Industry*, Bailey and Swinfen, 1953.
[B 14] W. S. Jevons, *The British Coal Trade*, Kegan Paul, 1920.
[B 15] M. G. Kendall (Editor), *The Sources and Nature of the Statistics of the United Kingdom*, Volume I, Oliver and Boyd, 1952.
[B 16] B. Lewis, *Coalmining in the Eighteenth and Nineteenth Centuries*, Longman, 1971.
[B 17] F. D. K. Liddell, 'Attendance in the Coal Mining Industry', *British Journal of Sociology*, Volume XI, pp. 78–86, 1954.
[B 18] S. Moos, 'The Statistics of Absenteeism in Coal Mining', *Manchester School for Economics and Social Studies*, Volume 19, pp. 89–108, 1951.
[B 19] J. U. Nef, *The Rise of the British Coal Industry*, Routledge (2 volumes), 1932.
[B 20] R. W. S. Pryke, *Public Enterprise in Practice: The British Experience of Nationalisation over Two Decades*, MacGibbon and Kee, 1971.
[B 21] C. A. Roberts in *National Coal Board: The First Ten Years*, edited by Sir Guy Nott-Bower and R. H. Walkerdine, Colliery Guardian, 1956.
[B 22] C. Robinson, 'The Energy "Crisis" and British Coal', *Hobart Papers*, 59, 1974.
[B 23] J. W. F. Rowe, *Wages in the Coal Industry*, King, 1923.
[B 24] E. F. Schumacher in *National Coal Board: The First Ten Years*, edited by Sir Guy Nott-Bower and R. H. Walkerdine, Colliery Guardian, 1956.
[B 25] H. Wilson, *New Deal for Coal*, Cole, 1945.
[B 26] National Coal Board, *Books on Coal*, NCB Public Relations, 1977.
[B 27] *British Fuel and Power Industries*, Political and Economic Planning, 1947.
[B 28] Parliament, *Children's Employment Commission, First Report, Mines*, 1842.
[B 29] Parliament, *Coal Industry Commission, Reports and Minutes of Evidence* (3 volumes), Cmd 359–361, 1919.
[B 30] Department of Energy, *Coal Industry: Final Report*, 1974.
[B 31] Ministry of Fuel and Power, *Coal Industry Nationalisation Act*, HMSO, 1946.
[B 32] Ministry of Fuel and Power, *Coal Mines Act*, 1911.

[B 33] Ministry of Fuel and Power, *Coal Mines Act*, 1930.
[B 34] Ministry of Fuel and Power, *Coal Mines Act*, 1938.
[B 35] Ministry of Fuel and Power, *Coal Mining, Report of the Technical Advisory Committee*, Cmd 6610, 1945.
[B 36] National Coal Board, *Coal News*, Monthly.
[B 37] National Board for Prices and Incomes, *Coal Prices*, Cmnd 4455, Report No. 153, HMSO, 1970, 1971.
[B 38] Department of Energy, *Energy Research and Development in the United Kingdom, A Discussion Paper*, Energy Paper No. 11, HMSO, 1976.
[B 39] Organisation for European Economic Cooperation, *Europe's Growing Needs for Energy: How can they be met?*, 1956.
[B 40] Treasury, *The Financial and Economic Obligations of the Nationalised Industries*, Cmnd 1337, HMSO, 1961.
[B 41] Government Statistical Service, *Government Statistics: A brief guide to sources*, HMSO, Annual.
[B 42] Government Statistical Service, *Guide to Official Statistics*, HMSO, 1977.
[B 43] National Coal Board, *Inbye*, Monthly.
[B 44] Department of Energy, *The Interim Report of the Coal Industry Examination*, 1974.
[B 45] National Coal Board, *Investing in Coal*, 1956.
[B 46] National Coal Board, *Management News*, Monthly.
[B 47] National Coal Board, *Plan for Coal*, 1949.
[B 48] National Coal Board, *Plan for Coal*, 1974.
[B 49] National Coal Board, *Plan 2000*, 1977.
[B 50] Ministry of Labour and National Service, *Rationing of Coal*, Cmd 6364, 1942.
[B 51] Ministry of Fuel and Power, *Regional Survey of Coalfields*, HMSO, 1946.
[B 52] National Coal Board, *Report of the Advisory Committee on Organisation*, 1955.
[B 53] *Report on the British Coal Industry*, Political and Economic Planning, 1936.
[B 54] Department of Employment, *Report of a Court of Inquiry into a Dispute between the National Coal Board and the National Union of Mineworkers*, HMSO, 1972.
[B 55] Price Commission, *Report No. 12: Distribution of Domestic Coal and Solid Smokeless Fuels*, 1969.
[B 56] Treasury, *A Review of the Economic and Financial Objectives of the Nationalised Industries*, Cmnd 3437, HMSO, 1967.
[B 57] National Coal Board, *Revised Plan for Coal*, 1959.
[B 58] Parliament, *Royal Commission on the Coal Industry*, Cmd 2600, 1926.
[B 59] Parliament, *Select Committee on Nationalised Industries, National Coal Board*, HMSO, 1969.
[B 60] Pay Board, *Special Report: Relative Pay of Mineworkers*, Cmnd 5567, HMSO, 1974.

SUBJECT INDEX TO COAL

Absence, 7.1.1; 7.1.4; 7.2.1
Absence percentage, 7.1.4; 7.4.1; 7.5
Accidents, 10
Accidents, causes of 10.1
Accounts, notes to the 8.5.1.4
Age distributions, 7.2.3
Agricultural consumption, 6.4.1; 6.6.1
Allowances in kind, 7.1.6; 7.2.1; 7.6
Anderton Shearer, 1.1
Anglo-American Combined Production and Resources Board, 9.1
Anthracite, 3.2.1; 5.4.1; 5.8; 6.1.4; 6.2.1; 6.4.1
Area Statistics Departments, 3.3.1; 4.2
Areas, manpower by 7.2.2; 7.4.4
Association of Coal in Europe, 4.5
Association of Coal Producers in the European Community, 4.5
Atomic power, 1.1; 9.1
Audit fees, 8.6.1.3
Average capital employed, 8.5.1.2
Average daily manshifts, 7.1.5

Balance of payments *see* Energy Review
Balance sheet, consolidated 8.5.1.3
Banking workers, winding and 7.2.5
Beans, 6.2.1
Benzole, gas 6.3; 8.2; 8.6.1.4
Bituminous coal, 3.2.1; 5.8
Bonus payments, 7.1.6
Brickmaking, 8.3; 8.6.1.1
British Coal Utilisation Research Association, 8.4; 11
British Gas, 11
British National Oil Corporation, 8.2
British Steel Corporation, 11
Builders' merchanting, 8.3; 8.6.1.1

Calendar year statistics, 4.3; 4.6
Calorific value *see* Energy Review
Capital, 8.5
Capital account, coal extracted on 5.1.2; 5.4.1
Capital employed, average 8.5.1.2
Capital expenditure, 8.5.2; 8.5.4
Capital expenditure, future 8.5.1.4
Cash balances, 8.5.1.4
Cash flow techniques, 8.1
Causes of accidents, 10.1
Causes of disputes, 7.3

Census of production for coal mining, 5.7; 8.5.2
Channel Islands consumption, 6.4.1
Chemicals from coal, 8.2; 8.6.1.1
Children's Employment Commission, 2
Clean Air Act 1956, 3.2.3
Coal Commission, 2
Coal, deep-mined 3.2.1
Coal equivalent *see* Energy Review
Coal extracted on capital account, 5.1.2; 5.4.1
Coal Industry Act 1965, 8.5.1
Coal Industry Acts 1973, 7.8.2; 8.5.1; 8.5.4
Coal Industry Nationalisation Act 1946, 2; 3.1; 8.1
Coal merchants, 6.1.4
Coal Mines Act 1911, 2
Coal Mines Act 1930, 2
Coal Mines Act 1938, 2
Coal Mines Reorganisation Commission, 2
Coal, open-cast 3.2.2
Coal preparation workers, 7.2.5
Coal recovered from tips, 3.2; 5.1.2; 5.1.3; 12
Coal Research Establishment, 11
Coal, sources of 3.2
Coalite, 3.2.3
Cobbles, 6.2.1
Coefficient *see* Energy Review, energy
Coke and manufactured fuel industries, manpower in the 7.9
Coke and manufactured fuel, stock of 8.5.1.4
Coke breeze consumption, 6.1.2
Coke breeze, hard 6.1.2
Coke consumption, 6.1.2; 6.4.1
Coke, manufactured fuel and 3.2.1; 3.2.3; 5.4.1; 6.1.2; 6.4.1; 8.2; 8.5.1.4; 8.5.2; 8.6.1.4
Coke oven consumption, 6.1.2; 6.3; 6.4.1
Coke ovens, 5.4.1
Coke sales, income from 6.3
Coking industry, 2
Collection of statistics, 4.1; 4.2
Collieries—numbers of, 5.2.1
Collieries, NCB 5.1.1
Colliery review procedure, 7
Comparability of fuels *see* Energy Review
Computing services, 8.3; 8.6.1.1
Confederation of British Industry *see* Energy Review
Consolidated balance sheet, 8.5.1.3
Consolidated profit and loss account, 8.6.1.3
Consultative committee, 7

COAL

Consumer categories, 6.1
Consumption, sales and 6
Conversion factors *see* Energy Review
Costs, 8.6.1.1; 8.6.1.4; 8.6.2
Countries' consumption 6.4.2
County Record Offices, 2
Crisis *see* Energy Review, Oil
Crude tar and tar products, 6.3; 8.2; 8.6.1.4
Current assets, 8.5.1.2; 8.5.1.3; 8.5.1.4
Customs, HM 6.1.7; 6.4.3

Daily output per face, 5.3
Death of workers, 7.2.4; 7.4.3
Deep-mined coal, 3.2.1
Definition of disposals, 6.1
Department of Energy, 1.1
Department of Energy *see* Energy Review
Depreciation of fixed assets, 8.5.1; 8.6.1.3
Depreciation of provisions, 8.5.1.5
Depreciation rates for plant machinery and equipment, 8.5.1
Development for fuel and power *see* Energy Review
Dismissals, 7.2.4; 7.4.3
Disposals, 6.1; 12
Disposals, definition of 6.1
Disputes, 1.1; 5.1.5; 5.2.1; 5.4.1; 5.5; 7.3
Distribution, solid fuel 8.3; 8.6.1.1
District selling schemes, 2
Domestic consumption, 6.1.4; 6.3; 6.4.1
Doubles, 6.2.1
Dry steam coal, 5.4.1; 6.1.4; 6.4.1

Earnings, 7.1.6; 7.1.7; 7.1.8; 7.2.1; 7.2.7; 7.6
Efficiency of a colliery, 5.1.3
Electricity cuts, 1.1
Electrification of pits, 3.4
Energy balances *see* Energy Review
Energy coefficient *see* Energy Review
Energy data, 6.1; 6.1.3; 6.4; 6.6.1
Energy model group *see* Energy Review
Energy modelling *see* Energy Review
Energy papers *see* Energy Review
Energy sector *see* Energy Review
Engineering services, 8.3; 8.6.1.1
Establishment of NCB, 1.1; 3
Estate and land management, 8.3; 8.6.1.1
Euraton, 9.1
Europe, Association of Coal in 4.5
European Coal and Steel Community, 4.5; 8.5.4; 8.6.1.3; 9.1; 11
European Coal Organisation, 9.1
European Community, Association of Coal Producers in the 4.5
European definitions, 5.10; 9.2.1
European Economic Community, 4.5; 9
European Energy Data *see* Energy Review
Expenditure, capital 8.5.2; 8.5.4
Expenditure, future capital 8.5.1.4

Expenditure on fuel and energy *see* Energy Review
Expenditure on revenue account, income and 8.6.1.4
Exports, 5.2.3; 6.1; 6.1.7; 6.2.1; 6.3; 6.4.3

Face output per manshift, 5.1.3; 5.2.1; 5.3; 5.5; 5.6
Face workers, 7.2.5
Fibrosis X-rays, 7.3; 10
Financial targets, 8.1
Financial year statistics, 4.3; 4.6
Fixed assets, 8.5.1; 8.5.1.3; 8.5.1.5
Fixed assets, depreciation of 8.5.1; 8.6.1.3
Fleck Committee, 1.1
Forecasts *see* Energy Review
Free coal, miners' 5.1.2; 6.1.4; 7.1.6
Freehold land, 8.5.1
Fuel conversion, 6.2.1; 6.4; 6.4.1
Future capital expenditure, 8.5.1.4

Gas and oil, North Sea 8.2
Gas benzole, 6.3; 8.2; 8.6.1.4
Gas, British 11
Gas coke breeze, 6.1.2
Gas works' consumption, 6.4.1
Geographical coverage of statistics, 4.7
Geological conditions, 1.1; 3.1; 5.1.3
Government fuel policy *see* Energy Review
Government intervention *see* Energy Review
Government publications, 4.3
Grades of coal, 6.2.1
Grains, 6.2.1
Grants, investment 8.5.1; 8.5.1.3
Grants, regional development 8.5.1; 8.5.1.3
Grants under Coal Industry Act, 8.6.1.1; 8.6.1.3; 8.6.1.4
Greene Commission, 2
Gross domestic product *see* Energy Review
Guaranteed wage, 7.1.6

Hard coke breeze, 6.1.2
Hartley Committee, 1.1; 9.1
Haulage in mines, 3.4
Health in mines, safety and 10
Heat supplied *see* Energy Review
Historical data, 2
HM Customs, 6.1.7; 6.4.3
Homefire, 3.2.3; 5.4.1
Hours worked, 7.6
House allowance, 7.1.6
House coal, 6.1.4
Hydro-electric power *see* Energy Review

Imported coal, 3.2; 5.6; 5.10; 6.1; 6.1.7; 6.2.1; 6.4.3
Income, 8.6.1.1; 8.6.1.4
Income and expenditure on revenue account, 8.6.1.4
Income from coke sales, 6.3
Incomes, National Board for Prices 4.3
Industrial consumption, 6.1.3; 6.3; 6.4.1; 6.6.1
Industrial grade colliery workers, 7.1.1
Industrial relations, 7.3

SUBJECT INDEX

Industrial revolution, 1.1
Input/output tables *see* Energy Review
Inspectorate, mines 2; 10
Institute of Occupational Medicine, 10.3; 11
Internal NCB Publications, 4.2
International data, 4.5; 5.10; 9
International Energy Agency, 8.4; 11
Investment grants, 8.5.1; 8.5.1.3
Investment in energy *see* Energy Review
Investment policy, pricing 8.1
Involuntary absentees, 7.4.1; 7.5
Involuntary wastage, 7.1.3
Iron and Steel Industry Consumption, 6.4.1
Iron casting, 6.4.1

Joint Advisory Committee, 7

Kent coalfield, 3.3.1
Key operating statistics, 8.5.1.2; 8.6.1.1; 8.6.1.2

Land management, estate 8.3; 8.6.1.1
Large coal, 6.2.1
Licensed mines, 5.1.1; 5.4.1; 7.4.2
Lift winding systems, 3.4
Local authority consumption, 6.4.1
Locomotives, 3.4
London Coal Committee, 9.1
Longwall method, 1.1; 5.1.3; 5.2.1
Low temperature carbonisation plants, 6.4.1
LS (Leasing) Ltd, 8.2
Lump sum payments, 7.8.2

Manpower, 7
Manpower by areas, 7.2.2; 7.4.4
Manpower in the coke and manufactured fuel industries, 7.9
Manshifts, 5.1.3; 7.1.5
Manshifts, average daily 7.1.5
Manufactured fuel and coke, 3.2.1; 3.2.3; 5.4.1; 6.1.2; 6.4.1; 8.2; 8.5.1.4; 8.5.2; 8.6.1.4
Manufactured fuel industries, manpower in the coke 7.9
Manufactured fuel, stock of coke 8.5.1.4
Market consumption, 6.6.2
Marketing, 3.3.4
Mechanisation, 1.1; 3.4; 5.1.4
Mechanised output, 5.1.4
Merchants, coal 6.1.4
Metrication, 4.2; 9.2.1
Miner's Federation—History, 2
Miners' free coal, 5.1.2; 6.1.4; 7.1.6
Mines inspectorate, 2; 10
Mineworkers' Pension Scheme, 8.1; 8.6.1.3
Mining Association of Great Britain, 2
Mining Research and Development Establishment, 11
Modelling *see* Energy Review, Energy
Multiheat, 5.4.1

National Board for Prices and Incomes, 4.3

National Consultative Council, 7.1.4
National Energy Research and Development *see* Energy Review
National Smokeless Fuels Ltd, 8.2
National Union of Mineworkers Executive Committee, 7.8.1; 7.8.2
Nationalisation, 1.1; 2; 3
Nationalisation Act 1946, Coal Industry 2; 3.1; 8.1
NCB (Ancillaries) Ltd, 3.3.3; 8.3; 8.6.1.1
NCB (Coal Products) Ltd, 3.3.3; 8.2; 8.6.1.1
NCB (Exploration) Ltd, 8.2
NCB (Hydrocarbons) Ltd, 8.2
NCB (IEA Services) Ltd, 8.4
NCB Collieries, 5.1.1
NCB, Establishment of 1.1; 3
NCB Library, 4.2
NCB Organisation, 3.3
NCB Public Relations Dept, 4.2
NCB Publications, 4.2
NCB Publications, Internal 4.2
Newly employed, 7.2.4; 7.4.3
North Sea Gas and Oil, 8.2
Northern Irish data, 4.7
Notes to the Accounts, 8.5.1.4
Numbers of workers, 7.2.6; 7.4.2
Nuts, 6.2.1

OECD, 4.5
OECD *see* Energy Review
Oil crisis, 1.1
Oil crisis *see* Energy Review
Oil equivalent *see* Energy Review
Oil, North Sea Gas and 8.2
Open-cast coal, 3.2.2
Open-cast executive, 3.3.2
Open-cast Mining Organisation, 3.3.2
Operating profit, 8.6.1.1
Operating statistics, key 8.5.1.2; 8.6.1.1; 8.6.1.2
Output by areas, 5.2.2; 5.3; 5.4.2; 5.9
Output, mechanised 5.1.4
Output per face, daily 5.3
Output per manshift, 5.1.3; 5.2.1; 5.3; 5.4.1; 5.5; 5.6
Output per man year, 5.1.3

Pay Board, 4.3
Petroleum and Submarine Pipe Act, 8.2
Petroleum industry *see* Energy Review
Phurnacite, 3.2.3; 5.4.1
Piecework, 7.1.6
Pits in operation, 5.2.1; 5.4.1; 7.4.2
Place of work of colliery employees, 7.2.5
Pneumoconiosis compensation, 8.6.1.3
Pneumoconiosis X-rays, 7.3; 10
Power loading machines, 3.4
Power station coal, 3.2.1
Power station consumption, 6.1.1; 6.3; 6.4.1
Price Commission, 4.3
Prices and Incomes, National Board for 4.3
Pricing and investment policy, 8.1
Primary fuels *see* Energy Review

Private mines, 3.2; 5.1.1
Production methods, 1.1; 3.4
Productivity indicators, 5.1.3
Profit and loss account, consolidated 8.6.1.3
Profit, operating 8.6.1.1
Public Record Office, 2
Public service consumption, 6.4.1

Railways' consumption, 6.4.1; 6.6.1
Re-enrolment, 7.2.4; 7.4.3
Recruitment, 7.1.2; 7.2.1; 7.2.4; 7.4.1; 7.4.2; 7.5
Redundancies, 7.2.4; 7.4.3; 7.6
Redundant mineworkers payment scheme, 7.3; 7.8.1
Regional development grants, 8.5.1; 8.5.1.3
Register of routine statistical statements, 4.2; 12
Reid Report, 2; 3.4
Rent Allowance, 7.1.6
Reporting of accidents, 2
Research and development, 11
Research and Development Establishment, Mining 11
Research and development for fuel and power see Energy Review
Research Establishment, Safety in Mines 10.2; 11
Research Establishment, Coal 11
Respirable dust regulations, 10
Retirements, 7.2.4; 7.4.3
Retreat mining, 5.1.2; 5.2.1
Revenue account, income and expenditure on 8.6.1.4
Rexco, 3.2.3
Roof supports, 3.4
Roomheat, 5.4.1
Royal Commission, 2

Safety and Health in Mines, 10
Safety in Mines Research Establishment, 10.2; 11
Saleable output, 5.1.2
Sales and consumption, 6
Sales regions, 3.3.4
Samuel Commission, 2
Sankey Commission, 2
Schedules, 8.5.1.5; 8.6.1.1; 8.6.1.4
Scottish data, 4.3
Screening losses, 5.1.2
Secondary fuels see Energy Review
Selby project, 1.1
Select Committee Reports, 4.3
Singles, 6.2.1
Slurry, 5.1.2; 5.1.3; 6.2.1
Small coal, 6.2.1
Smokeless fuel, 3.2.1; 3.2.3; 5.4.1; 6.4.1; 8.2

Solid fuel distribution, 8.3; 8.6.1.1
Sources of coal, 3.2
Steam raising coal, 3.2.1
Steel Corporation, British 11
Stock in stores, 8.5.1.4
Stock in trade, 8.5.1.4
Stock of coke and manufactured fuel, 8.5.1.4
Stock of products, 8.5.1.4
Stock, valuation of 8.5.1.1; 8.5.1.4
Stocks, undistributed 5.2.3; 5.4.1; 5.6; 5.7; 6.1.6
Substitutability of fuels see Energy Review
Sunbrite, 3.2.3
Superannuation scheme, 8.6.1.3
Surface maintenance workers, 7.2.5
Surface officials, 7.2.5
Surface output per manshift, 5.1.3; 5.2.1
Surface workers, 7.2.5

Tar products, crude tar and 6.3; 8.2; 8.6.1.4
Thermal content see Energy Review
Thomas Ness Ltd, 8.2
Three day week, 1.1
Tips, coal recovered from 3.2; 5.1.2; 5.1.3; 12
Tonnage lost, 5.1.5; 5.2.1; 5.4.1; 5.5
Transfer between collieries, 7.1.2; 7.1.3; 7.4.3
Trebles, 6.2.1
Turnover, 8.6.1.2; 8.6.1.3; 8.6.1.4

Underground engineering workers, 7.2.5
Underground officials, 7.2.5
Underground roadway workers, 7.2.5
Underground transport workers, 7.2.5
Undistributed stocks, 5.2.3; 5.4.1; 5.6; 5.7; 6.1.6
United Nations, 4.5
Units of measurement, 4.2; 5.2.1; 6.1.3; 6.4; 9.2.1
Units of measurement see Energy Review
Unscreened coal, 6.2.1
Useful energy see Energy Review
Uses of coal types, 3.2.1

Valuation of stock, 8.5.1.1; 8.5.1.4
Voluntary absentees, 7.4.1; 7.5
Voluntary wastage, 7.1.3

Wage earners on colliery books, 7.1.1; 7.4.1; 7.4.2; 7.5
Wastage, 7.1.3; 7.2.1; 7.2.4; 7.4.1; 7.4.2; 7.5
Water transport consumption, 6.4.1; 6.6.1
Welsh data, 4.3
Wilberforce Report, 4.3
Winding and banking workers, 7.2.5

20: GAS

H. Nabb

REFERENCE DATE OF SOURCES REVIEWED

This review is believed to represent the position, broadly speaking, as it obtained in August 1978. Later revisions, including the Addendum (page 104), have been inserted up to the proof reading stage, May 1979, taking account as far as possible of any major changes in the situation.

INDEX TO INITIALS USED IN THE TEXT

BGC	British Gas Corporation
DTI	Department of Trade and Industry
ECE	Economic Commission for Europe
HMSO	Her Majesty's Stationery Office
IGE	Institution of Gas Engineers
ILO	International Labour Organisation
IMSSOC	Institute of Manpower Studies System of Occupational Classification
NBPI	National Board for Prices and Incomes
PEP	Political and Economic Planning
SIC	Standard Industrial Classification
SOEC	Statistical Office of the European Communities

CONTENTS OF REVIEW 20

Addendum		104
1.	**Introduction**	105
2.	**Definition of the Gas Industry**	106
2.1.	*The Beginning of an Industry*	106
2.2.	*The Traditional Gas Industry*	106
2.3.	*The Natural Gas Industry*	107
2.4.	*The Organisation of the Industry before 1949*	108
2.5.	*Nationalisation, Rationalisation and a New Industry in Great Britain*	108
2.6.	*The Position in Northern Ireland*	109
3.	**Collection of Data**	110
3.1.	*Pre-Nationalisation*	110
3.2.	*Post-Nationalisation*	111
3.3.	*Definition and Measurement*	112
	3.3.1. Gas Measurement	112
	3.3.2. Periodicity of Meter Readings	113
	3.3.3. Thermal Values	113
	3.3.4. Load Factor	113
	3.3.5. Temperature Correction	114
3.4.	*Availability of Data*	114
4.	**Statistics in the Modern Gas Industry**	115
4.1.	*Production*	115
	4.1.1. Gas Output	115
	4.1.2. Coke and Breeze	116
	4.1.3. Other By-Products	116
4.2.	*Sales*	117
	4.2.1. Gas	117
	4.2.1.1. Domestic Sales	117
	4.2.1.2. Commercial Sales	119
	4.2.1.3. Industrial Sales	120
	4.2.1.4. Public Lighting	121
	4.2.1.5. Own Use	121
	4.2.2. Coke and Breeze	121
	4.2.3. Appliances	121
4.3.	*Comparisons with Other Fuels*	123

5.	**Manpower**	125
5.1.	*Employment*	125
5.2.	*Labour Turnover*	126
5.3.	*Sickness and Accidents*	127
5.4.	*Hours and Earnings*	128
5.5.	*Labour Costs*	129
5.6.	*Productivity*	130
5.7.	*Workload*	130
5.8.	*Education and Training*	131
6.	**Capital**	132
6.1.	*Plant Capacity*	132
6.2.	*Holders*	133
6.3.	*Mains and Services*	133
6.4.	*Meters*	134
6.5.	*Showrooms*	134
6.6.	*Financial Details*	135
7.	**Revenue and Expenditure**	136
7.1.	*Gas Billing*	137
8.	**Research and Development**	138
9.	**Natural Gas**	139
9.1.	*Discovery of North Sea Gas*	139
9.2.	*Conversion*	140
10.	**Public Interest**	141
10.1.	*Consultative Councils*	141
10.2.	*Safety*	141
11.	**Prices and Price Indices**	143
11.1.	*Consumers' Expenditure on Gas*	143
11.2.	*Retail Price Index*	143
11.3.	*Family Expenditure Surveys*	144
11.4.	*Retail Prices in Certain Large Towns*	144
11.5.	*Gas Used by Industry*	144
11.6.	*Average Delivered Prices of Fuels Used by the Gas Industry*	145
11.7.	*Index of Labour Costs*	145
12.	**Regional Statistics**	146
12.1.	*Pre-Nationalisation*	146
12.2.	*Post-Nationalisation*	146
13.	**International Gas Statistics**	148

14.	**Market Research**	149
14.1.	*Domestic Market*	149
14.2.	*Industrial Market*	151
14.3.	*Commercial Market*	151
15.	**Future Developments and Desirable Improvements**	152
15.1.	*The Impact of Corporate Planning and the Future*	152
15.2.	*Desirable Improvements*	153

Quick Reference List 155
    Key to Publications 176

Bibliography 181

Appendix: Reconciliation of Standard Regions with Boundaries of British Gas Corporation Regions 185

Subject Index 189

ADDENDUM

The following publications have become available since the work on the original draft of this review was done.

1. *UK Fuel Price Trends*

This is a quarterly bulletin available from the Department of Energy which has appeared as an Energy Commission paper. It shows current and "real" fuel price index numbers for domestic and industrial sectors. For domestic, the "real" fuel price indices are obtained after deflating by the Retail Price Index for all items excluding fuel. For industrial, the Wholesale Price Index of materials (excluding crude oil and carbonising coal) purchased by all manufacturing industry is used to deflate current prices. Quarterly and Annual Data $1970 = 100$.

2. *Price Index Numbers for Current Cost Accounting*

This is an occasional publication of the Central Statistical Office published by HMSO. It now contains indices from all domestic gas appliances, gas cookers, gas water heaters and wash boilers, gas fires and space heaters. Monthly price indices $1970 = 100$.

It also contains price indices for all stocks held by the gas industry on a quarterly basis using implied deflators from the national accounts. The estimates at constant prices consist of a figure for stocks of fuels valued at 1970 prices, plus an estimate for non-fuel stocks.

3. *"Marketing—extending success"*

This paper by E. A. Haynes (May 1979) is published as *The Institution of Gas Engineers* Communication 1085. It contains figures for exports of cookers, fires, wall heaters, central heating and water heaters for 1977/78 in thousands and as a percentage of total deliveries from manufacturers.

CHAPTER 1

INTRODUCTION

This study is concerned with statistical sources for the gas industry. It covers the production and sales of gas and by-products, manpower, capital, revenue and expenditure, prices and price indices and other relevant topics. Official statistics on the industry have been collected and published for many years. The revived *Guide to Official Statistics* [B 80] provides a broad indication of these together with their sources. In particular it refers at length to the *British Gas Corporation Annual Report and Accounts* [QRL 12] which deals extensively with the nationalised gas industry in Great Britain. Most of the official Department of Energy statistics relate to the gas supply industry in Great Britain [QRL 23] but certain tables do include additional details about Northern Ireland. The British Gas Corporation statistics [QRL 12] refer to Great Britain only. They include key information over a period of ten years whereas the tables in the *Digest of UK Energy Statistics* [QRL 23] are for varying numbers of years.

The *bona fide* researcher may be able to obtain additional information—not normally published—from the Department of Energy or the headquarters of the British Gas Corporation. Further statistics may be found in various proceedings of the Institution of Gas Engineers founded in 1863.

CHAPTER 2

DEFINITION OF THE GAS INDUSTRY

By-law 1 of the Institution of Gas Engineers states that:
"'The Gas Industry' means and includes:

(a) the exploration for, or the production, winning, treatment, transmission, distribution or utilisation of gas;
(b) the production, processing, distribution or use of the by-products of gas production;
(c) the design or construction of works, machinery, plant or apparatus in connection with any of the above purposes;
(d) related research or educational work in connection with any of the above purposes."

For the purposes of this review both coke-oven and low-temperature carbonisation industries as such have been excluded. Gases produced at gas works, purchased and reformed coke oven, refinery and natural gases distributed through mains and service pipes have been covered. In this respect it should be noted that since 1963 the *Energy Digest* [QRL 23] has been expanded to include the production, availability and consumption of gas from all sources.

2.1. The Beginning of an Industry

The "father" of the gas industry is regarded generally to be William Murdock who, in 1791, applied coal gas to light his house and office at Redruth, Cornwall. However, the supreme early publicist of the properties of gas was Frederick Albert Winsor and it was in no small measure due to his efforts that in 1812 a charter was granted to incorporate the London Gas Light and Coke Company, the first and largest of the gas undertakings.

Initially, gas was used for an illuminant for streets, public buildings and the homes of the wealthy—and it was not until the latter part of the nineteenth century that the domestic market extended to include cooking and heating.

A synoptic view of the growth of the industry is given graphically by Bell [B 5] in his Presidential Address to the Institution of Gas Engineers.

2.2. The Traditional Gas Industry

From its earliest years until the beginning of the 1960s a gas works was recognisable instantly by "its Sulphorous odour, mountains of coal and coke, and its smoke-blackened maze of pipes, buildings and boilers. These attributes were a function of the way in which gas was produced, by carbonization of certain types of coal" [B 54]. Oil-based processes had been developed as alternatives to coal-carbonisation in the formative years of the industry. However, even after carburetted water-gas became popular, coal was the basic feedstock. (Carburetted water-gas was obtained by passing steam over red-hot coke in a chamber and enriching by oil. It was more flexible than carbonisation and provided a means of using a by-product, coke.) Before being distributed the various gases needed to be washed and purified to remove ammonia, sulphur and other by-products. All gases then came together at the gas-holders where they were stored until required. From the holders to the consumers there was a network of pipes (mains), feeding at pressure into the services which went from the mains up to the gas meters. Internal installation pipes then took gas from the meters to the appliances.

The scarcity of suitable coal for carbonisation and the associated high capital costs led to developments in complete gasification of low grade coal (Lurgi process) and oil gasification. By 1967 more than half of the gas producing capacity was based on oil gasified in a number of ways whilst five years later carbonisation had disappeared almost completely.

There were several important consequences of the change to oil gasification. First, a substantial shift in raw materials occurred from coal to oil. Secondly, the new high pressure plants enabled gas to be transmitted economically over greater distances than the old coal-gas works, thereby assisting in the extension of gas grids and the concentration of production on fewer, larger sites. Thirdly a considerable impetus was given to gas sales which quadrupled between 1960 and 1973.

2.3. The Natural Gas Industry

Experiments had been approved by the Ministry of Power in 1967 regarding the importation of natural gas. These received a considerable boost when the true extent of the natural gas wells in Algeria became evident. In November 1961 official sanction was given to a project for receiving imported, natural gas at Canvey Island for distribution to the main cities between London and Leeds. Meanwhile, the discovery of a very large natural gas field at Groningen in the Netherlands had directed attention to the North Sea, where comparable geological formations exist. A search for gas began in the latter part of 1964 and by the end of 1970 five large gas fields and a number of smaller ones had been discovered in British waters.

Natural gas has a calorific value about twice that of manufactured town gas. It needs more air than manufactured gas to make it burn efficiently. Consequently, a fundamental decision had to be made whether the natural gas should be reformed, i.e. reduced in calorific value in existing gas manufacturing plant, or supplied direct, with appliances being converted to burn it. The second alternative was chosen to avoid large continuing expenditure on reforming plant as the demand for gas increased. Moreover, the transmission of natural gas to consumers enabled the carrying capacity of the existing storage and distribution system to be increased considerably due to the differences in calorific value and transmission pressures.

2.4. The Organisation of the Industry before 1949

After the formation of the Gas Light and Coke Company, other companies were established in London and the provinces. In the early days gas supply was a highly speculative business faced with strong opposition from those with vested interests in alternative fuels and operating under conditions of competition between rival gas undertakings serving the same areas.

Legislation soon gave local monopolies to statutory gas companies. Regulation of supply, quality and pressure of gas, and of prices and dividends, together with instances of municipal "take-overs", prevented the exploitation of these monopoly powers. As Daniel [B 16] indicated in his earlier work, some of the legislation had important consequences on the provision of statistical information. From 1920 co-operation and amalgamation of gas undertakings became easier initially through Special Orders issuable by the Board of Trade.

Later legislation, in 1933, fostered the development of holding companies which closed many of the smaller, less efficient works and provided gas from larger stations. Purchases of coke oven gas as an alternative to production also became more commonplace.

Nevertheless, in June 1944 the Minister of Fuel and Power considered it necessary to set up the Heyworth Committee [QRL 34] to review the structure and organisation of the gas industry, to advise what changes were necessary to develop and cheapen gas supplies and to make recommendations. This report formed the basis of the Gas Act 1948 by which the industry was nationalised.

2.5. Nationalisation, Rationalisation and a New Industry in Great Britain

On 1 May 1949 over 1000 gas undertakings were transferred to national ownership. About 700 of these were owned by companies and over 250 by Local Authorities, the remainder having been operated by Joint Boards, Electricity Boards, ancillary undertakings or non-corporate bodies. Some undertakings, mainly owned by railway and transport authorities, were not taken over. Information for these continued to be published by the Ministry of Fuel and Power [QRL 23] until the end of 1954 by which time most had been absorbed by the nationalised gas industry or closed.

The Gas Act 1948 provided for the constitution of twelve Area Gas Boards whose principal function was to develop and maintain an efficient, co-ordinated and economical system of gas supply and coke production (other than hard coke) in their areas. The first schedule of the Act gave a general description of the area of the individual Boards and the names by which they were to be known.

A Gas Council was established consisting of a Chairman and Deputy Chairman together with the Chairmen of all the twelve Area Gas Boards. The primary responsibility of the Gas Council was to issue British Gas Stock and to obtain agreements with the Area Boards over certain financial and other matters. Generally Area Boards were responsible to the Ministry rather than the Gas Council. The powers and duties of the Gas Council and Area Boards remained unchanged until 1965 when the former received additional powers and duties whereby full advantage could be taken of technical advances and new sources of gas which required development on a national scale. The Gas Act 1965 imposed on the Council a duty to promote and assist the co-ordinated development of gas supplies in Great Britain as a whole together with power to manufacture gas, to buy gas in bulk and to supply gas in bulk to Area Boards.

In order to expand gas sales following the discoveries of North Sea natural gas, the Gas Council carried out a major reorganisation of ifs own activities. The Area Boards adapted their organisations in a complementary manner pending the Gas Act 1972. On 1 January 1973 the British Gas Corporation replaced the Gas Council and the twelve Area Boards. Responsibility for Regional activity was taken over by the Corporation.

The main duty of the Corporation is to develop and maintain an efficient, co-ordinated and economical system of gas supply for Great Britain, and to satisfy, as far as it is economical to do so, all reasonable demands for gas in Great Britain. The Corporation has favoured a regional structure and decided that initially the regions should conform with the former Area Boards. Every Region is a complete management unit on its own under a Regional Chairman with responsibility for dealing with the sale of gas and the sale, installation and servicing of appliances. However, the new structure is more amenable to the development of uniform practices and standards throughout the industry.

The Gas Act 1972 also appointed a National Gas Consumers' Council. Its main duty is to consider any matter affecting the interests of gas consumers and they submit annual reports to the Secretary of State. Although it has a working relationship with the Gas Corporation, the Council is autonomous. Regional Councils replace the Gas Consultative Councils established under the Gas Act 1948.

2.6. The Position in Northern Ireland

At present there are 13 separate gas undertakings in Northern Ireland: 9 being municipally owned and 4 in private hands [B 3]. This fragmentation is akin to the position in Great Britain prior to nationalisation although there has been some integration over the years [B 44]. However, the problem is complicated by the dominance of Belfast which produces nearly 80% of all the gas made in the province. Throughout Northern Ireland the production of gas is derived from oil. In the larger undertakings a light petroleum feedstock is reformed in catalytic reforming plants whilst the smaller ones distribute a mixture of either butane or propane and air. So far natural gas deposits have not been found, despite success off Kinsale in Eire. The Department of Commerce commissioned the British Gas Corporation to undertake a survey of the Northern Ireland Gas Industry in May 1976.

CHAPTER 3

COLLECTION OF DATA

Originally a great deal of the statistical information on gas was collected to meet the requirements of outside bodies, whether official such as a Ministry or unofficial like Trade Associations and the technical press. More recently the emphasis has switched towards data required for various management purposes. This has resulted in the industry sometimes refusing to collect certain statistics for Government which clearly appeared to be useless to Management in the form suggested.

3.1. Pre-Nationalisation

Daniel (1950) [B 16] in his earlier study identified a number of distinct chronological periods relating to official gas statistics. He made little reference to details collected on a voluntary basis or to the shortcomings of the returns to the then Ministry of Fuel and Power. In order to link up with Daniel's paper—and indicate the progress made subsequently—it would seem sensible to go back to the Gas Regulation Act, 1920.

The Act of 1920 required undertakers to furnish annual accounts and statistics to the Board of Trade which followed closely the lines of previous Returns to Parliament. The main points of difference noted by Daniel [B 16] were the exclusion of Ireland, the substitution of details about calorific value for those dealing with illuminating power, and the addition of information about bulk sales between undertakings, bulk purchases from the coke ovens and the production of crude tar, coke and sulphate of ammonia.

The analyses of gas undertakings, accounts published privately by the *Gas World* [QRL 33] were improved considerably during this time. Information was given showing output by type of plant, gas consumers as a percentage of the population served, the manufacturing load factor, the distribution load factor, the date of maximum make and the date and hour of maximum demand. Holding companies, whose formation in the 1930s was an important feature in the organisation of the industry, also began to publish more accurate and extended statistics for their constituents.

Nevertheless, despite these improvements, Chantler [B 12] writing a preface in 1938 commented on the inadequacy of statistical information. In particular he noted:

"There are no official statistics collected annually relating to the 550 non-statutory undertakings and, as the majority of them employ ten or fewer workers, they do not even find a place in the Census of Production Returns. The Annual Return relating to all authorised gas undertakings in Great Britain, published by the Board of Trade since 1882, is a valuable source, but there are serious omissions. There is no record of the amount of gas sold for different uses (except street lighting). The information on price policy is of very limited value. Returns on transactions in gas utilisation apparatus are absent. Whether individual companies are independent concerns or are controlled by some outside agency is not shown."

Notwithstanding these shortcomings, Chantler's study and the report compiled by Political and Economic Planning [B 87] are the most comprehensive sources of statistical information prior to the Second World War.

The Returns for 1938–1944 were published in a composite volume by the Ministry of Power and were noteworthy for the inclusion for the first time in official statistics of information relating to non-statutory undertakers. The larger of these in England and Wales—those selling more than 30 million cubic feet of gas annually—were compelled to assume statutory powers and obligations under the terms of the Gas Undertakings Act of 1934. Those that remained non-statutory, over 400 in 1938, were required to submit an annual return of gas supplied. In the 1947 Return the particulars for non-statutory undertakers were given in the same detail as for statutory undertakers.

More detailed information was collected on the analysis of gas sales and details for 1943 to 1947 are contained in the *Ministry of Fuel and Power Statistical Digest for 1946 and 1947* [QRL 23]. Some financial statistics were published between 1945 and 1947 although the financial part of the old Board of Trade Returns last appeared in 1937.

For 1948 the statutory annual forms of return were revised and, so far as the special conditions of the industry permitted, were made comparable with the annual forms of return for the other fuel and power industries and with the schedules of the Census of Production Office. The Gas Act of 1948 provided that statistical information should be supplied to the Ministry of Fuel and Power by the Gas Council and Area Boards.

3.2. Post-Nationalisation

This provision of the Gas Act led a number of Area Boards to engage statisticians and in November 1949 the first meeting of gas industry Statistical Officers was held to arrange the transfer from the Ministry to the industry of the procedures for collecting routine statistical information. A pattern was established early on that data would be collected in the 12 Area Boards/Regions and submitted to the Gas Council for consolidation, recirculation within the industry and subsequent transmission (when required) to Ministries and other outside bodies. All requests for statistical information from outside the industry should be made to the Gas Council in the first instance.

Since 1949 the scope and content of statistical information required by the industry itself has expanded but the essentials remain of completing submissions daily, weekly, monthly, quarterly, annually or on an *ad hoc* basis. With telemetry established for grid control purposes, day to day operating instructions are coming to rely more on teleprinters and Visual Display Units than forms for data transmission. Similar developments are taking place in connection with appliance sales statistics and gas taken by industrial consumers of gas in large quantities. Experiments with mark-sensing documents to improve the analysis of data have been undertaken and more use is made of punched cards as a transmission medium.

One feature of the growth in routine statistical requirements has been a tendency recently towards the collection of data by the appropriate operating divisions, e.g. marketing, engineering, rather than through a central department. This process has been strengthened by the appearance of standard functional accounts, e.g. PROJECT MAC (Marketing Account Control), rendering and collection, production and supplies and personnel [B 21].

As far as market research is concerned, the process of information gathering is more complex. Some Regions have access to their own panels of part-time interviewers, others rely on agency staff. British Gas Corporation [BGC] HQ handles certain surveys directly whilst involving Regions with others. Postal questionnaires are employed extensively by Regions for simple projects (rarely by BGC HQ). The response rates achieved regularly reach the 75%–80% level after 2 reminders [B 62] which perhaps reflects the semi-official standing of a nationalised industry amongst the public.

Quite lengthy and detailed demographically interlaced analyses are made of the results, usually involving computer assistance. Presentations to management and staff of results are commonplace. The whole process is supported by cross-reference to internal and external data sources and syndicated studies like those of Audits of Great Britain [QRL 38].

3.3. Definition and Measurement

Particular problems of definition are dealt with, as appropriate, in Section 4. A British Standards Institution publication [B 79] on terms used in the gas industry may be a valuable supplement to readers requiring greater understanding of gas industry practice, or one by Shell International Petroleum Limited [B 86].

Useful explanatory notes can be found accompanying official published statistics, notably the *Annual Digest* [QRL 23], the annual supplement to the *Monthly Digest of Statistics* [QRL 40] and the March 1976 supplements of *Energy Trends* [QRL 30].

Statistics published in Great Britain are expressed still in the traditional units of measurement although in 1967 a booklet [B 84] was prepared showing particular aspects of moving towards SI standards Système International d'Unités). The present situation leads to difficulties in comparing one fuel industry with another in this country and between Great Britain and other countries. Further reference to some of the problems involved may be found in Sections 4 and 12.

3.3.1. *Gas Measurement*

The instruments used to measure gas range from the expensive, sophisticated devices on the national transmission system to the small credit and prepayment meters found on domestic premises. Typically the volume of gas which passes through the meter is converted into thermal equivalents by reference to the declared calorific value. However, in certain instances, e.g. large industrial consumers, the actual calorific values are maintained and used to calculate the bills.

On the statistical side, the tolerance for the official test is within the range 2% fast to 3% slow. Jewers [B 33] has evaluated the losses to the industry from meter inaccuracies.

3.3.2. *Periodicity of Meter Readings*

Although telemetry systems enable the gas taken by some large industrial consumers to be recorded daily, most meters are read quarterly over a cycle. This means that the precise amount of gas used by consumers in a given calendar period is subject to estimate since the meter registrations would normally include consumption from a previous period. The Institution of Gas Engineers published a method of dealing with the calculation of gas quantities as part of an investigation into unaccounted for gas which began in 1938 [B 88]. In recent years the British Gas Corporation has instituted a standard method for estimating unread gas which has regard to:
  (a) the consumption levels of individual consumers;
  (b) the number of days for which an estimate is required for each consumer;
  (c) an observed relationship between temperature and gas consumption levels obtained from a linear regression.

3.3.3. *Thermal Values*

The statutory heat unit by which gas has been sold in Great Britain since 1920 is the therm (1 therm = 100,000 British Thermal Units). The heating power of gas, its calorific value, is the number of British Thermal Units obtained by burning one cubic foot of it. To convert gas volumes into therms the equation used is:

$$\frac{\text{Volume (Cubic Feet)} \times \text{Calorific Value}}{100,000} = \text{Therms}$$

Alternative calorific values may be found on occasion—gross and net. The former relates to the British Thermal Units liberated by 1 cubic foot of gas when the products are cooled to the initial temperature of the gas and air (60°F). The latter is the value obtained when the water produced by combustion is assumed to remain as vapour. However, most official statistics of output relate to gross calorific values.

Gas supplied by undertakings has to conform to calorific values stipulated by them in advance—declared calorific values. Gas examiners were appointed officially to ensure that such standards were met. Not infrequently when gas was manufactured the actual calorific value recorded at the works exceeded that declared to the Ministry—the difference being regarded as part of that "unaccounted for" between production and consumption.

3.3.4. *Load Factor*

The relationship between maximum output and average output is known as the load factor. To assess plant utilisation the basis is between maximum day and average day whilst for gas distribution purposes the ratio between maximum hour and the daily demand is normally more significant. Official statistics refer to system load factor which expresses the average weekly gas available during the financial year as a percentage of the availability in the peak week during the same period.

3.3.5. *Temperature Correction*

The weather, especially the temperature component, has a significant effect on gas demand; figures are produced within the nationalised industry adjusting sales to normal temperature (see para. 15.1 for further details) but not published as yet.

A working party which had been set up in 1976 to review temperature correction methods within the industry found some inconsistencies in practice. These included the choice of temperature (whether weighted or not) and correction by market sector. However, one concept which has been applied generally to help assess temperature variation is the degree day. This is a measure of the extent to which the mean daily temperature falls below an assumed base. For many years the assumed base in the United Kingdom was 60°F as in the United States. Thus a temperature of 30°F would represent 30 degree days. In 1976, however, the temperature base was altered to 15.5°C which is more in line with European practice, and Regional figures are published now by the Department of Energy [B 72,76].

3.4. Availability of Data

The majority of sources quoted in the Quick Reference List relate to data which appear regularly. However, mention has been made of information which, although not always published, is collected either by a Ministry, the British Gas Corporation or a Trade Association on a routine or an *ad hoc* basis. This is because in many cases figures can be made available on request to the appropriate body—either in their entirety or in summary form—as indicated by some of the specific bibliographical entries.

CHAPTER 4

STATISTICS IN THE MODERN GAS INDUSTRY

From this point onwards it would seem convenient to consider the statistical information for the gas industry according to subject matter. Following such a convention will enable the developments which have taken place already since 1950 and possible future changes to be considered in some depth.

4.1. Production

For many years the information published in official statistics [QRL 23, QRL 40] related specifically to the operations of public gas supply. Later the coverage was extended to include the contributions of colliery methane, coke oven gas, blast furnace gas, liquefied petroleum gas, and other petroleum gas to the energy equation. Nevertheless, the most comprehensive analyses have continued to relate to the public supply gas industry.

4.1.1. *Gas Output*

Before the Second World War, the definition of gas made was not precise, but subsequently it was laid down that the figures should be corrected to a standard pressure of 30 inches of mercury and a standard temperature of 60°F. From the year 1943 undertakings were required, also, to measure the gas made before extracting benzole although since 1965 the gas equivalent of benzole has been excluded from the statistics [QRL 23]. After Vesting Date places supplied previously by non-statutory undertakings received gas on a thermal instead of a volumetric basis. (The early reports and accounts of the former Area Boards contain details of calorific value declarations.) Consequently, the output data for Great Britain were much more uniform than hitherto. Annual information was published on a financial year period (1 April to 31 March) in the *Annual Reports of the Gas Council* [QRL 13] and Area Boards (the first Annual Report covering an eleven month period from 1 May 1949 to 31 March 1950) and on a calendar year period in the Ministry publication [QRL 23]. Details were given initially for coal gas, water gas and other gases together with purchases from coke ovens. The analysis was extended to cover new processes, e.g. oil reforming plant, Lurgi, natural gas (imported and indigenous) and purchases from mines and oil refineries. In most cases the scope covered the volumes made, the thermal equivalents produced and the average calorific value appropriate. Soon after the outbreak of war in 1939, the Mines Department had begun to collect weekly returns from gas works in order to programme solid fuel. This practice has continued, to provide information for the industry's management and the Government. Summaries of key figures are circulated weekly within the industry and the Department although the practice of issuing a Weekly Statement on Fuel has been discontinued.

One useful result of collecting weekly information is the provision of data relating to availability under peak conditions. Published figures have distinguished between the maximum overall week and the week of maximum output of particular types of gases [QRL 23]. In practice, these need not coincide.

Within the industry considerable information is available daily, particularly since central control was established on the natural gas transmission system. Every daily period ends at 0600 hours—another relic of war-time—and information is available nationally and regionally in respect of natural gas distributed, used for gasmaking or sold direct to consumers. Within the 24 hour period much information now exists on the variations in demand which is essential for the operation and control of gas distribution [B 63]. Sometimes these short-term figures require to be adjusted for metering accuracy, changes in holder stock levels or other reasons. An illustration of variations in the hourly consumption of gas on selected days in 1967-8 for the West Midlands has been published in Figure II of Appendix A of the *National Board for Prices and Incomes Report No. 102* [QRL 51].

4.1.2. *Coke and Breeze*

Coke made at gas works usually is referred to as gas coke as distinct from hard coke produced at coke ovens. Small coke of sizes below ½ inch is regarded as breeze. Much of this was used for steam-raising at traditional gas works and consequently did not always feature in published statistics. Before nationalisation a number of regional associations had been formed for coke marketing (e.g. London and Counties, Midland, NE Coast).

The objects of the Associations were to develop markets for gas coke, to improve standards of quality and to co-ordinate prices. In 1939 they were united to form the National Federation of Gas Coke Associations. To meet their objectives the Coke Associations had begun to collect regular statistical information, in addition to that required by the Board of Trade. This practice was extended during the war—as part of the controls associated with fuel—and continued after nationalisation. Weekly data were collected regularly in the industry until March 1972 after which a quarterly cycle was adopted.

Published statistics [QRL 13, 23] covered the gross production of coke and breeze, the quantities consumed in heating retorts and used in other processes on the works. The peak of coke and breeze production was reached about 1955.

4.1.3. *Other By-Products*

Whilst gas continued to be produced primarily from coal carbonisation, several by-products were of particular importance, especially ammonium sulphate, spent oxide, tar and benzole. Official statistics [QRL 23] for the gas industry recorded the production of such by-products long before nationalisation, sometimes in considerable detail. Since many of the larger carbonising works used to operate their own tar distilleries and benzole plants, figures were available showing oxide outputs and the principal refined products obtained, e.g. road tar, creosote/pitch, naphthalene and phenol. Gas Council records [QRL 13] extended the coverage to include some details of sales and stock levels.

Trade associations had been formed to deal with some of these by-products before the war. In 1919 the National Benzole Association was formed, in 1920 the British Sulphate of Ammonia Federation Limited and in 1945 the British Road Tar Association and British Tar Confederation (now merged in the British Tar Industry Association). Arrangements were made with the Gas Council to continue to supply these Associations with statistical data. The most comprehensive requirements were those of the British Tar Association [QRL 18]. Data were published in great detail for individual gas undertakings, showing coal carbonised, crude coal tar produced and crude oil tar produced. Sales also were analysed between Tar Distillers, Co-operative Schemes and Miscellaneous. Since 1969 the scope has been reduced to some extent, reflecting the change from gas manufacturing (with by-products) to a mainly gas distributing industry.

It is worth noting, however, that certain of the by-products figures were appropriate estimates. Many gas undertakings did not have means for dividing tar production between coal-tar and oil-tar, especially if all tar went into a common tank. Usually a proportion of the gas oil used in water gas manufacture was taken as a basis for quantifying the output of oil tar. Similarly, ammoniacal liquor and spent oxide referred usually to output for sale and did not include liquor which went as effluent or oxide which was wholly waste. Moreover, the standards used for quantifying these by-products were changed over time.

4.2. Sales

4.2.1. *Gas*

The quantity of gas sold differs from the total availability of gas, not only because of benzole extraction, but a number of other factors. These include losses in transmission, differences arising from temperature and pressure variations between the supply points and consumers' premises, gas used in gas works, offices, etc. and delays in reading meters. Since nationalisation the financial year figures (1 April–31 March) as published with the *Annual Accounts* have included an adjustment of the quantities billed to consumers to allow for the estimated consumption remaining unread at the year-end [QRL 12, 23]. Calendar year data from 1966 have been adjusted similarly but for earlier years the figures [QRL 23] are aggregates of the quantities charged quarterly to consumers.

4.2.1.1. *Domestic Sales*
Before 1945 official statistics did not identify the whole of the domestic market for gas—only that part supplied through prepayment meters. (Although even here

some slight qualification is needed as certain commercial-type premises, e.g. fish and chip shops, took gas from prepayment meters.) After 1945 a more useful definition was established in the annual returns for the gas industry whereby every meter connected to a service pipe, the gas from which is used mainly for private or residential purposes, was to be regarded as domestic. Even this guide-line was to cause problems. It became necessary to ensure that the number of domestic consumers was restricted to those having main meters, i.e. excluding tenants who paid for their gas on secondary (or sub-)meters. Moreover, with the growth of communal heat schemes, it became possible for domestic consumers to receive a gas supply without the necessity of having a meter such that further qualification to the basic concept was unavoidable. This quite ignores the element of uncertainty arising from split domestic/commercial premises, e.g. doctors' waiting rooms, retail shops with living accommodation, where the determination of wholly or mainly may be subjective and liable to the influence of tariff availability. In this respect gas is quite unlike electricity where many of the Area Boards have recognised a dual Domestic/Commercial class. The figures quoted [QRL 23] for the domestic market normally distinguish between the type of main meter used, i.e. prepayment or credit. Prepayment meters became very popular after 1890 as a means of promoting gas sales, especially in conjunction with the hire of domestic appliances, such as cookers and water heaters.

Subsequently, the growth of space heating has brought about a marked switch from prepayment to credit meters, fostered by the industry itself.

Total sales to domestic consumers tended to decline in the early years of nationalisation but from 1959/60 an upward trend became apparent. Although to some degree this change was brought about by increased numbers of consumers, the more significant factor was the rise in the average level of consumption per domestic consumer due to the increased use of gas for space heating. Government statistics have tabulated therms per consumer [QRL 23] from 1943 onwards (see for example 1963 *Ministry of Power Digest*). The *British Gas Corporation Reports* [QRL 12] also contain information of relevance. Buckley [B 11] has given some idea of the pattern of gas consumption for domestic consumers.

Average sales per head of population are shown also in the Department figures [QRL 23] but one point which is vital to assessing the growth of gas relates to the area of gas supply. Electricity is regarded now as being available generally to nearly all domestic households in the country, but this is not so with piped gas. Official statistics have not covered this aspect, although even before the war certain unofficial statistical records did attempt to deal with it, and the form prescribed and supplied by the Ministry of Fuel and Power to gas undertakings for 1943 and 1944 included questions on the authorised area of supply, the availability of gas, total premises in the area of supply and the number using gas. Lists of Towns and Villages supplied with gas were required as well. However, certain comparisons prepared for international bodies have attempted to evaluate the proportion of households which could be (as opposed to are) supplied with gas from the existing mains network. A report presented to the International Colloquium on Marketing Gas in 1967 [QRL 24] assessed that in 1965 some 88% of dwellings were in the gas supply area—a proportion higher than for other European countries or the United States. (More recently the share has been given by Hetherington as 86%)

[B 29]. Unpublished estimates have been made within the industry to assess the significance of "gas supply area" in different Regions. The commonly adopted standard within the Marketing Division of the British Gas Corporation for existing dwellings is whether or not they are located within 100 yards of an existing gas main. As far as projected new dwellings are concerned, an alternative concept is used which relates to the economic viability of supplying them with gas.

4.2.1.2. *Commercial Sales*

Commercial consumers were not identified separately in official statistics until 1943 [QRL 23]. They include shops, offices (other than Government offices), hotels, catering establishments, licensed premises, banks, hospitals, schools, churches and more especially before 1949, railway station lighting. Central and Local Government sales have been shown separately, jointly as "Public Administration" or sometimes included as part of the Commercial market [QRL 12]. Official statistics on the general analysis of consumption within the United Kingdom [QRL 23] have shown another alternative, i.e. hospitals and educational establishments being included with Central and Local Government as "Public Services" and other commercial consumers shown as "Miscellaneous". The basis of counting consumers is rather different from the convention adopted for Domestic. It is taken as the number of meters directly connected to a service pipe supplying gas to premises which are used wholly or mainly for commercial purposes, except that all meters in the same name within the same premises should be regarded as one consumer.

Total sales to Commercial and Public Administration consumers increased considerably in recent years. As with domestic a significant factor was the increase in the average level of consumption per consumer.

Within the nationalised part of the industry, Commercial sales have been analysed in some detail over various headings listed in the Standard Industrial Classification. One or two undertakings, e.g. Gas Light and Coke Co. [B 24], had begun this practice before nationalisation, but data were not collected generally until 1967 and have had a restricted circulation. For the year 1966/7 the scope was limited to therms sold, value and average price received for 11 categories—to which a balancing item was added in respect of "unclassified" Commercial consumers. Subsequently the breakdown was extended to 22 categories plus separate figures for National and Central Government, with additional data for numbers of consumers and for natural gas. Thackray [B 61] has published details of how these categories match up with the Minimum List Heading of the 1968 Standard Industrial Classification. A particular weakness of the SIC for gas marketing purposes is that it is based on type of business. Since gas competes with gas oil for bulk commercial heating a new category classified as "office block" would be particularly advantageous. Offices normally are classed in the SIC as part of a local establishment—the exception being Central Offices not allocable elsewhere—so that their fuel consumptions are often mixed up with those of manufacturing departments although the usage pattern may be very different.

Johnson [QRL 8] has given national details about the composition of the total Commercial fuel market according to process and of the appropriate gas share.

He has indicated, also, the variation which exists between establishments and thermal consumption amongst different groups.

Apart from the annual figures, which are adjusted for unbilled gas, the British Gas Corporation collects quarterly details of Commercial sales according to meters read. These not only relate to sales in the different market sectors, but provide a further breakdown according to the type of tariff concerned, i.e. published tariff, firm contract or interruptible contract, which later permits gas supplied to be cut off at short notice.

4.2.1.3. *Industrial Sales*

Industrial consumers include factories, workshops and other premises where goods, commodities or articles are produced, manufactured or processed. The basis of counting consumers is similar to that adopted for Commercial, and there is reason to believe that a large part of the apparent decline in numbers of Industrial consumers from 1949 to March 1975 was due to a more rigorous application of the rules relating to main meters in the same curtilage.

Total industrial sales, which had grown steadily to 1959/60, expanded more rapidly with the introduction of natural gas from the North Sea. A new development since 1967 was its use as a primary feedstock in both power stations and petro-chemical plants producing ammonia.

An analysis over 14 market sectors has been published in the official statistics since 1963/4 [QRL 12, 23] although internal British Gas Corporation records go back to 1957 and some companies before nationalisation (Garrud, 1949 [B 24]. Thackray [B 61] has produced details of how the SIC headings can be reconciled with market sectors used in the gas industry together with figures of competitive fuel consumption. Further information on this latter topic can be found in *Industrial Fuel Markets 1973–74* [QRL 39] and *Energy for Industry 1976* [QRL 28].

The scope of the data for Industrial is similar to Commercial, but it is worth noting that unlike other types of gas sales where the nationalised industry total is the sum of the figures for all the 12 Regions, in the case of Industrial the British Gas Corporation HQ undertakes some sales directly. A good example of a bulk industrial sale is the fifteen-year contract signed with ICI in 1969 given by Reid, Allen and Harris [B 54]. Certain of these very large contracts involve feedstocks for petro-chemical plants and the gas involved is not analysed in the official statistics in an identical manner to oil used for similar purposes.

For 1946 and 1947 the Ministry returns [QRL 23] asked for particulars of sales in excess of 50,000 therms per annum to industrial consumers and the published figures analysed such sales over 9 industrial headings. Details about the size of individual loads have been collected on occasion in the industry (usually as a special exercise) and some idea of the pattern can be found in papers given by Hayman [B 28] and Buckley [B 11].

Comparisons of the sizes and numbers of industrial consumers compared with commercial and domestic for the West Midlands have been shown graphically by Goode [B 25].

4.2.1.4. *Public Lighting*

For its first general acceptance, gas is indebted to the authorities concerned for public order after dark in the rapidly growing centres of population following the Napoleonic Wars.

Despite the competition from electricity, sales for this purpose were still significant before the Second World War. During hostilities all street lighting was curtailed and although it returned afterwards gas usage for this purpose had all but disappeared by 1968. Certainly, from that time onwards sales in this market tend to be included under "Public Administration" in official statistics.

Details of lighting contracts were normally not collected although statistics of the number of lamps available to use gas were. The switch to natural gas speeded up replacement of the lamps.

4.2.1.5. *Own Use*

Traditionally gas has been used by the supply industry in its own works, offices, showrooms, etc. and recorded as such. The gas equivalent of benzole extracted was shown separately until March 1965 [QRL 23].

Gases used as feedstocks for gas manufacturing plant have been included where appropriate in the published data [QRL 12, 23]. Also account has been taken of losses incurred in the process of reforming [QRL 12, 13, 23].

4.2.2. *Coke and Breeze*

Coke and breeze sales statistics generally have been included in official publications along with those relating to hard coke from coke ovens [QRL 23]. Little information about consumption and disposals, other than exports, was collected before the last war but details have been available since 1940, originally as a result of fuel programming.

Inland consumption has been analysed over a number of headings, i.e.

Domestic
Industry—divided between Iron and Steel and "Other"
Public Services
Miscellaneous

Gas industry statistics [QRL 13] analysed these sales over slightly different headings (Domestic, Industrial, Non-Industrial, and Merchants), providing further details by size of coke. Once carbonisation ceased to be the major gas manufacturing process, such figures were not collected.

4.2.3. *Appliances*

The supply of gas is of no value to the consumer without an appliance in which to use it. In the twentieth century the major supplier of gas appliances in this country usually has been the gas industry, but official statistics [QRL 23] have related only to income from the sales of appliances. (Annual returns circulated by the Ministry of Fuel and Power between 1945 and Vesting Date had asked for details about cookers installed and in use.) This deficiency in respect of numbers and type of gas appliances has been made good for the nationalised sector by the Gas Council (and later British Gas Corporation) [QRL 12, QRL 13].

Although prior to 1953/4 some details were provided by certain Area Boards of the appliances they sold, in that year basic statistics for all Boards began to be collected. At first the appliances covered were

   Cookers
   Space heaters—gas
   Space heaters—coke
   Water heaters
   Wash boilers
   Washing machines
   Refrigerators

figures being provided separately for hire purchase and cash or credit sales. The following year the coverage was extended to include appliances sent out on and returned from hire—a practice which had been common before Vesting Date. In 1959/60, the list of appliances was extended to include gas central heating appliances and warm air units and in 1961/2 to show incinerators and tumbler dryers. In 1962/3 gas space heaters were divided between flued and flueless appliances and from 1963/4 onwards into flued heaters, fixed flued heaters and others. Later they were analysed between (i) those integral with back boiler units, (ii) unit heaters and (iii) others. From 1968/9 onwards water heaters were split between multipoints and single-points and in the next year central heating boilers began to be divided into back boilers and conventional boilers. In the latter case the analysis was extended to apply to the output rating of installations which had been collected originally in 1966/7, albeit on a "best estimate" basis. Shilton greenhouse heaters were added to the list of appliances in 1971/2 whilst the following year saw the end of coke space heaters, incinerators and tumbler dryers.

With the growing popularity of gas central heating an increasing amount of business began to be undertaken by outside contractors and merchants. (In June 1974 a particularly significant development was the acquisition of Gas Trend Limited by Comet Radiovision Services Ltd, to produce the first national competitor to BGC in retailing gas appliances.) Consequently, from 1962/3 attempts were made to estimate the numbers of central heating installations sold indirectly; in 1971/2 the list was extended to include outside sales of cookers, space heaters and water heaters. This is a very difficult problem to cover and despite extensive market research and data on deliveries provided to subscribers by the Society of British Gas Industries, it is not one that has been solved satisfactorily to date.

The contribution of gas appliance manufacturers to the British economy is difficult to assess. PEP [B 83] gave some details before nationalisation. Corley [B 15] has referred to the situation in the 1930s when electric competition became more severe, especially for cookers. More recently, Hoare and Co. Investments Research [QRL 19] have produced estimates of turnover, net output and the labour force employed. They analysed the extent to which production of various appliance types were distributed between the various producers and how the profit levels varied over time.

Internal sales statistics within the British Gas Corporation have been elaborated much further as part of a total information plan for marketing decision-making. In 1971 this was introduced as PROJECT MAC—a management accounting and control system with a number of objectives, one being to provide data in a form more comparable with that produced by private enterprise firms. Fisher [B 21] provides a full description of the system and it is referred to in later sections of this review.

In addition to information on appliance sales, estimates of the numbers in use have been made annually since 1963. Normally such data are circulated only within the industry but figures can be found in the annual reports of the International Collequium on Marketing Gas (see [QRL 24] of the saturation levels for cookers, water heaters, space heaters, washing machines and refrigerators. Although details of appliances sales by models had been collected at operational level for some time, these were only collated centrally at first in a somewhat haphazard manner. From April 1975, however, standard formats were adopted for cookers, space heaters, water heaters and refrigerators.

One interesting feature relating to appliances concerns quality control. Webb [B 67] has commented particularly on the subject of enamel damage in North Thames. Further work in this direction has been done at the Watson House research station of the British Gas Corporation and a National Defect Monitoring Scheme introduced. At present results have not been published, though they are available within the Gas Corporation.

4.3. Comparisons with Other Fuels

When assessing the relative contribution made by gas to total energy usage, a complication arises, due to differences in the original units of measurement for the various fuels. Two alternative bases have been adopted in official statistics:

(*i*) primary fuel input before allowing for conversion and distribution losses and expressed either in terms of coal or oil equivalent;
(*ii*) thermal content of primary fuels consumed directly by final consumers and secondary fuels produced by the fuel conversion industries from primary fuels and supplied to final consumers.

As the Department of Energy says in its introduction to *Digest of UK Energy Statistics 1976* [QRL 23] the relative weights of the fuels are quite different according to the method of aggregation chosen and it depends on the purpose in view which is the more appropriate to use.

The shortcomings of coal equivalent are well-known; basically they reflect the difficulty of expressing the value of non-coal fuel in terms of coal had the latter been used for a similar purpose. Thus, an overall value of 1 ton of oil equal to 1.7 tons of coal need not reflect accurately the real situation but more precise values are not possible due to difficulties of measurement in many instances.

The "heat supplied" basis overcomes some of the shortcomings associated with coal equivalents, but still presents problems where the efficiency in use of one form of energy is greatly different from another. Another possibility referred to by the DTI is the "useful heat" basis which does take account of the efficiency with which various fuels are used. The relative weightings are different again but no figures are given in the *Digest* [QRL 23] owing to lack of precise data on utilisation efficiencies and the different purposes for which fuel is used by some sectors. In November 1972 an article by G. F. Ray in the *National Institute Economic Review* [B 50] contained some estimates for domestic efficiency factors (estimated with the help of the DTI).

However, as was pointed out in the article, these figures represent the difference between input and output to the consumer. From the national point of view the situation is different because of losses incurred when converting primary to secondary energy as well as further losses in transmission. Further details on the ratio between energy received and the primary energy involved have appeared in a Building Research Establishment report on Energy Conservation [QRL 27]. A more detailed account of the problems involved in producing aggregates of fuel consumption appear in the review on Energy.

Differences of opinion about the relative efficiencies of various fuels have existed for many years. *Postwar Building Studies No. 19* [QRL 37] contain a good deal of information about the pre-Second World War situation, whilst the Ridley Report [QRL 56] gives the post-war arguments of the rival fuel interests. The recent report (1974) [QRL 26] by the National Economic Development Office would appear to be the nearest approach yet to an impartial official view of the matter. The major differences continue to be in the Industrial and Commercial markets where the precise interpretation of "efficiency" can be very important.

CHAPTER 5

MANPOWER

5.1. Employment

Certain basic details about the numbers employed in the industry began to be collected regularly during the Second World War. Before that time the *Census of Production* return is probably the best source for assessing employment in the industry, together with the *Census of Population*. The occupational analysis has been extended considerably in recent years, especially in the nationalised sector of the industry. Ministry figures for 1939 (see *Ministry of Fuel and Power Statistical Digests for 1946 and 1947* [QRL 23]), for instance, did a simple analysis, by sexes, over

    Administrative, technical, clerical, etc.
    Total works and plant
    Total distribution

A few years later meter readers and collectors began to be identified separately, together with retort house workers, transport workers and gas fitters, plumbers and service layers. Further refinements were made to the analyses such that by 1967 [QRL 23] Ministry of Power could publish a detailed table based on a Bi-annual Census of Manpower, compiled by the Gas Council. Thereafter an Annual Census, taken in October, operated until 1972.

However, this was the last occasion on which such a comprehensive picture appeared although the subsequent issue of the *Digest* stated that extracts for later years could be obtained on application to the Ministry. Such employment data as did appear showed the average number per annum of (i) Operatives, (ii) Administrative, technical and clerical employees separately for England, Wales, Scotland, Northern Ireland and Total.

Nevertheless, it is possible to obtain a more comprehensive picture of employment in the nationalised sector. Details are given both for Manual grades and Staff grades engaged on different activities at the end of every financial year. Figures are shown also for 5 grade categories of the numbers employed in the various Regions together with the total (including HQ) [QRL 12]. Appendix A of *Report No. 86 by the National Board for Prices and Incomes on "Pay of Staff Workers in the Gas Industry"* contains details of the occupations covered by the various staff grades, e.g. secretaries, foremen and supervisors, clerks and different types of engineers [QRL 50]. When making a detailed study of employment care must be taken with the definitions employed at different times. The early Ministry statistics counted part-time female workers as half units only whereas later practice was to treat all persons on the payroll as full-time employees [QRL 23]. Moreover, the definitions (now incorporated in the Annual Census of Production handled by the Business Statistics Office [QRL 17]) distinguished "Excluded employees", i.e. those engaged in canteens, sports groundsmen, bandsmen, gardeners, convalescent home employees and others engaged on any business other than in showrooms and offices and in the production, distribution and sale of products. In total such employees did not exceed 1% of the workforce. Information has been supplied also in October every year to the Department of Employment on Building and Civil Engineering craftsmen employed in the industry. Details required relate to the numbers in certain trades, e.g. carpenters and joiners, bricklayers, masons, and those apprentices having verbal or written indentures. The industry has been involved as well in other general inquiries like those relating to shift workers in 1954 and 1964 [QRL 20].

More recently, since 1971, the Department of Employment has conducted an annual census of employment which requests the number of employees at the separate postal addresses from which they operate broken down between males and females, full-time and part-time. This is believed to make good the information loss associated with changes in National Insurance administration. The results appear in the *Department of Employment Gazette* [QRL 20] and the *British Labour Statistics Yearbook* [QRL 16].

In addition to the normal classification, the industry provided the Gas Industry Training Board with a partial cross-analysis by age in 1966. More comprehensive figures have been collected since then by the British Gas Corporation as a basis for planning manpower requirements but not published. Further evidence of this interest is provided by the decision to introduce the Institute of Manpower Studies System of Occupational Classification (IMSSOC) which employs a number of axes for classifying jobs as part of a Personnel Management Information System, namely

    Job Activity
    Job Activity Level
    Job Authority Level
    Job Knowledge
    Job Knowledge Level

Urwin [B 64] has provided a full account of developments in this field. Finally, it is worth noting that some information does exist on the size of working units as opposed to occupational and age breakdowns. Early issues of the Ministry of Power *Statistical Digest* [QRL 23] analysed undertakings by the numbers of people employed at specific dates and after nationalisation figures were submitted showing employment at individual gas works.

5.2. Labour Turnover

Labour turnover statistics—expressed as a percentage of numbers employed at the beginning of year—have been published for British Gas Corporation as a whole since 1953/4 [QRL 12 and 13]. Separate recruitment and wastage rates have been given for manual workers, staff and all employees. Similar figures for the various Regions of British Gas Corporation exist at HQ but have not always been published. More extensive statistics have been calculated within British Gas Corporation analysing the results for specific occupation groups at quarterly intervals. Research has been done also into variations of turnover according to age, sex and length of service whilst some estimates of a Stability Index have been made on occasion. An example of how this index and another method of measuring wastage—"the half-life"—can be used in manpower planning has been given by Bramham [B 9] in respect of gas converters in the North East.

In using turnover statistics it must be appreciated that they have been influenced by organisational practices. A policy of engaging temporary staff—especially during summer holidays—can have a significant effect on the figures. Similarly, until 1974 the turnover was inflated by not excluding movements between different Regions of British Gas Corporation and its HQ, although subsequently internal transfers have been eliminated within the Regional data.

It is worth noting also that since 1956 details have been kept at BGC HQ specially of the recruitment and wastage of all university graduates recruited by the British Gas Corporation.

5.3. Sickness and Accidents

The man-days lost for sickness and accidents, expressed as a percentage of total possible man-days, have been issued by British Gas Corporation since 1953/4 [QRL 12, 13]. Published data analyse sickness for male manual workers and male and female staff grades whilst accident statistics refer to male manual grades alone. Some limited data on accidents amongst staff grades exist but are not published. Certain Regions have more complete information on sickness over an abridged ILO classification. The basis adopted by them for internal comparisons has been usually that of expressing the days lost per 100 people employed. In practice, this standard has been used when collecting data in the industry, generally, the conversion to a percentage of possible man-days being undertaken centrally. Also details have been collected every November on the duration of sickness spells associated with employees absent during that month. Information has been collected for many years in British Gas Corporation on time lost from trade disputes and for absence without permission but these have not been widely published. Similarly, considerable analysis of accidents on duty has been made internally. Accidents for manual workers have been classified by cause of injury, e.g. road vehicles, falling objects, and over certain broad occupational groupings. Frequency and duration rates also exist at HQ in respect of such accidents. Details of reported accidents in calendar years can be found in the *Annual Report of HM Chief Inspector of Factories* (now part of the Health and Safety Executive) [QRL 14]. However, it must be appreciated that whereas an accident is notifiable to HM Inspector of Factories, if it disables any person for three days from earning full wages at work, the gas industry records relate to absences of one day or more, not including the day or shift on which the accident occurred. Fuszard [QRL 3] has commented on different aspects of safety in gas, demonstrating that 80% of accidents are caused by falls, striking objects, falling objects, handling objects and hand tools. His paper probably contains the most comprehensive summary of accidents statistics readily available from 1965/6 to 1969/70.

5.4. Hours and Earnings

Before nationalisation wages, hours and working conditions were dealt with by the National Joint Council and its eleven Regional Councils. Rates of wages for basic occupations were agreed nationally and the undertakings graded at regional level according to size, character and economic environment to fit into the national pattern.

For a number of years wages were regulated on a sliding scale basis in accordance with the Ministry of Labour costs of living index. Co-partnership and profit-sharing schemes were strongly developed in the private companies—details being given in issues of the *Gas World* [QRL 33] Yearbooks of the schemes, years in operation and employees participating.

The statistical appendix to the British Gas Corporation annual reports contain summary results of the earnings and hours surveys carried out in April and October every year [QRL 12]. These summaries relate to adult manual workers only and show average weekly earnings, hours worked per week and pence earned per hour The Department of Employment [QRL 20] publish additional details and additional figures for female workers and young males. The *Historical Abstract of British Labour Statistics* [QRL 15] provides much earlier data on gas workers. Information appears therein for 1924, 1928 and 1931, together with a series of years from 1947 to 1968. This book is valuable in providing past details of the basic weekly rates paid to Gas Fitters and Labourers in the industry which are up-dated in the *British Labour Statistics Yearbook* [QRL 16].

Until 1974 statistics of the wages and salaries paid per annum in England, Wales, Scotland and Northern Ireland for Operatives and Administrative, Technical and Clerical employees appear in the official *Digest of UK Energy Statistics* [QRL 23]. Figures are collected also as part of the Census of Production and published in *Business Monitor* PA 601 [QRL 17]. The salaries and wages bill of British Gas Corporation appears every year in their annual report [QRL 12].

British Gas Corporation have collected figures internally for a number of years in respect of clerical grades and other staff. These usually relate to October and differentiate weekly paid from monthly paid employees. The details relate to males and females, full-time and part-time, identifying separately total salaries, overtime payments and incentive payments. (On these returns "part-time" denotes staff who work less than 30 hours per week although casual workers, working less than 9 hours per week, are excluded.)

Since 1963 the industry has been called upon to provide the Department of Employment every month with supplementary information. The following details are collected now. In the process of meeting the Ministry requirements, the Gas Corporation extended the coverage to provide additional data for its own purposes.

1. *Weekly Paid Employees*
   (i) Total amount of wages and salaries paid in the last pay week of the month
   (ii) of which overtime payment (for BGC information)
   (iii) Total number of employees included in 1(i)

2. *Monthly Paid Employees*
   (i) Total amount of wages and salaries paid in the month
   (ii) of which overtime payment (for BGC information)
   (iii) Total number of employees included in 2(i)

3. *Total Employees*—Equivalent annual rate (all for BGC information)
   (i) Total wages and salaries
   (ii) of which overtime
   (iii) Wages and salaries per head

In addition to these regular returns 1 in 15 samples have been extracted from the manual worker payroll for the month of April and October to provide details of the make-up of pay packets. Specific items covered include hours worked, overtime hours worked at different rates, basic pay, shift allowances, incentive payments and other payments. The earnings associated with manual workers covered by Work Study schemes have been recorded twice a year in April and October. Details are available for different functional categories of occupations. A recent innovation by the British Gas Corporation is to show the emoluments received by the Chairman and other Members, together with details of employees receiving more than £10,000 per annum [QRL 12].

5.5. Labour Costs

The gas industry has been involved in Surveys of Labour Costs made in 1964, 1968, 1973 and 1975 for the Department of Employment. Details were required separately for Operatives and Administrative, Technical and Clerical workers of gross annual earnings, holiday bonuses, sickness and injury payments and payments incurred during attendance at training classes. National insurance contributions, provisions for redundancy, employers' liability insurance and voluntary social welfare had to be itemised. The object has been to evaluate total labour costs for comparison particularly with other countries. Surveys of labour costs are to continue under a regulation of the European Economic Commission. Results so far have been published in [QRL 20] December 1966, March 1967, August and October 1970, January 1971, September and October 1975 and September and December 1977.

Various Reports of the National Board for Prices and Incomes have contained further relevant information [QRL 49–52]. Report No. 86 [QRL 50] recommended that more statistics should be collected on the grades, relative positions on salary scales, etc. of staff. Its authors noted the tendency for manual workers to move to salaried status whilst white-collar workers were tending more towards payment-by-results. A later Report *No. 155 Costs and Efficiency in the Gas Industry* [QRL 52] devoted considerable attention to work-studied incentive payment schemes and their development over time.

5.6. Productivity

A ratio of sales of gas per employee in Great Britain appeared in the official *Energy Statistics* [QRL 23] for many years. This is no longer published since, as Ray and Jones [B 51] pointed out, the industry changed from a maker to a distributor of gas. Nevertheless it was indicative of the exploitation of the innovations made possible by the North Sea discoveries.

Recent issues of the *Energy Digest* [QRL 23] have shown also comparative values of net output (£) per employee in the introductory section dealing with Key Energy Statistics. The British Gas Corporation give details of the relationship between capital and manpower [QRL 12]. Comparable Regional figures for the most recent year can be found in the *British Gas Corporation Annual Report and Accounts* [QRL 12]. A considerable number of comparative ratios for various types of manpower have been produced internally within British Gas Corporation. Sales staff are commonly related to the customers served whilst those on transmission and distribution of gas to the length of the mains system. Such ratios are derived not merely from historic data but also from future projections to measure performances. NBPI Report No. 155 (1970) devoted an Appendix to Performance Indicators [QRL 52] suggesting such measures as

Trench yards (on distribution) per man-day.
Number of manual workers per first-line supervisor.

Specific examples of improved staff productivity without incentive payments can be found in Appendix F of the NBPI Report No. 86 [QRL 50]. Volume II of the *Report from the Select Committee on Nationalised Industries* (1961) [QRL 48] contains some figures for Scottish Gas relating to productivity by meter readers and collectors. (This activity had been explored earlier by the Weir Committee [B 70] when trying to assess any potential benefits obtainable from increased co-operation between the gas and electricity industries.) Phillips and Hodge [B 46] have described other improvements which can be obtained in customer service.

Pryke [B 49] has given details of productivity in the gas industry compared with other public enterprises and manufacturing. Even after allowing for additional capital employed he concluded that there had been substantial improvements in gas.

5.7. Workload

A fairly recent development when dealing with manpower planning and utilisation has been the concept of workload measurement, i.e. a derived figure obtained from applying a work factor to a job count. This developed originally in Customer Service and has been documented by Jones [QRL 9] and Hill [QRL 6]. Jones referred particularly to the need for maximum definition in job counting according to job type, location and season and the importance of separating out the impact of conversion related tasks.

In 1977/8 Regional Service Departments of the British Gas Corporation completed 14.1 million jobs in customers' homes [QRL 12]. The mix of jobs has changed over time with regular servicing assuming greater importance. Since the time taken for a service visit can be very different from an installation job the original 41 categories of job adopted by HQ have been expanded in many Regions to enable more accurate local assessments of the hours required to meet customers' requirements to be related to available manpower. To help in the matching process a basic model has been produced for job forecasting and workload calculation known as SWIM (Service Workload Investigation Model). Similar ideas have been extended to distribution and now form a familiar part of planning and operations monitoring procedures.

5.8. Education and Training

Education and training activities are of considerable importance in the industry. Although internal statistics are maintained these are not published normally in great detail. However the Select Committee on Gas (1961) [QRL 48] did produce a detailed picture by Area Boards for 1959/60. Since that time more attention has been devoted to these matters and attempts made to provide a more comprehensive statistical appreciation of the overall picture. Specific details of the qualifications possessed by Senior Officers and other staff are collected periodically by BGC HQ and this coverage will be extended once the computer-based Personnel Management Information System is operating.

CHAPTER 6

CAPITAL

The *National Income and Expenditure Blue Book* [QRL 43] contains summary information on capital but more detailed statistical and financial information has been collected by the industry for a number of years on the assets employed. It would seem appropriate to distinguish the different kinds of records.

6.1. Plant Capacity

Certain pre-nationalisation publications, e.g. *Gas World Year Book* [QRL 33], did contain details of the types of plant used at the various undertakings. However, the first comprehensive analysis was that made in December 1946, summarised by Daniel (1950) [B 16].

Official statistics of plant capacity began to appear annually after Vesting Date [QRL 13, QRL 12]. The details given relate to "effective capacity", i.e. the output after allowing for limitations of ancillary plant, etc. These figures were made more valuable by the appearance of load factors which appeared variously for types of plant and size of gas works [QRL 23]. The nationalised industry began to publish details from 1953/4 [QRL 13, QRL 12] although steps had been taken to establish a comprehensive Plant Register before that time. Plant capacity was given before benzole extraction and allowance made for scurfing although not repairs. As technology developed, provision was made to show alternative capacities where more than one feedstock could be used. Alternative capacities became necessary as well with plants equipped for (1) carrier gas or (2) light oil, etc. injection. Lurgi plant capacity was stated for (a) coal only, including ballast gas and (b) including enrichment. Oil gasification plant began to be classified as

    Cyclic—Non-Catalytic, e.g. Hall, Jones
    Cyclic—Catalytic, e.g. Onia Gegi, Micro-Simplex
    Continuous—Non-Catalytic, e.g. Shell partial oxidation process
    Continuous—Catalytic, e.g. I.C.I. reformers, Power Gas (Girdler).

Total plant capacity in the nationalised sector reached a maximum around March 1969. By that time carbonising plant accounted for less than 6% of all capacity.

From 1953/4 the Gas Council *Annual Report and Accounts* [QRL 13] also contained details of new plant brought into use and plant scrapped and abandoned, not to mention the occasional retorts recommissioned. These reports showed at the end of every year the number of works in operation, supplementary details appearing for the individual Area Boards of the size of works by annual make. In addition to the annual details, figures have been submitted quarterly to the Gas Council (and later British Gas Corporation) on variations in plant capacity. These are used partly to monitor progress against forward plans submitted previously.

6.2. Holders

Here again only sketchy information prior to nationalisation can be obtained from unofficial sources. Daniel [B 16] produced details at the end of 1946 whilst other figures began to be published regularly for Great Britain after Vesting Date [QRL 23], relating both to numbers of gas holders and their effective capacity. The industry's Statistical Officers agreed in 1953 that capacity should relate to effective working capacity such that relief water gas holders merely used to accommodate fluctuations in gas pressure and production through the cyclic operation of water-gas plant would be excluded.

After 1967/8 Ministry statistics ceased to record gas holder capacity. However, low-pressure holders were ceasing to be the traditional form of storage used in the gas industry. Clarke, Cribb and Walters [B 13] refer to high-pressure vessels, linepack in super-grid systems, storage mains, etc. as means of providing storage. This paper is valuable for explaining clearly the concept of diurnal variation which arises from comparison between gas availability and demand in a 24 hour period. Later work by Bouch and Thomas [B 8] has shown how diurnal demand has been varying over the years in the Northern Region.

6.3. Mains and Services

Although information on mains can be found in some form from both official and unofficial sources prior to 1949, since that time published details appear only in the reports of the nationalised industry. Between Vesting Date and March 1975 the miles of main in public ownership nearly doubled. During this same period the number of consumers served per mile of main declined considerably, in part because some mains laid were for high pressure transmission as opposed to distribution purposes [QRL 12, 13]. In recent years BGC internal statistics have distinguished mains operating at 100 lb/sq in and above from the remainder.

Details of services have never been collected officially. However, for many years BGC has obtained unpublished figures for new services laid, relaid and disconnected both quarterly and annually. The definition of a service pipe was a problem for a time, especially with regard to supplies into flats and public lamps, but from 1958 a ruling was accepted which generally equated services with consumers, actual or potential. What is subject to uncertainty is the total number of services in existence.

Certain international standards have been adopted with reference to mains utilisation which do not appear in general use here. At the 10th International Gas Conference held in 1967 [B 81] comparative figures were circulated relating domestic and total gas sales to lengths of main whilst "lost" gas (i.e. unaccounted for) was expressed per length of main per day.

One aspect of the mains which has been studied in some detail by the Institution of Gas Engineers (Gas Distribution Committee) has concerned pipe breakages. The information has been analysed exhaustively according to the location of the pipe, the depth of cover, the type of joint used, type of fracture and condition of soil around the break. Severe weather conditions have been found to be a major factor. This information has not so far been published but is referred to in the King Report [QRL 57]. Four factors which are considered to have an effect on the level of escapes reported by the general public are:

1. renewal activity on mains and services.
2. system leakage control treatment.
3. extent of leakage survey.
4. conversion to natural gas.

Internal statistics supporting these conclusions have been prepared by British Gas Corporation, although variations in data collection before April 1973 have precluded both a detailed analysis and the identification of definite trends.

6.4. Meters

Meters are important for many reasons. Most consumers obtain their gas through a meter and about 10% of the work of fitters concerns meters one way or another. Unpublished figures have been collected centrally at BGC for many years on meters fixed and removed although not for meters exchanged or repaired. However, this kind of analysis is necessary at Regional (formerly Board) level since forward forecasts of meter requirements are essential for forward planning.

6.5. Showrooms

Showrooms have served many purposes in the gas industry, e.g. enquiry centres, cash receipt agencies, in addition to their main function of selling. The National Board for Prices and Incomes Report No. 155 [QRL 52] devoted considerable attention to showroom efficiency, producing supporting evidence on turnover, floor area, type of ownership, levels of bill payments, etc. They advocated that the industry should undertake a thorough examination of the viability of showrooms and their suggestions can be seen to be reflected in some of the ideas embodied in PROJECT MAC [B 21].

Details on turnover, purchases, margins, stock levels and employment have appeared in various reports on the *Census of Distribution* [QRL 53, 54].

Differences of treatment in installation, maintenance and repair of appliances have occurred and been noted.

6.6. Financial Details

The Ministry publish details for Great Britain [QRL 23] showing acquisitions and disposals of capital assets and also separately the value of the output of the industry's own employees concerned with new construction. Capital expenditure on plant, etc., road vehicles and vessels and new building work appears also for the different parts of the UK.

The *Annual Report and Accounts* [QRL 12] for the BGC contains more detailed figures.

Before Vesting Date although some figures of capitalisation can be found they need considerable care in interpretation. Differences in the capital structures of Company and Local Authority undertakings had resulted in the former selling on average 6.5 therms for every £1 of share and loan capital whilst the latter sold 20 therms per £1 of outstanding debt. Bailey [B 4] has pointed out that there was no common practice in the accounting treatment of fixed assets in the accounts for Gas Companies, many operating wholly or partially on the renewal method. Undertakings owned by Local Authorities, however, tended to favour a depreciation approach.

Details on borrowing and financing of the industry's operations—both capital and revenue—have been given by Smith [B 58]. Table 4 of his paper contains an example of the type of monthly performance against agreed objectives.

McKnight [B 43] supplemented the picture by providing additional facts on working capital.

CHAPTER 7

REVENUE AND EXPENDITURE

Details of Gross and Net Output have appeared for many years in the official statistics. [QRL 23] and Stone and Wigley [B 59] have produced estimates at constant prices.

Although separate figures are published for England, Wales, Scotland and Northern Ireland, the Regional information collected by BGC is not available generally. Nevertheless income from gas sales—the major element of Gross Output—is shown for individual Regions in the BGC *Annual Report* [QRL 12]. The consolidated trading and profit and loss account of BGC cross-analyses costs between operating and support activities and between prime materials and a variety of other headings. A number of changes in accounting practice adopted by BGC prevent any absolute comparisons with figures for the former Area Boards and Gas Council. Reference is made to these variations in the Notes to the Accounts in the 1973/4 *Annual Report* of BGC [QRL 12].

The procedure for reconciling information required for Annual Reports with the needs of the appropriate Ministries has been well-established, Gross Output, for instance, being the income shown in the revenue account less "other payments including payments to contractors". Reference to specific account headings tends to ensure uniformity.

Installation and contracting and Appliance Marketing accounted for over a fifth of the trading costs so that it is not surprising they had been subject to scrutiny by the NBPI. Report No. 102 on "*Gas Prices*" [QRL 51] contains comparative costs of these activities in 1976/8 and a number of strictures on management accounting standards then extant. Most accounting information was considered at that time to be geared too closely to the form of annual accounts with the result that the costs shown for services were not true indicators. The treatment of overhead expenses was too arbitrary. These have been remedied subsequently by such developmeans as Project MAC [B 21], although other differences in cost noted by Cooper [B 14] due to variations in service levels, customers, staff, history, habits, unions and consumer councils still make it difficult to use the accountancy results as an entirely satisfactory measure of real management achievement.

The benefits of the new systems are:

(1) the facility for inter-regional comparisons, particularly in terms of unit costs;
(2) the ability to set functional targets on specific activities and to monitor achievements against targets;
(3) a greater awareness in management of the costs and/or benefits that follow decisions;

(4) a broad guide in the assessment of pricing policy for such as service charges and other rechargeable work; and
(5) the involvement of line management in a reassessment of their needs in the way of management accounting information.

Before nationalisation the paucity of data was even worse than that pertaining in the 1960s. The *Report of the Committee of Inquiry into the Gas Industry* (1945) [QRL 34] commented that such accounts as were published did not give the layman a clear picture nor did they provide means of comparison between one undertaking and another. Nevertheless some attempts were made to study costs and revenue, notably by Sleeman [B 57] in respect of 38 municipal undertakings in 1938/9 and 1946/7 and Lomax [B 40] for different size groups. Under Section 41 of the Gas Act, 1948, income was supposed to be not less than sufficient to meet outgoings properly chargeable to the revenue account taking one year with another. The 1961 White Paper on *The Financial and Economic Obligations of the Nationalised Industries* [QRL 32] received the comparative results for gas and other industries and made new suggestions regarding financial objectives. These gave rise to financial target being calculated for the industry and component Boards. NBPI Report No. 57 (1968) [QRL 49] contains details of such targets expressed as a percentage of net assets.

Smith [B 58] has referred to the limitations inherent in calculating returns on capital employed. The latter figure comprises unadjusted book values—a mixture of historical costs, due to the differing age of assets, and sharp changes in prices.

Changes in the accounting system prompted by a need to take inflation into account when replacing assets and for building up reserves to help pay for dearer gas in the future affected the published profit in 1976/7. Consequently it must be accepted that pre-tax profits are not always a good measure of financial performance so that alternative indicators may need to be developed, e.g. comparisons with public utilities elsewhere. Indeed the re-introduction of financial targets might receive renewed support.

7.1. Gas Billing

In very many businesses no information is collected either to analyse customer reaction to accounts or to establish the reasons for non-payment. McKnight [B 43] has produced some figures for the Scottish Region relating to credit gas bill enquiries, whether received from correspondence, showrooms, telephone calls or personal visits. Every week an analysis is made for 28 types of enquiry. Somewhat earlier (1972) North Eastern [B 78] carried out a major market research investigation amongst customers who had queried some part of an account or similar document. Amongst various aspects dealt with were the length of time before a full answer was obtained, acceptability of estimated bills for gas consumption and arrangements for the Budget Plan method of payment.

CHAPTER 8

RESEARCH AND DEVELOPMENT

Because of the widespread nature of the problems associated with the production, transmission, distribution and utilisation of gas, there has been a long tradition of co-operation with other industries and research associations. Before nationalisation Regional Centres had developed to pool technical information in the industry and overcome the lack of adequate technical staff at many of the smaller undertakings. Subsequently, the Annual Reports of the nationalised body included very full accounts of research and development activities [QRL 12]. Ray and Jones [B 51] have shown the trend of expenditure related to turnover at constant prices. In 1974–5 the relevant expenditure was apportioned between the Research and Development Division of BGC, Regional laboratories and in operating the Westfield Development Centre. The latter is concerned with developing a high-pressure slagging gasifier for coal gasification. Income from external sources is shown separately as well, including the total cost of the Westfield operation.

A great deal of research aimed at producing a synthetic natural gas from coal is done not by the British Gas Corporation but by the National Coal Board. Proposals have been made for coal liquefaction and gasification involving the use of solvents, more sophisticated forms of coal carbonisation and a fluidised bed gasifier which could produce a gas capable of driving both gas and steam turbines.

Modern high-efficiency processes exist already for producing a substitute natural gas from oil.

CHAPTER 9

NATURAL GAS

Exploration for oil and natural gas on land in the United Kingdom has been carried on for many years. Initially this was done under the terms of the Petroleum (Production) Act, 1918 and later under the Petroleum (Production) Regulations 1934.

The Select Committee on the Gas Industry, 1961 recorded how much money had been spent unsuccessfully—on searching for additional sources. At that time the importations of liquefied natural gas from Algeria to Canvey Island seemed to be the most likely way of acquiring natural gas. (Indirectly this project helped the construction of a natural gas grid later used for the transmission of natural gas from the North Sea.)

Jones [B 37] calculated that at full load two tankers could deliver about 10% of the existing total requirements of gas which would be used mainly to enrich lean gases produced either in the Lurgi plant at Coleshill or in some of the reformers.

9.1. Discovery of North Sea Gas

The 1958 Geneva Convention on the Continental Shelf established that a coastal state has the right to the natural resources of its sector of the Continental Shelf. In 1964 the United Kingdom Parliament passed an Act which gave the Government power to grant licences to search for and extract petroleum (oil or gas). Drilling in the United Kingdom sector of the North Sea began on 26 December 1964 and gas was found in the autumn of 1965. Supplies from the West Sole Field began to flow into the natural gas pipeline system in July 1967. The petroleum industry is mainly responsible for the extraction of natural gas from the wells and its despatch to the beachhead where it enters the Gas Corporation transmission system. An exception is the Morecambe Field drilled by a wholly-owned subsidiary of the British Gas Corporation.

In the *Energy Digest* [QRL 23] for 1966 a section appeared for the first time dealing exclusively with natural gas. Figures were shown in respect of licences issued, the area licensed, wells drilled and completed, wells drilling at end of year and production during the year. In August 1971 a generally unpopular move was the introduction of licensing by cash bid. Fifteen blocks were selected for award to the highest cash bidder, sealed bids having to be submitted before 30 August. A list of blocks and successful bidders has been compiled by Hinde [B 30].

By 1973 official statistics [QRL 23] had been expanded considerably. Information published covered rigs employed and wells drilled, an analysis of the supply and disposal of natural gas and estimates of the recoverable reserves. Certain of these figures are abstracts from the annual report to Parliament on *Development of the Oil and Gas Resources of the United Kingdom* [QRL 21]. The report presented in May 1975 indicated the scale of production which could be supported from known reserves plus the addition to be expected from the Frigg Field. Details relating to the beachhead price and supply conditions for some major natural gas contracts have been summarised in a convenient form by Reid, Allen and Harris [B 54].

9.2. Conversion

During the summer of 1966, the appliances of consumers on Canvey Island were converted to burn natural gas. This operation was followed in the summer of 1967 by the conversion of Burton-on-Trent and the start in earnest of the national programme.

Details of the customers converted in a year and the total numbers using natural gas direct are published by the British Gas Corporation. The first Region to complete conversion—Wales—had done so in June 1974 and the entire programme was finished by September 1977. Information as to rates of conversion, numbers of components required and so forth have appeared in the texts of various industry *Annual Reports* [QRL 12]. NBPI Report No. 155 [QRL 52] contains some information as to the costs of the operation, whilst further data for Wales only have been released by Griffiths [B 27].

CHAPTER 10

PUBLIC INTEREST

As a major part of the gas industry in the United Kingdom is nationalised, it has given rise to a greater concern with the public interest than many other industries. This has been reflected in studies made into public views on nationalised industries, such as that compiled by Abrams (1960) in *Socialist Commentary* [B 1]. However, as so many of these enquiries had strong political overtones it is difficult to treat them as wholly objective.

10.1. Consultative Councils

Perhaps more valid indications as to consumer interest can be obtained from the work of Gas Consultative Councils. These were established under the Gas Act 1948, to consider matters affecting the supply of gas and the services and facilities provided. Details appeared in their Annual Reports in respect of the total numbers of representations made analysed over various categories and they are consolidated now in the Report of the National Gas Consumers' Council [QRL 11].

The total complaints represented only 2 per 1000 consumers in a year which may not reflect a high standard of consumer satisfaction so much as a lack of awareness about Consumer Councils.

One of the first acts of the North Western Council after its reconstitution under the Gas Act 1972 was to commission a piece of research with Manchester University on public awareness and degree of satisfaction provided by such bodies [B 74]. The Second Report of the National Gas Consumers' Council for 1974/5 listed a number of crucial topics requiring detailed research [QRL 11] and reported on its own investigations into public awareness in 1975 and 1976.

10.2. Safety

During the carbonisation era, there were certain hazards associated with the use of coal gas, notably carbon monoxide. Statistics of accidental deaths attributed to gas appear in the *Registrar-General's Statistical Review* [QRL 47] although there are grounds for believing that on occasion some "suicides" have been regarded as "accidents" to spare family feelings.

In July 1970, Professor Frank Morton published a comprehensive report on the safety of natural gas as a fuel [QRL 55]. Both the Registrar-General's Statistics and details collected by the industry, which were included in the report, indicated a dramatic decline in deaths from gas poisoning. Professor Morton also dealt with other hazards, namely fire and explosion, referring to data published by the Fire Research Station for 1969 (Appendix 6 of the Morton Report) which assessed material damage and injuries resulting from gas explosions in dwellings both for manufactured gas and natural gas.

The conclusions of the Report indicated that natural gas was non-toxic and its substitution for manufactured gas will reduce and possibly eliminate poisoning accidents from unburnt gas. The most serious dangers encountered in the enquiry were lack of adequate ventilation and flueing, especially the use of unflued appliances in unventilated rooms. These aspects featured prominently in the publicity attendant upon a report issued by a team of the Medical Research Division of the Health Education Council regarding water heaters in Bristol in 1972. A lengthy section of the first report of the South Western Gas Consumers' Council [B 75] is devoted to the matter, comment being made that the team's conclusions did not appear to have been accepted by the Health Education Council itself. The Institution of Gas Engineers 39th Autumn Research Meeting held in 1973 devoted considerable attention to different aspects of safety in the industry. Frith and Smith [B 22] updated the records relating to accidental deaths, giving details of the variations in appliance establishment with which to obtain a yard-stick for improvement. Alexander and Taylor [B 2] presented a paper on 'The Frequency and Severity of Gaseous Explosions" dealing with incidents reported from 1 April 1971 to 31 March 1973 and which involved piped gas. However, as only 122 incidents were regarded as being "significant", 98 of these being attributed to piped gas, any conclusions were bound to be tentative. Consequently, the authors recommended that further work should be undertaken.

In June 1977 a further report commissioned by the Department of Energy [QRL 57] into serious gas explosions was produced by Dr. P. J. King, who had assisted Professor Morton in the earlier enquiry.

CHAPTER 11

PRICES AND PRICE INDICES

11.1. Consumers' Expenditure on Gas

The National Income statistics [QRL 43] estimate personal consumption of gas in Great Britain to be the domestic sales—as shown in published statistics—plus an allowance to represent the domestic element in sales to commercial and public administration. (This allowance was given as 1% in *1956 Sources and Methods* [B 85] and confirmed in the 1968 edition.) A further 1½% was added to cater for Northern Ireland but since 1969 sales estimates provided by the Ministry of Commerce have been used. The average price for valuation is the average revenue per therm for domestic supply sales of gas to domestic consumers in Great Britain. Expenditure at constant prices was obtained by applying the average receipts in the base year to the number of therms used in each year which did not seem ideal with the growth in popularity of two-part tariffs. Consequently current price estimates are now deflated by movements in the gas component of the retail price index, thus recognising that gas sold on different tariffs represents sales of separate "products".

11.2. Retail Price Index

Information about retail prices including the price of gas has been collected on a continuous basis since 1914 when the weights used were based on a family budget enquiry made in 1904. Since then there have been changes in the composition of the index and the relative importance attached to gas. The index for gas is available monthly from the Department of Employment [QRL 20].

When the interim Index of Retail Prices was started in 1947, information on gas prices was obtained for 200 towns throughout the United Kingdom. The data related to the standard flat rate charge per therm for supplies by credit meters and meter rents. If block rate tariffs were in operation the rate for the initial block was used. Subsequently, the charges were related to a standard consumption of 25 therms per quarter in the separate gas Regions. With the growing popularity of two-part tariffs the Department of Employment endeavoured to match their index calculations to consumption patterns by collecting annual details for separate domestic tariffs in respect of:

(*a*) the numbers of consumers
(*b*) average therms per consumer
(*c*) the aggregate annual expenditure

As an extension of a study of the domestic market for fuel (1968) [B 59] Wigley had a national annual series for the marginal price, or commodity rate, for gas. In this context he used the levels and dates of tariff changes since 1952 allied to the gas sold at standard rate or by two-part tariff.

11.3. Family Expenditure Surveys

The weights used in the retail price index are derived from family budget enquiries. Although gas was used in the pre-war index it related to the pattern of working-class expenditure in 1904. The Department of Applied Economics at Cambridge has attempted to estimate the records back even before this date, to 1900. In 1937–8 a family budget enquiry covering manual workers in general and non-manual workers with earnings not exceeding £250 p.a. was held to up-date the weights of the retail price index (results were published in [QRL 20] Dec. 1940 and Jan. 1941). The results did not become available until after the war and were used to estimate weights in the interim index introduced in 1947. The next comprehensive enquiry was in 1953–4 whilst in 1957 the continuous Family Expenditure Survey commenced [QRL 31]. Results of these studies have been used by economists in the gas industry and outside (e.g. S. J. Prais) [B 48] to assess the elasticity of demand for gas.

More recent published estimates of expenditure elasticity and price elasticity are given by Stone and Wigley (1968) [B 59] together with some alternative projections associated with different price assumptions.

11.4. Retail Prices in Certain Large Towns

Since 1966 the annual publication on fuel and power statistics [QRL 23] has included typical retail price of gas for different consumption levels in 14 large towns. The usual practice is for the *Digest* to give figures for the three latest years (December).

The annual levels of consumption chosen are 80, 250, 400, 800 and 1200 therms. The prices are based on the most economical domestic tariffs for the appropriate consumption level. Standing charges have been taken into account where applicable. In recent issues the adjustment associated with natural gas has been shown in respect of those towns partly converted; for complete conversions the price relates to natural gas only.

Watson (1969) [B 66] adapted this retail price information to show comparative costs of using different kinds of appliance.

11.5. Gas Used by Industry

An official series is published showing the average revenue received by the gas industry from sales to industrial consumers [QRL 23]. From the beginning of 1974 unit values have been calculated quarterly by a panel of about 800 large fuel consumers within manufacturing industry in Great Britain. From April 1976 figures have appeared in *Energy Trends* [QRL 30] as well. These differ from the figures produced by BGC [QRL 12] which relate to *all* industrial consumers. Year to year variations in the value received per therm sold reflect not merely tariff changes but also alterations in the pattern and scale of consumption.

11.6. Average Delivered Prices of Fuels Used by the Gas Industry

Information on the average delivered prices of the fuels used by the gas industry has been published for a number of years [QRL 23]. The items covered are coal for gas-making (and other purposes prior to 1958/9), light oil, gas oil, heavy oil and natural gas. Figures are collected also by the industry showing the cost of liquefied petroleum gases purchased. A useful synopsis of raw material prices movements for 1938/9 and 1949–1959 inclusive can be found in the Appendices to the Minutes of Evidence taken before the Select Committee in 1961 [QRL 48].

11.7. Index of Labour Costs

In addition to information on labour costs referred to earlier in the Manpower section, a number of indices have been published on weekly wage rates. Perhaps the most interesting one is that published by the *Guardian* newspaper based originally on 1948 as 100 [QRL 2].

CHAPTER 12

REGIONAL STATISTICS

12.1. Pre-Nationalisation

The *Ministry of Fuel and Power Statistical Digest* [QRL 23] for 1946 and 1947 refers in its Preface to the definition of Regions adopted at that time. However, the only table on gas which gives a Regional analysis is in respect of sales to industrial consumers using 50,000 therms per annum or more.

The *Gas World Yearbooks* [QRL 33] did produce details for separate counties of the numbers and sizes of gas undertakings and the PEP Report on the industry in 1939 [B 87] contained a map of the main centres of gas production in England and Wales.

12.2. Post-Nationalisation

The Standard Regions used for statistical purposes form the basis of certain final energy consumption tables published since 1962. These tables appear both in original units of measurement and on a heat supplied basis for industry, domestic and all classes of final consumers.

Although Wales and Scottish Regions of the British Gas Corporation conform with the Standard Regions, this is not so with the remaining 10 English Regions. In some cases, e.g. West Midlands, the differences are not too significant but it does mean that some approximations may be necessary when producing figures for Standard Regions. Details on appliance sales—as required for the *Census of Distribution*—can be obtained by proper allocation of showroom details, for instance, whilst gas can be treated somewhat similarly since data have to be collected for individual Local Authorities under the formula used for paying rates.

Nevertheless, the position remains that the most detailed information below national level refers to the operating management divisions and not the Standard Regions. In this respect, however, gas is no different from other nationalised industries, such as electricity. Prior to the formation of the British Gas Corporation on 1 January 1973, the previously autonomous Area Boards had issued their own Annual Reports containing a wealth of data which supplemented the national statistics. Now there are signs that this practice is being revived by certain Regions of the British Gas Corporation although the content and style of presentation is undergoing considerable revision.

The Yearbooks published by the gas technical press have continued to show Area Board/Gas Region statistics although again the tendency in recent years has been towards a reduction in the coverage [QRL 33]. Figures relating to component undertakings—which continued to appear for a while for some Area Boards, both in the Yearbooks and their own Annual Reports—have disappeared. With the evolution of a new management structure, based more on consumers than former gas works' areas of supply, it is anticipated that new bases for statistical comparisons will emerge. Since it is by no means impossible that changes could be made to existing Regional boundaries, in time this might affect any analysis which can be made of variations below the national level.

CHAPTER 13

INTERNATIONAL GAS STATISTICS

Although the scope of this review is limited to UK Statistics, it may be worth noting that a considerable amount of useful summary information can be found in comparative international source books. Much of this is expressed in metric standards.

The International Gas Union has published figures on a world-wide basis [B 81]. A Gas Committee established by the Council of the Organisation for European Economic Co-operation in 1956 co-operated with the International Gas Union in providing information for Europe. The Department of Energy's *Digest of United Kingdom Energy Statistics* [QRL 23] gives reconciliations between EEC and UK figures. The United Nations also has included gas data in statistics of World Energy Supplies whilst the International Colloquium on Marketing Gas reports on the Domestic Gas Market in different European countries and the United States [QRL 24].

An *Energy Statistics Yearbook* is published by the Statistical Office of the European Communities (SOEC) and an *Annual Bulletin of Gas Statistics* is issued by the Economic Commission for Europe (ECE).

International Gas Union analyses especially are useful in respect of providing details of imports and exports of gas—notably liquid petroleum gas—by reference to the particular countries involved.

CHAPTER 14

MARKET RESEARCH

The emphasis in the preceding sections has been on data produced regularly and published for general use. However, a great mass of additional information has been collected, especially in recent years, by market researchers. Certain of their findings have been released and it would seem desirable to refer to such information.

14.1. Domestic Market

The first market research section in the gas industry was almost certainly that established by the Gas Light and Coke Company in 1946. Reece [B 52, 53] has produced a record of methods they adopted. Before that time, however, some details had been published, mainly by Government departments, on the numbers and patterns of use of gas-burning appliances.

In 1947–8 an enquiry was instituted into domestic hot water supply in Great Britain with the collaboration of the Social Survey. The results appeared in the National Building Studies Series as Special Reports Nos. 8 and 14 printed in 1950 and 1952 respectively [QRL 41, 42].

A few years previously, in 1942, the Department of Scientific and Industrial Research had commissioned an enquiry into the heating of working-class dwellings. Details published in 1945 related to cooking, central heating and laundry requirements over the 5 geographical regions used in the National Building Studies [QRL 37]. Somewhat later, in 1948/9, The Social Survey produced more facts on *Domestic Utilisation of Heating Appliances and Expenditures on Fuels* in a report by Wilkins [B 68]. Additional reports followed by Gray (1954, 1955) [QRL 4, 5] into heating appliances in urban households of medium and low rateable values. Aspects covered included hours and time of usage, together with ancillary details on cooking and water heating.

Research being carried out about this time by the British Electrical and Allied Industries Research Association (1948, 1949) [B 69, 82] was useful as providing further information upon the popularity of certain gas appliances, e.g. cookers, space heaters, wash boilers, amongst electricity users. Comparable figures can be found in later reports produced by the Electricity Council, e.g. for 1955 and 1961 [B 71, 89, 90]. Other research into domestic appliances was being undertaken by independent organisations. *Woman* magazine published a series of reports on gas appliances comparing ownership patterns of all housewives with those of their readers [QRL 45, 58, 61, 62]. These reports are interesting insofar as they analyse brand popularity of different appliances. The Economist Intelligence Unit/British

Market Research Bureau began about the same time a service of economic forecasting and market research on space heating appliances and gas and electric cookers [QRL 25]. Audits of Great Britain inaugurated a continuing sample of 35,000 homes to assess sales and changes in establishment of central heating, cookers, space heaters, refrigerators and water heaters [QRL 38]. Since their analyses covered all fuels as well as gas they were useful in showing how the gas market share was behaving as well as absolute sales—an example appearing in Fulop and Harris [B 23].

At the same time the gas industry itself was expanding its market research activities. In 1950 the East Midlands' first survey examined the gas cooker market, its location, type and size. In 1959 the Scottish Gas Board conducted a motivation survey of the reasons why people changed from gas to electricity in their Glasgow and Western Division [B 73].

Everard (1960) [B 20] produced extracts from a number of North Thames and South Eastern investigations into cooker gas consumption, refrigerators, water heaters, central heating and minor appliances. The following year Bone [B 7] provided further data on appliance establishments in the South East whilst Polanyi gave some results from surveys completed in the North West [QRL 10]. Johnson (1963) [B 34] presented data dealing particularly with gas fires in the East Midlands and Evans (1963) [B 17] dealt with some figures for Wales and Tilley (1973) [B 62] with North Eastern. However, the support given to the market research varied considerably in different parts of the industry and although a national approach had begun to evolve in 1959, the first large-scale survey involving appliance establishments did not occur until 1969. Since that time as Johnson (1971) [QRL 8] has shown, the scope and size of the activity has increased appreciably.

A specialist type of research which began to assume increasing importance around 1960 was Load Research based on the individual metering of specified types of appliances in the customers' premises (Johnson [QRL 7]). Polanyi and Berrisford [B 47] indicated that the need arose, especially in the domestic market, from the growth of the new type gas space heating which was producing greatly increased gas demands at peak hour and peak day periods.

In recent years as Johnson [QRL 8] has reported, the conversion exercise has been monitored by market research techniques. Moreover, the industry has extended its interest into customer service activities and public relations. These latter aspects have been of concern also to members of the Consumer Association as shown in *Which?* [B 91].

Details of the initial surveys into the "image" of gas were given by Sir Kenneth Hutchinson in 1964 [B 31]. These compared gas with other fuels and sought opinions on service and the competence of personnel. The results influenced the new advertising policy documented by Green (1967) [B 26]. More recently, Tilley [B 62] has reproduced a specimen table showing consumers' price expectations.

Jones and Olssen [B 38] have referred in some detail to two major national surveys into customer service conducted early in 1968 and late 1969.

An idea of how far the gas industry has itself progressed in recent years can be obtained from Bone (1976) [QRL 1]. In a paper presented in 1975 he summarised work done in Northern Gas between 1965/6 and 1973/4 on appliance establishments and acquisitions.

14.2. Industrial Market

This market was not so well served with research data as the domestic one. Johnson [QRL 8] has given a full account of the development of a national policy in this sector with the employment of Merrett Cyriax in 1968 to assess industrial fuel usage throughout the country. When the original study was completed the total industrial fuel market was segmented into three:

1. Upper premium—high price—electricity, gas, oil, light fuel oil and liquefied petroleum gas.
2. Lower premium—medium price—medium fuel oil.
3. Non-premium—low price—heavy fuel oil and solid fuel used for crude heat.

The relative size of the segments was evaluated by Johnson [QRL 8]. At that time the figures reconciled with those published officially. Since then, differences in interpretation, e.g. regarding natural gas used as feedstock in chemical plants, has made it necessary to look more closely at the definitions employed.

In October 1973 the Confederation of British Industry [QRL 59] decided to undertake jointly with the Department of Trade and Industry a wide-spread and detailed survey of fuel used in industry. The questionnaires were issued in July 1974 and some 1269 were analysed (63 relating to non-manufacturing industries). Quite apart from providing data by SIC orders interesting details were collected about changeover to gas from other fuels. The *National Institute Economic Review* of May 1975 produced further information on such movements as part of its study into industry's reaction to the energy crisis [QRL 44].

Further work on industrial markets has been published by the Gower Press in *Industrial Fuel Markets 1973/74* [QRL 39]. Johnson [B 35] has supplemented earlier papers with regard to marketing segmentation and pricing research.

14.3. Commercial Market

Pioneering work had been done in a part of the Commercial market—doctors' waiting rooms—as long ago as 1907 by the Gas Light and Coke Company. The results appeared in a paper to the British Commercial Gas Association in 1912 entitled "A Campaign amongst the doctors". Despite this early interest, however, there had been little effort devoted to assessing the Commercial market. Johnson (1971) [QRL 8] refers to a national survey commissioned in 1969 which sought to provide details for different parts of the market. These covered the types and quantities of fuels used, the processes for which they were employed, market shares and prices paid. To some degree the information supplemented data collected from an earlier national study (by another agency) in 1966 and sporadic studies made by some of the then Area Gas Boards.

Subsequently, attention has been devoted in this market to evaluating the image of gas and other fuels (see Johnson [B 36] to more detailed studies of particular sectors, e.g. hotels and price-elasticity investigations. Thackray [B 61] has illustrated the usefulness of such surveys for decision-making taking as a specific example the Badged Catering Equipment Programme.

CHAPTER 15

FUTURE DEVELOPMENTS AND DESIRABLE IMPROVEMENTS

15.1. The Impact of Corporate Planning and the Future

Increasing attention to the needs of corporate planning and capital investment have had considerable impact on statistics in the nationalised industry.

Kelf-Cohen [B 39] referred to the first programme of development published in 1954—*Fuel for the Nation*—and criticised the performance achieved against expectation. Subsequently steps were taken to improve the bases of information and the rigour of the statistical analyses underlying such future plans. In order to obtain data for making effective inter-Regional comparisons new systems have had to be introduced and measures taken to extend the records. A good example is to do with workload, where the need to plan for better utilisation of manpower resulted in a control being introduced to assess the existing situation and measure future performance against planned performance.

Changes such as these are significant for the gas industry. Until comparatively recently the main impetus for collecting statistics had come from outside, e.g. Ministries, but now the emphasis has switched to the needs of internal management. In this respect the installation of computers has been significant, providing the means to satisfy the new requirements. Although at present there are varieties of computer installations and operating systems to be found, greater emphasis is being given towards the achievement of more uniformity. Such a tendency should have considerable repercussions on the accuracy, consistency and comparability of management data.

A considerable literature has grown up in recent years on the use of data for forecasting, the problems of forecasting and whether or not it should be attempted. Buckley (1965) [B 10] has referred to the impact of appliance sales on gas demand whilst Watson (1965) [B 65] concentrated on the relationship between gas and fuel in general. Two years later, Watson in collaboration with Hyde and Lewis [B 32] discussed types of forecast errors, the development of domestic space heating using logistic curves and the data requirements for long-term planning. In that same year Natural Gas Co-ordination, Shell Centre, prepared a résumé of basic parameters associated with long-range forecasting, e.g. design temperatures, appliance consumption, load factors and diversity factors. Nabb (1970) [B 45] and Rodger, Rawlings and Simpson (1971) [B 55] have given examples of how they can be applied in actual situations.

Certain of these papers elaborated previous investigations. Rose (1949) [B 56]

15.2 FUTURE DEVELOPMENTS AND DESIRABLE IMPROVEMENTS

had been an early researcher into the correlation between gas consumption and atmospheric temperature and his analysis was improved further by Berrisford (1965) [B 6]. Everard (1948, 1949) [B 18, 19] established the importance of family size, economic and social changes, illness, etc. as influencing gas requirements. Recent workers have tended to adopt more sophisticated analytical methods. Lyness and Badger (1970) [B 42] applied the lognormal distribution to accumulated temperature as a measure of winter severity and discussed certain sources of uncertainty, e.g. changing consumer habits, in translating temperature into gas demand. Taylor (1972) [B 60] developed a stochastic model to generate pseudo daily mean temperatures for planning problems. Turton and Harper (1973) [B 63] studied the accuracy of weather forecasts and short-term gas demand prediction. Lyness (1970) [B 41] attempted to quantify the relative vulnerability of the national high-pressure gas transmission system referring particularly to the large number of unknown factors involved in the problem. In practice, Lyness had to relate many assumptions to American transmission network experience as there was a lack of data in this country. It would thus appear that if more rigorous statistical analysis is to be adopted as a more common practice in the gas industry to aid decision-making, then the basic information bases must be extended and even further improved. Such a conclusion should not in itself be regarded as a criticism of the considerable improvements made already since nationalisation, but as an indication of how statistical requirements are changing to meet new circumstances.

The extent to which management in the gas industry has been aware of the position was typified by the organisation of an entire course of *Management Data in Action* through the Institution of Gas Engineers in 1973. The tone of these discussions was set in an introduction by Smith (1973) [B 58] calling for a "war on paper" and a real attempt to produce only those data which could be used effectively by management. In part, these may well have influenced a passage in the 1974/5 *Annual Report of the British Gas Corporation* [QRL 12] which stated: "The present statistical systems are being examined to see what modifications are needed to meet the changing needs of the industry."

15.2. Desirable Improvements

Despite a greater appreciation of the importance of accurate information for management in the gas industry, statistics published regularly by the Department of Energy [QRL 23] are, in certain aspects, less informative than before. Details on holder capacity, peak weekly demands and system load factor (the relationship between average and peak demand), for example, which appeared regularly for some years are no longer shown in the annual *Digest*. Although some of these figures are obtainable on request, other data, like numbers of consumers disconnected for non-payment of gas accounts, have to be elicited by Parliamentary Question (*Hansard* 20 and 25 May 1976). The situation in France provides an interesting contrast. Statistics are issued regularly showing industrial usage over sectors by region, numbers of domestic consumers on different tariffs and appliances in use per 1000 consumers.

Similarly in the USA the American Gas Association produce very detailed figures for separate states, including such items as numbers of consumers with gas heating.

It is quite probable that a more comprehensive publication of such data would be resisted here as being useful to competing interests. However, this is to ignore the fact that the *Handbook of Electricity Supply Statistics* prepared annually by the Electricity Council does provide a very useful detailed summary for another nationalised fuel industry. Even so, it is worth noting that in 1976 the Public Relations Department of the British Gas Corporation did begin issuing an annual summary leaflet of "Facts and Figures". Certain of these tables can be identified readily in the BGC *Annual Report and Accounts* [QRL 12]. Other data on profits, gas prices related to weekly earnings and so forth are more conveniently covered in this new publication than the original sources.

Another criticism against producing more statistics relates to the amount of time and effort involved. Some people in the gas industry already consider that too much is being collected. Nevertheless one proposal likely to find support would be the production of truly comparable data for all fuels. This could lead to not merely greater uniformity in basic definitions, such as consumer classifications, but the acceptance of agreed standards for measuring the heat used by consumers for different purposes. Such statistics might assist in the framing of a National Fuel Policy.

A more basic problem relates to the efficiency of any nationalised undertaking. Changes in accounting practice may alter the published profit or loss. Financial targets can lead to policies of profit maximisation rather than cost minimisation. The lack of competition in the United Kingdom has led to comparisons being attempted with gas undertakings in other countries. These cause difficulties in respect of price comparisons, differences in the services offered and the validity of the performance indicators which are chosen.

Moreover, there are problems related to how the aims of an industry—especially one that is nationalised—are viewed. The Green Paper on *The Future of Company Reports* Cmnd 6888 (1977) [B 77] indicated that more information should be disclosed to reflect the "wider accountability of directors and cover the interests of people other than shareholders". Specific possibilities include separate identification of school-leavers joining and leaving, information about education and training, numbers retiring and made redundant and a value added statement on the creation and distribution of company wealth.

Corporate social reporting generally would seem to be a matter in which nationalised industries might take a lead. Certain data collected already, e.g. on service standards, customer satisfaction, might then appear in the Annual Report and Accounts. However one drawback is the production of ever-weightier volumes destined for the waste-paper basket.

A benefit of studying such concepts as social reporting is that attention is devoted within an organisation to the overall collation of material. Within the BGC a report from an internal working party on information flows in 1976/7 has meant an improved system for the co-ordinated gathering and processing of information. This should mean that the outside researcher can more easily find out what information is collected and may be made available in the nationalised gas industry.

QUICK REFERENCE LIST—TABLE OF CONTENTS

Gas Output	156
Coke and Breeze Output	157
Other By-Products	157
Gas Sales	157
Coke and Breeze Sales	161
Appliances	161
Comparison with Other Fuels	163
Employment	163
Labour Turnover	164
Sickness and Accidents	164
Hours and Earnings	165
Productivity	165
Workload	166
Education and Training	166
Plant Capacity	166
Mains	167
Services	167
Capital	167
Revenue and Expenditure	168
Gas Billing	169
Natural Gas	169
Conversion	171
Public Interest/Consultative Councils	171
Safety	171
Prices and Price Indices	172
Market Research	173
Domestic Market	173
Industrial Market	175
Commercial Market	175
Organisation of the Industry before 1949	175

QUICK REFERENCE LIST

Descriptive Title	Breakdown/Detail of Analysis	Area	Frequency or Data	Publication (see QRL Key)	Text Reference and Remarks
Gas output					
Town gas made	By type of fuel used	GB	Annual	[QRL 23]	4.1.1
	By type of fuel used	Former area boards	Annual	[QRL 13]	Available from 1 May 1949 until the formation of the British Gas Corporation 1973
Natural gas	Gross production, importation and availability for natural gas and colliery methane	UK	Annual	[QRL 23]	
Other gases	Breakdown for natural gas repeated for coke oven gas, blast furnace gas, liquefied petroleum and other petroleum gas	UK	Annual	[QRL 23]	
Gas available	By type of gas	UK	Annual	[QRL 23]	Gas available comprises gas made together with reformed purchased gas and gas purchased and resold as such
	Manufactured gas and natural gas for direct supply	Regions of BGC	Annual	[QRL 12]	
Gas sent out	Public supply system	UK	Annual	[QRL 23]	Relates to gas actually delivered From May 1978 a new natural gas series based on a method of temperature correction developed by the British Gas Corporation is included (see also 3.3.5)
	Public supply system	UK	Monthly	[QRL 30]	
System load factor	Public supply system	UK	Weekly averages	[QRL 40]	
	Public supply system	GB	Annual	[QRL 23]	3.3.4 and 4.1.1
Peak availability	Public supply system	GB	Peak week	[QRL 23]	
Materials used for gas making	Coal, coke, breeze, light oil, gas oil, heavy oil used by public supply system	GB	Annual	[QRL 23]	
	Coal, oil and LPG	Regions of BGC	Annual	[QRL 12]	

QUICK REFERENCE LIST

Coke and breeze output				
Coke made for sale	Public supply system	UK	Annual	[QRL 23]	4.1.2. Coke made less used on work, etc. for gas making and other purposes
Coke used	Public supply system: for all purposes	GB	Annual	[QRL 23]	Details for the former Area Boards were published by the the then Gas Council until 1971/2
Gas coke breeze	Production stocks and change in undistributed stocks	UK	Annual	[QRL 23]	
Coke breeze made for sale	Public supply system	UK	Annual	[QRL 23]	
Coke breeze used	Public supply system: for all purposes	GB	Annual	[QRL 23]	
Other by-products					
Other by-products made	Coal tar, oil gas tar, crude benzole and spent oxide	GB	Annual	[QRL 13]	4.1.3. Details for the former Area Boards were published by the then Gas Council until 1971/2
Coal tar made	Coal tar made according to type of gas making plant	Regions of BGC	Annual	[QRL 18]	The diminished output of gasworks tar has reduced considerably the published details
Gas sales					
Domestic sales	Liquefied petroleum gas	UK	Annual	[QRL 23]	
	All gases	UK	Annual	[QRL 23]	
	Public supply: town gas and natural gas	UK	Annual	[QRL 23]	
	Public supply: prepayment and credit meter	GB	Annual	[QRL 23]	4.2.1.1
	Public supply: total domestic	Regions of BGC	Annual	[QRL 12]	
	Public supply: total domestic	Regions of BGC and NI	Annual	[QRL 23]	
	Public supply: total domestic	UK	Quarterly	[QRL 30]	
Domestic consumers	Public supply: prepayment and credit meter	GB	Annual	[QRL 23]	
	Public supply: total domestic	Regions of BGC	Annual	[QRL 12]	

Descriptive Title	Breakdown/Detail of Analysis	Area	Frequency or Date	Publication (see QRL Key)	Text Reference and Remarks
Gas sales (*Contd.*)					
Domestic consumers' (*Contd.*)	Public supply: total domestic	Regions of BGC and NI	Annual	[QRL 23]	
Average sales per domestic consumer	Public supply: converted to natural gas by end-year	GB	Annual	[QRL 12]	9.2
	Public supply: prepayment and credit meter	GB	Annual	[QRL 23]	
	Public supply: total domestic	Regions of BGC	Annual	[QRL 12]	
Total net selling value—domestic	Public supply: Prepayment and credit meter	GB	Annual	[QRL 23]	Excludes prepayment supplements and meter rents where charged separately from gas supplied
	Public supply: total domestic	Regions of BGC	Annual	[QRL 12]	
Average net selling value per therm sold to domestic consumers	Public supply: prepayment and credit meters	GB	Annual	[QRL 23]	
	Public supply: total domestic	Regions of BGC	Annual	[QRL 12]	
	Public supply: total domestic	Regions of BGC and NI	Annual	[QRL 23]	
Commercial sales	Public supply: town gas and natural gas by Public Administration and Commercial Sectors	UK	Annual	[QRL 23]	4.2.1.2
	Public supply: commercial, National and Local Government	GB	Annual	[QRL 23]	
	Public supply: total commercial	Regions of BGC	Annual	[QRL 12]	
	Public supply: total commercial	Regions of BGC and NI	Annual	[QRL 23]	
	Public supply: total commercial	UK	Quarterly	[QRL 30]	

QUICK REFERENCE LIST

Commercial consumers	Public supply: commercial, National and Local Government	GB	Annual	[QRL 23]	
	Public supply: total commercial	Regions of BGC	Annual	[QRL 12]	
	Public supply: converted to natural gas by end-year	GB	Annual	[QRL 12]	
Average sales per commercial consumer	Public supply: commercial, National and Local Government	GB	Annual	[QRL 23]	
Total net selling value—commercial	Public supply: commercial, National and Local Government	GB	Annual	[QRL 23]	
Average net selling value per therm sold to commercial consumers	Public supply: commercial, National and Local Government	GB	Annual	[QRL 23]	
	Public supply: total commercial	Regions of BGC	Annual	[QRL 12]	
	Public supply: total commercial	Regions of BGC and NI	Annual	[QRL 23]	
Industrial sales	Public supply: town gas for iron and steel industry and other industries	UK	Annual	[QRL 23]	4.2.1.3
	Public supply: natural gas for power stations, iron and steel industry, petro-chemical plants and other industries	UK	Annual	[QRL 23]	Petro-chemical figures include direct sales by producers
	Coke oven gas: iron and steel and other industries	UK	Annual	[QRL 23]	
	Blast furnace gas: iron and steel industry	UK	Annual	[QRL 23]	
	Liquefied petroleum gas: refineries, iron and steel industry, petro-chemical plants and other industries	UK	Annual	[QRL 23]	
	Other petroleum gas: refineries and petro-chemical plants	UK	Annual	[QRL 23]	

160   GAS

Descriptive Title	Breakdown/Detail of Analysis	Area	Frequency or Date	Publication (see QRL Key)	Text Reference and Remarks
Gas sales (*Contd.*)					
Industrial Sales (*Contd.*)	Public supply: over 14 industrial headings: China and earthenware Bricks, cement, etc.	GB	Annual	[QRL 12]	A split between "Bricks and Building Materials" and "Cement" may be found in *Energy for Industry* [QRL 28]
	Glass and glass containers Chemicals and allied trades Ferrous metals Non-ferrous metals Engineering and ship-building Electrical goods Vehicles Metal goods not elsewhere specified Textiles, leather and clothing Food, drink and tobacco Paper and printing Miscellaneous and unallocated				
	Public supply: total industrial	Regions of BGC and NI	Annual	[QRL 23]	Until 1970/71 "Miscellaneous" shown separately from "Unallocated"
	Public supply: power stations, iron and steel and other industries	UK	Quarterly	[QRL 30]	
Industrial consumers	Public supply: total industrial	GB	Annual	[QRL 23]	
	Public supply: total industrial	Regions of BGC	Annual	[QRL 12]	
	Public supply: converted to natural gas by end-year	GB	Annual	[QRL 12]	

QUICK REFERENCE LIST

Average sales per industrial consumer	Public supply: total industrial	GB	Annual	[QRL 23]	4.2.1.3. Details of the distribution of sales by individual consumers can be found from Hayman [B 28[and Buckley [B 11]
Total net selling value—industrial	Public supply: total industrial	GB	Annual	[QRL 23]	
Average net selling value per therm sold to industrial consumers	Public supply: total industrial	GB	Annual	[QRL 23]	
	Public supply: total industrial	Regions of BGC	Annual	[QRL 12]	
	Public supply: total industrial	Regions of BGC and NI	Annual	[QRL 23]	
Public lighting sales	Public supply: total industrial	GB	Annual	[QRL 23]	4.2.1.4. Included with Commercial and Public Administration since 1968. Prior to that data details on numbers of gas lamps were collected as well
Own use	Public supply: works, offices, showrooms, etc.	UK	Annual	[QRL 23]	4.2.1.5
	Public supply: works, offices, showrooms, etc.	GB	Annual	[QRL 23]	
	Gas used for own purposes	Regions of BGC	Annual	[QRL 12]	
Losses in distribution, reforming, etc.	Public supply	UK	Annual	[QRL 23]	4.2.1. Regional figures can be estimated by deducting sales from gas available
Coke and breeze sales					
Coke sold	Disposals to merchants for the domestic market of premium smokeless fuels and gas coke	UK	Annual	[QRL 23]	4.2.2. Figures since June 1975 have assumed negligible proportions
Coke breeze sold	Inland consumption of gas coke breeze in iron and steel sinter plants, power stations, gas works and other	UK	Annual	[QRL 23]	
Appliances					
Appliances sold	Exports of gas coke breeze	UK	Annual	[QRL 23]	4.2.3
	Number sold (including estimates of sales through other outlets): Cookers	GB	Annual	[QRL 12]	

162   GAS

Descriptive Title	Breakdown/Detail of Analysis	Area	Frequency or Date	Publication (see QRL key)	Text Reference and Remarks
Appliances (*contd.*) Number sold (*contd.*):	Water heaters Space heaters Warm air central heating Central heating boilers				
	Number sold direct: Cookers Water heaters Space heaters	Regions of BGC	Annual	[QRL 12]	
	New acquisitions: Cookers Water heaters Space heaters Central heating Refrigerators cross-analysed by age of dwelling, social class, etc.	Regions of BGC	Quarterly	[QRL 38]	14.1. There have been difficulties in reconciling AGB information with production and delivery statistics for certain gas appliances, notably central heating
Appliances in use	Homes owning: Cookers Water heaters Space heaters Central heating Refrigerators/freezers cross-analysed by age of dwelling, type of tenure, age of housewife, availability of gas	Regions of BGC	Annual	[QRL 38]	14.1
	The market for gas appliances: Cooking apparatuses Water heating Room heating Gas washing machines Freezers	GB	1960–1965	[QRL 24]	

QUICK REFERENCE LIST

Comparisons with other fuels

Shares of UK energy market on the basis of heat supplied to final users	Domestic, non-domestic and total for solid fuel, gas, electricity and petroleum	UK	Annual	[QRL 12]	4.3. The market shares are based on figures contained in the *Energy Digest* and *Energy Trends*
Inland consumption of natural gas	Expressed as (i) coal equivalent, (ii) oil equivalent, actual and seasonally adjusted	UK	Monthly	[QRL 40] & [QRL 30]	For a more detailed account of total energy comparisons see the companion review on Energy and an article on "Energy Balances" in *Statistical Notes*, Nov. 1976. Note the use of metric terms (tonnes) instead of statute tons in official statistics from May 1978
Appliance efficiency	Different forms of continuous and intermittent space heating and water heating. Varying calculations of production, test-bed and appliance efficiencies		1945	[QRL 37]	
	Comparisons of gas and electricity in the provision of domestic heat services—cooking, water heating and space heating		1952	[QRL 56]	It is interesting to see differences in the submission of different fuel interests regarding appliance efficiencies for comparable purposes
	Household utilisation efficiency—central heating, other space heating, water heating, cooking	UK	1974	[QRL 26]	Although the work is more pertinent to the Energy Review, it contains details on energy overheads, conversion and utilisation efficiencies which do not appear elsewhere
	Thermal efficiency of main forms of domestic space and water heating		27.7.77	[QRL 36]	

Employment

Numbers employed at 31 March	Manual and staff grades separately for Production and products Distribution of gas Conversion General customer service Customer accounting Administration and general services	GB	Annual	[QRL 12]	5.1

Descriptive Title	Breakdown/Detail of Analysis	Area	Frequency or Date	Publication (see QRL Key)	Text Reference and Remarks
Employment (*contd.*)					
Total employees at 31 March	Analysed by: Craftsmen, Other manual grades, Office grades, Other staff grades, Senior officers	Regions of BGC	Annual	[QRL 12]	5.1
Staff at July 1968	Categories and numbers of staff at July 1968—details for some 56 groups of Office grades, part-time staff, etc.	GB		[QRL 50]	5.1
Average levels of employment	Average number on the payroll	GB	Annual	[QRL 12]	A note to the annual accounts refers to average number on payroll of BGC and its subsidiaries during the year
Shift workers	As part of material enquiry	UK	1954, 1964	[QRL 20]	5.1
Analysis by age	By occupation, sex and age	UK	1966	[QRL 35]	5.1. The Gas Industry Training Board was formed in 1965 and obtained considerable information for planning manpower requirements. Even more detail exists in the industry under its Personnel Management Information System
Numbers employed at June	Males and females, part-time and full-time	UK and Standard Regions	Annual	[QRL 16] & Dec. issue of [QRL 20]	5.1. Figures for males and females are available also for March, September and December
Labour turnover	Recruitment and wastage rates for Manual grades, Staff grades, All employees	GB	Annual	[QRL 12]	5.2
Sickness and accidents					
Sickness and accidents (man-days lost as % of total possible man-days)	Sickness for Manual grades—male, Staff grades—male, Staff grades—female, Accidents for Manual grades—male	GB	Annual	[QRL 12]	5.3. Fuszard [QRL 3] has produced more detailed figures on accidents illustrating the scope of the gas industry internal reporting system

Fatal accidents	Number	GB	Occasional	[QRL 36]	5.3. Details are made available, e.g. for 1966–76 in a written reply in *Hansard* 25.7.77
Unemployment in the gas industry	Males and females	GB and UK	Quarterly	[QRL 16]	
Hours and earnings					
Adult male manual workers	Weekly earnings Hours worked per week Hourly earnings in pence for April and October	GB	Annual	[QRL 12]	5.3. This is information collected for the Department of Employment. More comprehensive details, e.g. for women and young males, can be found in the regular statistics of the Department of Employment [QRL 20]
Employees' emoluments	Remuneration in excess of £10,000 p.a.	GB	Annual	[QRL 12]	See "Notes to the Accounts"
Members' emoluments	Chairman and other members	GB	Annual	[QRL 12]	See "Notes to the Accounts"
Average weekly hours and make-up of average weekly earnings of full-time adult male manual workers—October 1966, 1968 and 1969	Details of basic, overtime, service increments, shift incentive and other earnings for craftsmen, labourers, shift workers and others	GB	1970	[QRL 52]	See also 5.6 and 5.7
Comparison of average weekly earnings and hours for full-time adult male manual workers on WSIP schemes with those not on WSIP schemes	Pay week including 31 October 1969. Craftsmen, labourers, other manual and total	GB	1970	[QRL 52]	See also 5.6 and 5.7. An earlier NBPI Report No. 29 also contained details of the distribution of earnings
Wage rates	Gas fitters and labourers	GB	Annual	[QRL 16]	5.4. A separate series of wage rate indexes for 1948–65 by E. Devons, J. R. Crossley and W. F. Maunder appears in *Economica*, November 1968 [QRL 2]. Variations between regions for certain occupations are to be found in QRL.
Productivity					
Net capital employed per employee	Public supply	Regions of BGC	Annual	[QRL 12]	5.6
Staff incentive schemes—October 1968	Proportions of meter readers and collectors, computer, showroom and sales staff covered by incentive schemes	Former Area Boards	1968	[QRL 50]	Details of the total number of BGC employees covered by WSIP schemes are shown in the BGC *Annual Report and Accounts*

Descriptive Title	Breakdown/Detail of Analysis	Area	Frequency or Date	Publication (see QRL Key)	Text Reference and Remarks
Productivity (*contd.*) Staff on SPM schemes	April 1970 and forecasts for 1971, 1972 and 1973	Former Area Boards	1970	[QRL 52]	
Workload	Total customer service jobs	GB	Annual	[QRL 12]	5.7. Some idea of the composition of those jobs can be obtained from Jones [QRL 9] and Hill [QRL 6]. The details quoted by Jones are a summary of the detailed activity headings listed by him which underly the published total customer service jobs
	Proportion of work-load devoted to on-demand service, installation, regular servicing, conversion related work, meters, escapes	GB	1971/72	[QRL 9]	
Education and training	Numbers engaged in Management training, Technologists and Technician training, Apprentice training, etc.	GB	Annual	[QRL 12]	5.8. Although details are still collected they have not been published since 1965/6. The Select Committee on Gas produced an Area Board analysis for 1959/60 [QRL 48]
Plant capacity	Daily capacity of all plant—million cubic feet	GB	Annual	[QRL 23]	6.1. The capacity of carbonising plant was measured after allowing for normal scurfing. This was the process of removing periodically the layer of carbon formed on the inner surfaces of high-temperature carbonising vessels as a result of the decomposition of hydrocarbons during carbonisation
	Daily capacity of all plant—million cubic feet and thermal equivalent	Regions of BGC	Annual	[QRL 12]	

QUICK REFERENCE LIST

Works in operation	Maximum daily capacity in million cubic feet for carbonising plant, Lurgi, oil gasification, water gas and other gas plant	GB	Annual	[QRL 12]
	Number at end of year	GB	Annual	[QRL 23]
	Number at end of year	Regions of BGC	Annual	[QRL 12]
Mains	Mileage of new mains laid, mains relaid and total in use at end of year	GB	Annual	[QRL 12]	6.3
	Mains (including transmission mains) in use at end of year	Regions of BGC	Annual	[QRL 12]
Services	New services laid and numbers relaid	GB	Annual	[QRL 12]
Capital—Financial details	Public supply: net assets	GB	Annual	[QRL 23]	6 and 6.6
	Public supply: average net assets employed	GB	Annual	[QRL 23]
	Public supply: return on average net assets employed (per cent)	GB	Annual	[QRL 23]
	Public supply: capital requirements	GB	Annual	[QRL 23]
	Public supply: self-financing ratio	GB	Annual	[QRL 23]
	Public supply: net capital employed per employee	GB	Annual	[QRL 12]	5.6
	Public supply: additions, transfers, disposals and balances for fixed assets over: Land and buildings—freehold and leasehold Mains Services Gasholders and other storage Plant and machinery Meters Motor vehicles and mobile plant	GB	Annual	[QRL 12]	Balance sheet of BGC

167

Descriptive Title	Breakdown/Detail of Analysis	Area	Frequency or Date	Publication (see QRL Key)	Text Reference and Remarks
Capital—Financial details (*contd.*)	Furniture, fittings and office machinery Miscellaneous Subsidiary companies *and* cross-analysed by activity: Gas Installation and contracting Appliance marketing				
	Public supply: new capital investment	Regions of BGC	Annual	[QRL 12]	
	Public supply: net capital employed per employee	Regions of BGC	Annual	[QRL 12]	5.6
	Public supply: forecasts of capital expenditure	GB	Annual	[QRL 46]	
	Public supply: gross capital stock at constant replacement cost	UK	Annual	[QRL 43]	
Revenue and expenditure					
Consolidated trading and profit and loss account of the British Gas Corporation	Turnover and operating costs cross-analysed by operating and support activities	GB	Annual	[QRL 12]	7. These figures needed to be studied in conjunction with the detailed Notes to the Accounts
Gross output	Value of sales and work done plus/less variation in stock for sale or work in progress	UK	Annual	[QRL 17] (although [QRL 23] for many years)	7. The precise definition of gross output may be found in the notes. The undertakings covered are those classified to the gas industry, minimum list heading 601 of the Standard Industrial Classification (revised 1968)
Net output	Gross output less materials and fuels used, payments for work done and transport	UK	Annual	[QRL 17] (again [QRL 23] for a period)	7

QUICK REFERENCE LIST 169

Net output per head	Gross output less materials and fuels used, payments for work done and transport	UK	Annual	[QRL 17]	7. Details of average numbers employed and net output given in the *Business Monitor* enables averages to be calculated separately for England, Wales, Scotland, Great Britain and Northern Ireland
Wages and salaries per head	For operators and other employees	UK	Annual	[QRL 17]	7
Gas billing					
Disconnection	For non-payment of gas accounts	GB		[QRL 36]	7. This has been a matter of some ministerial interest and figures have appeared in *Hansard*, e.g. 11th July 1977
Natural gas					
Gasfields in production or under development	Field name, block number, licensees, company interest, date discovered, date of production start-up	UK	Annual	[QRL 21]	9.1
Other significant gas and gas condensate discoveries	Field name, block number, discovered by, date discovered	UK	Annual	[QRL 21]	9.1. "Significant" relates to the flow rates achieved in well tests and this is not necessarily an indicator of the potential commercial value of the find
Natural gas production	By field, million cubic metres, oil equivalent in million tonnes	UK	Annual	[QRL 21]	9.1
Supply and disposal of methane (natural gas)	Production on land and off-shore by field, total production and own use, arrivals of liquefied natural gas, direct supply to petro-chemical industry and available for public supply to the gas industry. Million therms	UK	Annual	[QRL 23]	"Own use" here means for drilling, production and pumping operations see also 4.1.1. Natural gas from the Southern Basin which is predominantly methane is sometimes referred to as Dry Gas, because it contains only small quantities of hydrocarbons which can be easily liquefied
Supply and disposal of gaseous and liquid products	Production and disposals of methane, ethane, propane, butane and condensates	UK	Annual	[QRL 23]	

Descriptive Title	Breakdown/Detail of Analysis	Area	Frequency or Date	Publication (see QRL Key)	Text Reference and Remarks
Natural gas (*contd.*)					
Natural gas and crude oil	Production monthly of methane, associated gas and condensates on land and off-shore	UK	Annual	[QRL 23]	Excludes gas flared or re-injected. Applications to flare or re-inject gas must be made at least two years in advance to the Secretary of State. However gas being flared off at Flotta in the Orkneys is being donated free of charge to produce domestic electricity
Major North Sea pipelines	Length, diameter, operator and year commissioned of natural gas and associated gas pipelines	UK	Annual	[QRL 21]	
Estimated Continental Shelf gas reserves	Proven, probable and possible for Northern and Southern Basins and showing those under contract to the British Gas Corporation	UK	Annual	[QRL 23]	There are reasons to believe some of the estimates are conservative. Many gas fields have been drilled to moderate depths and if it becomes worthwhile to drill deeper, further reserves may be discovered as has happened in U.S.A.
Natural gas supply	Total into the public gas supply system, indigenous and imported	UK	Monthly	[QRL 30]	Figures differ from production and imports respectively because of stock changes and small quantities not entering the public supply system
Value of imports of natural gas	Value (c.i.f.) as derived from returns made to H.M. Customs and Excise	UK UK	Annual Monthly	[QRL 23] [QRL 30]	Includes liquefied gases other than natural gas and petroleum products not used as a fuel, e.g. lubricant
Corporation Tax and Royalties	Collected on North Sea natural gas	UK	Annual	[QRL 21]	An article in *Statistical News* No. 32 (1976) refers specifically to differences in the time distribution between Exchequer receipts and operators' gross profits. Although mainly concerned with North Sea oil many points in the article are relevant to gas activities as well

QUICK REFERENCE LIST

Conversion					
Customers: converted in year and at end year	Public supply	Regions of BGC	Annual	[QRL 12]	4.2.1 and 9.2
	Public supply by class of customer	GB	Annual	[QRL 12]	
Deferred charges: conversion to natural gas		GB	Annual	[QRL 12]	Notes on the Accounts contain details of costs
Forecasts of conversion costs	Costs per small conversion: actual quarter to December 1969, annual forecasts 1970/1 to 1973/4	Regions of BGC	1970	[QRL 52]	
Public interest/Consultative Councils					
Representations from individual gas consumers	Sales and service, conversion, disputed gas accounts, other disputed charges, central heating problems, meter problems and miscellaneous	GB	Annual	[QRL 11]	10.1. Regional information can be found in the reports of the Regional Gas Consumers' Councils
Safety					
Deaths attributed to gas	Accidental deaths and suicides by gases in domestic use	England and Wales	Annual	[QRL 47]	10.2
Accidental deaths and serious accidents attributed to gas	Deaths from poisoning by unburnt gas, deaths and serious accidents by products of combustion, deaths from fires and explosions attributed to gas	GB	1970	[QRL 55]	10.2 This is a summary of information from the Registrar-General's and Fire Research Station Statistics [QRL 60]
Fires in buildings and dwellings	Public supply gas: propane and butane	UK	1970	[QRL 55]	
Gas escapes in natural gas and manufactured gas areas of supply	Escapes per 10,000 domestic consumers, location of escapes	5 Area Boards	1970	[QRL 55]	
Town and natural gas explosions in dwellings	Material damage and injuries	GB	1969	[QRL 55]	Data from the Fire Research Station [QRL 60]

Descriptive Title	Breakdown/Detail of Analysis	Area	Frequency or Date	Publication (see QRL Key)	Text Reference and Remarks
Safety (*contd.*)					
Serious explosions caused by gas	Yearly 1972/3 to 1976/7—separate details for fatalities and "severe" damage. Analysis by source, cause and month	GB	1977	[QRL 57]	Serious explosions are those producing fatalities and/or damage valued at at least £100. The definition of "severe" damage is rather arbitrary
Explosion rates	Per thousand million therms of gas sold to domestic consumers, per million domestic consumers and per million appliances	GB	1977	[QRL 57]	
Prices and price indices					
Consumers' expenditure on gas	At current and constant market prices	UK	Annual	[QRL 43]	11.1
Retail price index	Domestic gas	UK	Monthly	[QRL 20]	11.2
Family expenditure survey	Gas and hire of gas appliances: average weekly household expenditure by: Weekly income of household Quarters of the year Size of household Administrative area Regions	UK	Annual	[QRL 31]	11.3. A similar survey has been produced for Northern Ireland since 1967. In April 1978 the Economics and Statistics Division of the Department of Energy published a document on fuel expenditure which is available free of charge from their library. This provides tables, charts and a commentary
Price elasticity	Domestic gas		1977	[QRL 29]	11.3. This Report of the Working Group on Energy Elasticities summarises recent work commencing with Stone and Wigley [B 59]
Retail prices in certain large towns	Average price at December for 80, 250, 400, 800 and 1200 therms of gas per annum in Aberdeen, Birmingham, Brighton, Cardiff, Edinburgh, Ipswich, Leeds, Liverpool, London,		Annual	[QRL 23]	11.4

QUICK REFERENCE LIST

		Area	Period	Reference	Remarks
Price of gas used by industry	Manchester, Newcastle-upon-Tyne, Nottingham, Plymouth and Portsmouth Gas used by large manufacturing firms	GB GB	Annual Quarterly	[QRL 23] [QRL 30]	11.5
Average delivered prices of fuel used by the gas industry	Annual prices for coal, light oil, gas oil, heavy oil, natural gas	GB	Annual	[QRL 23]	11.6
Market research					
Domestic market					
Domestic hot water supply	Proportions of households with different types of gas water heating appliances: by economic groups, opinion on use, purpose of use, hot water consumption 1947–8	GB and some sub-analysis	1950, 1952	[QRL 41] & [QRL 42]	14.1. These studies were primarily concerned with domestic hot water. The information on gas was to a degree incidental
Gas fires	Urban households of medium and low rateable values: average hours, usage per week, therms used and levels of usage. Subsidiary details available on gas cookers and water heaters	England and Wales: North and South	1954, 1955	[QRL 4] & [QRL 5]	Full details of sampling unit and questionnaires used are included in these reports, together with instructions for interviewers
Gas appliances	Market shares for gas cookers, fires, water heaters and refrigerators by age of housewife, social class, size of family, age of appliance	GB— Urban and Rural	Ad hoc	[QRL 45], [QRL 58], [QRL 61] & [QRL 62]	Purpose to make comparisons between the readers of *Woman* and housewives in general
Appliances in use and new acquisitions	Homes owning various appliances analysed by age of dwelling, type of tenure, etc.	Regions of BGC		[QRL 38]	14.1 and 4.2.3 with associated text reference
Market survey of domestic customers	Housing/social analysis of appliance and fuel use; gas consumption distribution for prepayment customers	North West Gas	1956/7	[QRL 10]	

Descriptive Title	Breakdown/Detail of Analysis	Area	Frequency or Date	Publication (see QRL Key)	Text Reference and Remarks
Market research (contd.) Domestic market (contd.)					
Domestic appliance consumptions	Annual usage for cookers, fires, wash boilers, water heaters	East Midlands	1965	[QRL 7]	The details are incidental to a detailed evaluation of different methods for obtaining appliance consumption levels
Peak day appliance consumptions	Average daily gas usage for gas fires, warm air units, and central heating boilers at various temperatures for week days and week-ends	East Midlands	1965	[QRL 7]	The report enumerates difficulties in obtaining and analysing data. See also 15.1
Durable consumer goods: gas and electric cookers	Ownership by social class, age of housewife, regional distribution, years housewife married. Make of cooker, characteristics, brand, awareness. Means of payment. Intentions to purchase	GB	6 monthly	[QRL 25]	14.1. These publications were part of a service for forecasting and market research. They reproduce the questionnaires used by the British Market Research Bureau to obtain the relevant information. Details also are given for electric and solid fuel cookers
Durable consumer goods: space heating	Fuels used by household type, e.g. with or without children. Reasons for choice of fuel. Central heating. Intentions to purchase	GB	6 monthly	[QRL 25]	14.1. See above. Details are given for competing fuels—oil, electricity and solid fuel
General domestic surveys	Interviews. Basic characteristics including availability of gas and smokeless zones. Age of housewife. Construction and ownership of dwellings. Appliances using various fuels. Main living room heating	Northern Gas	1965/6, 1969/70 and 1973/4. Some figures also for 1967/8 and 1971/2	[QRL 1]	14.1. The information is particularly interesting since it covers a reasonable time span. The methodology used is described more fully in other publications mentioned in the Bibliography

QUICK REFERENCE LIST   175

Purchasers of gas fires	Completed interviews. Purchasers. Reasons for choosing gas. Fuels displaced. Performance of fires	Northern Gas	Biennial	[QRL 1]	14.1. The information is particularly interesting since it covers a reasonable time span. The methodology used is described more fully in other publications mentioned in the Bibliography
Industrial market					
Industrial fuel and energy use	Gas and other fuels by S.I.C., size of establishment, purpose	UK	1974	[QRL 59]	14.2. Details of the coverage and validity of the results appear in the survey. A copy of the questionnaire appears at the end of the report
Industrial fuel markets	Gas and other fuels. Details for 9 industrial groupings for 1965 and 1971	GB	1965, 1971	[QRL 39]	A great deal of the information is abstracted from the *Energy Digest*
Energy for industry	Gas and other fuels	GB	Annual	[QRL 28]	Up-dates the information for the industrial groupings shown in [QRL 39]. Quarterly supplements have been available from 1977
Commercial market					
Process shares	Importance of gas for catering, water heating, space heating and other processes	GB		[QRL 8]	14.3. Limited data
Organisation of the industry before 1949					
Structure of the industry	Undertakings, gas sales, numbers of consumers, capital investment and proposals for re-organisation	GB	*Ad hoc*	[QRL 34]	2.4
Individual undertakings	Gas made, type of plant, consumers, manufacturing load factor, distribution load factor, date and hour of maximum demand	Selected undertakings in GB	Annual	[QRL 33]	3.1

Quick Reference List Key to Publications

Reference Number	Author/Organisation Responsible	Title	Publisher	Frequency or Date	Remarks
[QRL 1]	Bone, M. R.	'Trends in the Domestic Fuel Markets' in *Gas Engineering and Management*, Vol. 16, No. 10		Oct. 1976	
[QRL 2]	Devons, E., Crossley, J. R. and Maunder, W. F.	'Wage Rate Indexes by Industry, 1948–1965' in *Economica*		Nov. 1968	
[QRL 3]	Fuszard, W. R.	'Aspects of Safety' in *Journal of the Institution of Gas Engineers*, Vol. 12, No. 2		Feb. 1972	
[QRL 4]	Gray, P. G.	'The Use of Heating Appliances and the Expenditure of Fuel by Urban Households living in Dwellings of Medium and Low Rateable Values', *The Social Survey*		1954	
[QRL 5]	Gray, P. G.	'Domestic Heating', *The Social Survey*, SS. 237		1955	
[QRL 6]	Hill, R. W.	'A Career in Customer Service' in *Gas Engineering and Management*, Vol. 15		Apr. 1975	
[QRL 7]	Johnson, F. J.	'Forecasting' presented to Midland Section of the *Institution of Gas Engineers*		Nov. 1965	
[QRL 8]	Johnson, F. J.	'Marketing Research in the Natural Gas Industry', *Institution of Gas Engineers* Communication 864		1971	
[QRL 9]	Jones, R. J.	'A Future for Customer Service' in *Journal of the Institution of Gas Engineers*, Vol. 13, No. 7		July 1973	
[QRL 10]	Polanyi, G. M.	'Gas in the Domestic Market' presented to Manchester and District Section of the *Institution of Gas Engineers*		1961	
[QRL 11]	National Gas Consumers' Council	*Annual Report*	HMSO, London	Annual	
[QRL 12]	British Gas Corporation	*Annual Report and Accounts*	HMSO, London	Annual	
[QRL 13]	The Gas Council (former)	*Annual Report and Accounts*	HMSO, London	Annual from 1949/50 to 1971/72	

QUICK REFERENCE LIST

[QRL 14]	Department of Employment	*Annual Report of HM Chief Inspector of Factories*	HMSO, London	Annual	
[QRL 15]	Department of Employment	*British Labour Statistics—Historical Abstract 1886–1968*	HMSO, London	1971	
[QRL 16]	Department of Employment	*British Labour Statistics Yearbook*	HMSO, London	Annual	
[QRL 17]	Business Statistics Office	*Business Monitor PA 601*	HMSO, London	Annual	Quarterly information available in PQ 601
[QRL 18]	British Tar Association	*Coal Tar Statistics*	British Tar Association	Annual	Available on application
[QRL 19]	Hoare and Co. Investments Research	*Consumer Durables: I Domestic Appliances*	Hoare and Co., London	1968	Available on application
[QRL 20]	Department of Employment	*Department of Employment Gazette*	HMSO, London	Monthly	Formerly the *Employment and Productivity Gazette* and the *Ministry of Labour Gazette*
[QRL 21]	Department of Energy	*Development of the Oil and Gas Resources of the United Kingdom*	HMSO, London	Annual	
[QRL 22]	Business Statistics Office, Northern Ireland	*Digest of Statistics Northern Ireland*	HMSO, Belfast	Biannual	
[QRL 23]	Department of Energy	*Digest of United Kingdom Energy Statistics*	HMSO, London	Annual	Formerly produced by Dept. of Trade and Industry 1971/3, Ministry of Technology 1969, Ministry of Power 1956/69, Ministry of Fuel and Power 1946/55
[QRL 24]	International Colloquium on Marketing Gas	*The Domestic Gas Market: Statistical Record 1960–1965*	International Colloquium on Marketing Gas	1967	
[QRL 25]	The Economist Intelligence Unit Ltd.	*Durable Consumer Goods Reports*	Economist Intelligence Unit	1958–1968 half yearly	
[QRL 26]	National Economic Development Office	*Energy Conservation in the United Kingdom, Achievement, Aims and Options*	HMSO, London	1974	
[QRL 27]	Department of the Environment, Building Research Establishment	*Energy Conservation: A Study of Energy Consumption in Buildings and Possible Means of saving Energy in Housing CP 56/75*	BRE, Garston, Watford	1975	
[QRL 28]	Cambridge Information and Research Services Ltd. (in association with the School of Fuel Management)	*Energy for Industry 1976. The Executive's Guide to Fuel Supplies, Pricing and Suitability*	Cambridge Information and Research Services Ltd.	1976	

GAS

Reference Number	Author Organisation Responsible	Title	Publisher	Frequency or Date	Remarks
[QRL 29]	Department of Energy	*Energy Paper No. 17*	HMSO, London	1977	Available from Information Division, Dept. of Energy
[QRL 30]	Department of Energy	*Energy Trends—A Statistical Bulletin*	HMSO, London	Monthly	
[QRL 31]	Department of Employment	*Family Expenditure Survey*	HMSO, London	Annual	
[QRL 32]	White Paper	*The Financial and Economic Obligations of the Nationalised Industries* Cmnd. 1337	HMSO, London	1961	
[QRL 33]	Benn Brothers Ltd.	*Gas Directory and Who's Who*	Benn Brothers Ltd.	Annual	Incorporates publications formerly produced by *Gas Times*, *Gas World* and *Gas Journal*
[QRL 34]	Ministry of Fuel and Power (Heyworth Committee)	*The Gas Industry—Report of the Committee of Inquiry* Cmd. 6699	HMSO, London	1945	
[QRL 35]		Gas Industry Training Board data	Unpublished		British Gas Corporation took over responsibilities of Gas Industry Training Board and should be approached for data collected but unpublished
[QRL 36]		*Hansard*	HMSO, London		Abstracts of relevance to the gas industry are issued by the Press and PR section of BGC, e.g. 30.10.75 CO gas poisoning attributable to unburnt or burnt gas
[QRL 37]	Department of Scientific and Industrial Research	*Heating and Ventilation of Dwellings. Postwar Building Studies No. 19*	HMSO, London	1945	
[QRL 38]	Audits of Great Britain	*Home Audit*	AGB Ltd.	Quarterly	
[QRL 39]	Gower Economic Publications	*Industrial Fuel Markets 1973–74—A Guide to Supply and Pricing Conditions in Great Britain*	Gower Economic Publications	1973	
[QRL 40]	Central Statistical Office	*Monthly Digest of Statistics*	HMSO, London	Monthly	
[QRL 41]	Ministry of Works	*National Building Studies: An Inquiry into Domestic Hot Water Supply in Great Britain (Part I)*	HMSO, London	1950	

[QRL 42]	Department of Scientific and Industrial Research	*National Building Studies: An Inquiry into Domestic Hot Water Supply in Great Britain* (Part II)	HMSO, London	1952	
[QRL 43]	Central Statistical Office	*National Income and Expenditure—Blue Book*	HMSO, London	Annual	
[QRL 44]	National Institute for Economic and Social Research	*National Institute Economic Review*, No. 72 (Appendix: 'The re-action of Industry to the Energy Crisis')		May 1975	
[QRL 45]	*Woman Magazine*	*The Power of Woman—Domestic Appliances*	Odhams Press Ltd.	1957	
[QRL 46]	White Paper	*Public Expenditure White Paper*	HMSO, London	Annual	
[QRL 47]	Office of Population Censuses and Surveys	*Registrar-General's Statistical Review of England and Wales*	HMSO, London	Annual	Since 1973 data appear in series of OPCS *Monitors* (DH2 and DH4 for mortality) although figures for Scotland still appear in *Annual Report of the Registrar-General, Scotland*
[QRL 48]	House of Commons	*Report from the Select Committee on Nationalised Industries, The Gas Industry.* Vol. II. Minutes of Evidence, Appendices and Index	HMSO, London	1961	
[QRL 49]	National Board for Prices and Incomes	*Report No. 57 Gas Prices* (First Report) Cmnd. 3567	HMSO, London	1968	
[QRL 50]	National Board for Prices and Incomes	*Report No. 86 Pay of Staff Workers in the Gas Industry* Cmnd. 3795	HMSO, London	1968	
[QRL 51]	National Board for Prices and Incomes	*Report No. 102 Gas Prices* (Second Report) Cmnd. 3924	HMSO, London	1969	
[QRL 52]	National Board for Prices and Incomes	*Report No. 155 Costs and Efficiency in the Gas Industry* Cmnd. 4458	HMSO, London	1970	
[QRL 53]	Business Statistics Office	*Report of the Census of Distribution and other Services*	HMSO, London	1966	
[QRL 54]	Board of Trade	*Report of the Census of Distribution and other Services*	HMSO, London	1957	
[QRL 55]	Ministry of Technology	*Report of the Committee of Inquiry into the Safety of Natural Gas as a Fuel* (Morton Report)	HMSO, London	1970	
[QRL 56]	Ministry of Fuel and Power	*Report of the Committee on National Policy for the Use of Fuel and Power Resources* Cmnd. 8647 (Ridley Report)	HMSO, London	1952	

Reference Number	Author/Organisation Responsible	Title	Publisher	Frequency or Date	Remarks
[QRL 57]	Department of Energy	*Report of the Inquiry into Serious Gas Explosions* (King Report)	HMSO, London	1977	
[QRL 58]	*Woman* Magazine	*Space Heating: New Woman and the National Market Survey*	Odhams Press Research Division	1964	
[QRL 59]	Confederation of British Industry and the Dept. of Energy	*A Statistical Survey of Industrial Fuel and Energy Use July–December 1974*	CBI	1975	
[QRL 60]	Fire Research Station	*United Kingdom Fire and Loss Statistics*	BRE, Garston, Watford	Annual	
[QRL 61]	*Woman* Magazine	*Woman and the National Market—Gas and Miscellaneous Domestic Appliances*	Odhams Press Ltd.	1959	
[QRL 62]	*Woman* Magazine	*Woman and the National Market—Gas and Miscellaneous Domestic Appliances*	Odhams Press Ltd.	1961	

BIBLIOGRAPHY

[B 1] Abrams, M., 'Why Labour has lost Elections', *Socialist Commentary*, June 1960.
[B 2] Alexander, S. J. and Taylor, N., 'The Frequency and Severity of Gaseous Explosions', *Institution of Gas Engineers* Communication 925, 1973.
[B 3] Anderson, R. S. *et al.*, 'The Northern Ireland Gas Industry', *Energy World*, 39, July 1977.
[B 4] Bailey, W., 'Gas Industry Finance', *Institution of Gas Engineers* Communication 508, 1957.
[B 5] Bell, F., Presidential Address, *Institution of Gas Engineers* Communication 842, 1972.
[B 6] Berrisford, H. G., 'The Relationship between Gas Demand and Temperature', *Operational Research Quarterly*, June 1965.
[B 7] Bone, M. R., 'An Eye to the Future', *Gas Journal*, 11 October 1961.
[B 8] Bouch, W. E. and Thomas, B. E., 'Developments in Gas Storage', *Gas Engineering and Management*, Vol. 15, March 1975.
[B 9] Bramham, J. T., 'Manpower Planning—A Briefing', *Yorkshire Junior Gas Association*, 10 November 1971.
[B 10] Buckley, J. A., 'Gas Load Forecasting—A Marketing Contribution', *Institution of Gas Engineers* Communication 694, 1965.
[B 11] Buckley, J. A., 'The Customer and Industry', Paper presented to 16th Residential Course at Pembroke College and reproduced in *Journal of Institution of Gas Engineers*, Vol. 12, No. 12, December 1972.
[B 12] Chantler, P., *The British Gas Industry: An Economic Study*, Manchester University Press, Manchester, 1938.
[B 13] Clarke, D. J., Cribb, G. S. and Walters, W. J., 'The Philosophy of Gas Storage', *Institution of Gas Engineers* Communication 845, 1971.
[B 14] Cooper, G. E., 'Data in Management Action', Paper presented to Residential Course on Management Data in Action, *Institution of Gas Engineers*, 1973.
[B 15] Corley, T. A. B., *Domestic Electrical Appliances: Studies in British Industry No. 1*, Jonathan Cape, 1966.
[B 16] Daniel, G. H., 'Electricity and Gas Statistics', *Journal of the Royal Statistical Society*, Vol. CXIII, Part IV, 1950, reproduced in *The Sources and Nature of the Statistics of the UK*, ed. Kendall, M. G., Oliver and Boyd, London, 1952.
[B 17] Evans, D., 'Consumer Surveys as an Aid to Sales Development', *Gas Service*, February 1963.
[B 18] Everard, S., 'A Survey of the Uses of Gas for Domestic and Industrial Purposes together with Factors Influencing Future Trends', *Institution of Gas Engineers* Communication 338/152, 1948.
[B 19] Everard, S., 'Some Factors Controlling the Demand of Gas', *International Gas Union* IGU/6, 1949.
[B 20] Everard, S., 'Live Gas', *Institution of Gas Engineers* Publication No. 573, 1960.
[B 21] Fisher, D. H., 'Management Data in Action', *Institution of Gas Engineers* Communication 895, 1973.
[B 22] Frith, A. I. D. and Smith, B. G., 'Safety—the Marketing Role', *Institution of Gas Engineers* Communication 918, 1973.
[B 23] Fulop, C. and Harris, R., 'Marketing for Central Heating', *Institute of Economic Affairs* Research Monograph No. 4, 1966.
[B 24] Garrud, T. V., 'An Industrial and Commercial Gas Sales Organisation', Paper presented to London and Southern Junior Gas Association, 1949.
[B 25] Goode, J. S., 'Understanding the Commercial Market', *Gas Engineering and Management*, Vol. 15, No. 2, February 1975.
[B 26] Green, R. F. D., 'Gas Burns Brighter' in *A Penguin Survey of Business and Industry*, Penguin Books, 1967.
[B 27] Griffiths, D. H., 'Management by Objectives and Conversion', Paper presented to Residential Course on Management Data in Action, *Institution of Gas Engineers*, 1973.

[B 28] Hayman, R. F., Presidential Address, *Journal of the Institute of Fuel*, 1968.
[B 29] Hetherington, A., 'The Role of Gas in Britain's Energy Market', *Coal and Energy Quarterly*, July 1975.
[B 30] Hinde, P., *The Exploration Scene*, Foulis, 1972.
[B 31] Hutchinson, K., 'Creative Marketing', *Gas Journal*, 28 October 1964.
[B 32] Hyde, W., Lewis, P. O. and Watson, T. B., 'What is the Use of Forecasting?', 10th International Gas Conference, Hamburg, 1967.
[B 33] Jewers, W. G., 'The Financial Implications of Measurement', Second Seminar on Gas Measurement, 1971, reproduced in *Journal of the Institute of Gas Engineering*, Vol. 12, No. 2, February 1972.
[B 34] Johnson, F. J., 'Market Research and the Gas Industry', *Institution of Gas Engineers*, Eastern Section, 1963.
[B 35] Johnson, F. J., 'Market Segmentation and Pricing Research in an Industrial Market', ESOMAR Conference, 1974.
[B 36] Johnson, F. J., 'Marketing Research used in Tactical Decision Making', Market Research Society Annual Conference, 1974.
[B 37] Jones, H., 'The Gas Industry', *National Provincial Bank Review*, No. 69, 1965.
[B 38] Jones, K. E. and Olssen, W. V., 'Computers, Communications and Customers', *Institution of Gas Engineers* Communication 843, 1971.
[B 39] Kelf-Cohen, R., *Nationalisation in Britain—The End of a Dogma*, Macmillan, 1958.
[B 40] Lomax, K. S., 'Cost Curves for Gas Supply', *Bulletin of the Oxford University Institute of Statistics*, 1951.
[B 41] Lyness, F. K., 'Security of Supply in a Gas Transmission System', *Applied Statistics*, Vol. 19, No. 1, 1970.
[B 42] Lyness, F. K. and Badger, E. H. M., 'A Measure of Winter Severity', *Applied Statistics*, Vol. 19, No. 2, 1970.
[B 43] McKnight, S. E., 'Control of Working Capital', Paper presented to Residential Course on Management Data in Action, *Institution of Gas Engineers*, 1973.
[B 44] McVitty, D., 'Northern Ireland Energy Resources', *Energy World*, No. 18, July 1975.
[B 45] Nabb, H., 'Some Uses of Statistics in a Nationalised Gas Undertaking', *The Statistician*, Vol. 19, No. 4, 1970.
[B 46] Phillips, W. G. and Hodge, L. R., 'Developments in Eastern Gas Customer Service', *Institution of Gas Engineers* Communication 745, 1967.
[B 47] Polanyi, G. M. and Berrisford, H. G., 'Economic and Statistical Research: Some Applications in the Gas Industry', *Institution of Gas Engineers*, Communication 656, 1964.
[B 48] Prais, S. J. and Houthakker, H. S., *The Analysis of Family Budgets*, Cambridge University Press, Cambridge, 1955.
[B 49] Pryke, R. W. S., 'Are Nationalised Industries becoming more efficient?', *Moorgate and Wall Street Journal*, Spring 1970.
[B 50] Ray, G. F., 'Medium-term Forecasts Reassessed: III Energy', *National Institute Economic Review*, No. 62, 1972.
[B 51] Ray, G. F. and Jones, D. T., 'The Innovation Process in the Gas Industry', *National Institute Economic Review*, No. 73, 1975.
[B 52] Reece, J. A., 'Market Research in the Gas Industry', *Gas World*, 25 November 1950.
[B 53] Reece, J. A., 'Some Details of Market Research by the North Thames Gas Board', *The Incorporated Statistician*, Vol. 2, No. 1, 1951.
[B 54] Reid, G. L., Allen, K. and Harris, D. J., *The Nationalised Fuel Industries*, Heinemann Educational Books, London, 1973.
[B 55] Rodger, A. A. S., Rawlings, W. J. and Simpson, J. M., 'Forecasting in an Area Gas Board', *The Statistician*, Vol. 20, No. 3, 1971.
[B 56] Rose, D. G., 'A Background to some Economic Problems in the Gas Industry', *Institution of Gas Engineers* Communication 352, 1949.
[B 57] Sleeman, J F., 'Municipal Gas Costs and Revenue', *The Manchester School of Economic and Social Studies*, Vol. XVIII, No. 1, 1950.
[B 58] Smith, J. H., 'Management Data in the British Gas Corporation', Paper presented to Residential Course on Management Data in Action, *Institution of Gas Engineers*, 1973.
[B 59] Stone, R. and Wigley, K., The Demand for Fuel 1948–1975, A Sub-Model for the British Fuel Economy, Department of Applied Economics, Cambridge University, Chapman & Hall, 1968.
[B 60] Taylor, C. J., 'A Stochastic Model of Temperature Variations at Weather Stations in Britain', *Applied Statistics*, Vol. 21, No. 3, 1972.

[B 61] Thackray, G. N., 'CEMUS and Other Strange Animals—Market Research for Decision Making in Commercial and Industrial Markets', *Midland Junior Gas Association*, 12 November 1974.
[B 62] Tilley, J. G., 'Management Data in the Marketing Function', Paper presented to Residential Course on Management Data in Action, *Institution of Gas Engineers*, 1973.
[B 63] Turton, P. S. and Harper, M. D., 'Weather Forecast Evaluation and its Role in Short-term Gas Demand Prediction', *Institution of Gas Engineers* Communication 907, 1973.
[B 64] Urwin, N. J., 'Personnel Management Information Systems', Paper presented to Residential Course on Management Data in Action, *Institution of Gas Engineers*, 1973.
[B 65] Watson, T. C. B., 'Aspects of Planning Problems: Part II—Forecasting', *Institution of Gas Engineers* Communication 681, 1965.
[B 66] Watson, T. C. B., 'The Role of the Gas Industry in the British Energy Market in the 1970s', *Economic Studies*, Vol. 4, No. 1/2, 1969.
[B 67] Webb, F., 'You've Had Your Chips', *Bulletin of the Institute of Vitreous Enamellers*, 1962.
[B 68] Wilkins, L. T., 'Domestic Utilisation of Heating Appliances and Expenditures on Fuels in 1948/49', *The Social Survey*, 1949.
[B 69] The British Electrical and Allied Industries Research Association, *A Condensed Repeat Survey of Domestic Consumers for 1948*, 1949.
[B 70] Weir Committee, *Co-operation between Electricity and Gas Boards*, Cmnd. 695, HMSO, London, 1959.
[B 71] The Electricity Council, *A Domestic Heating Survey of England and Wales*, Utilisation Report No. 18, 1961.
[B 72] Department of Energy, *Energy Management*, Obtainable on mailing list by application to 'Degree Days, Energy Conservation Unit, Department of Energy', Monthly.
[B 73] Scottish Gas Board, *An Inquiry into the Reasons why People change from Gas to Electricity in the Home*, 1959.
[B 74] North Western Gas Consumers' Council, *First Report for the Period January 1st 1973 to March 31st 1974*, 1974.
[B 75] South Western Gas Consumers' Council, *First Report for the Period January 1st 1973 to March 31st 1974*, 1974.
[B 76] Department of Energy, *Fuel Efficiency Booklet No. 7; Degree Days*, 1977.
[B 77] Green Paper, *The Future of Company Reports*, Cmnd. 6888, HMSO, London, 1977.
[B 78] North Eastern Gas, *Gas Bills and Customer Queries*, 1972.
[B 79] British Standards 1179: 1961, *Glossary of Terms used in the Gas Industry*, British Standards Institution, 1944, revised 1961.
[B 80] Central Statistical Office, *Guide to Official Statistics No. 1*, HMSO, London, 1976.
[B 81] International Gas Union, *International Statistics of the Gas Industry*, 10th International Gas Conference, Hamburg, 1967.
[B 82] The British Electrical and Allied Industries Research Association, *A Large-Scale Sampling Survey of Domestic Consumers*, 1948.
[B 83] Political and Economic Planning, *The Market for Household Appliances*, PEP, 1945.
[B 84] Gas Council, *Metrication: the International System of Metric Units*, 1967.
[B 85] Central Statistical Office, *National Income Statistics: Sources and Methods*, HMSO, London, 1956.
[B 86] Planning Division, Natural Gas Co-ordination, Shell Centre, *Natural Gas Terms and Measurements* (NG/68/2), Shell International Petroleum Co. Ltd., 4th Edition, 1968.
[B 87] Political and Economic Planning, *Report on the Gas Industry in Great Britain*, PEP, 1939.
[B 88] The Institution of Gas Engineers, *Report of the Sub-Committee on Unaccounted for Gas*, Publication No. 380, July 1951.
[B 89] The Electricity Council, *The 1955 Sample Survey of Domestic Consumers*, Utilisation Report No. 7, 1958.
[B 90] The Electricity Council, *The 1961 Sample Survey of Domestic Consumers*, Utilisation Report No. 42, 1964.
[B 91] Consumers' Association, *Which?*, Sept. 1975.

APPENDIX

RECONCILIATION OF STANDARD REGIONS WITH BOUNDARIES OF BRITISH GAS CORPORATION REGIONS
(PER CENT OF HOME POPULATION 1974)

STANDARD REGIONS 1 APRIL 1974	REGIONS OF BRITISH GAS CORPORATION											
	Scottish	Northern	North Western	North Eastern	East Midlands	West Midlands	Wales	Eastern	North Thames	South Eastern	Southern	South Western
SCOTLAND	100											
NORTH												
Tyne and Wear		100										
Cleveland		100										
Cumbria		62	38									
Durham		100										
Northumberland		100										
NORTH WEST												
Greater Manchester			100									
Merseyside			100									
Cheshire			95			5						
Lancashire			100									
YORKSHIRE & HUMBERSIDE												
South Yorkshire				5	95							
West Yorkshire				100								
Humberside				63	37							
North Yorkshire		14	2	84								
EAST MIDLANDS												
Derbyshire			9		91							
Leicestershire					93	7						
Lincolnshire					100							
Northamptonshire					95						5	
Nottinghamshire					100							
WEST MIDLANDS												
West Midlands						89						11
Hereford and Worcester						98						
Salop			2		8	92						
Staffordshire						99						1
Warwickshire												
WALES							100					

APPENDIX

REGIONS OF BRITISH GAS CORPORATION

STANDARD REGIONS 1 APRIL 1974	Scottish	Northern	North Western	North Eastern	East Midlands	West Midlands	Wales	Eastern	North Thames	South Eastern	Southern	South Western
EAST ANGLIA												
Cambridgeshire					<½			99+				
Norfolk								100				
Suffolk								100				
SOUTH EAST												
Greater London								7	57	36		
Bedfordshire					1			93			6	
Berkshire									43		55	
Buckinghamshire					4			6	50		40	
East Sussex										100		2
Essex								49	51			
Hampshire											100	
Hertfordshire												
Isle of Wight											100	
Kent										100		
Oxfordshire											93	7
Surrey									18	70	12	
West Sussex										78	22	
SOUTH WEST												
Avon												100
Cornwall												100
Devon											<½	99+
Dorset											100	
Gloucestershire												100
Somerset											1	99
Wiltshire											20	80

SPECIMEN

SUBJECT INDEX TO GAS

Accidental deaths caused by gas, 10.2
Accidents, 5.3
Accidents, causes of 5.3
Adjustment of figures, 4.1.1; 4.2.1; 4.2.1.2
Algerian natural gas, 2.3; 9
American Gas Association, 15.2
Ammonia Federation Limited, British Sulphate of 4.1.3
Ammonia production, sulphate of 3.1; 4.1.3
Appliance installation, 7
Appliance manufacture in the economy, 4.2.3
Appliance marketing, 7
Appliances for natural gas, conversion of 2.3; 9.2; 14.1
Appliances, hire of domestic 4.2.1.1; 4.2.3
Appliances, hire purchase of 4.2.3
Appliances in use, 4.2.3; 14.1
Appliances, quality control in 4.2.3
Appliances, sales of 4.2.3; 14.1
Area Gas Boards, 2.5; 2.25
Area, gas supply 4.2.1.1
Assets, capital 6.6
Audits of Great Britain, 3.2; 14.1
Availability of gas, 4.2.1.1
Average day, 3.3.4
Average output, 3.3.4

Back boiler units, 4.2.3
Balance of payments *see* Energy Review
Benzole Association, National 4.1.3
Benzole, extraction of 4.1.1; 4.1.3; 4.2.1; 4.2.1.5
Benzole, gas equivalent of 4.1.1; 4.2.1.5
Bills, gas 7.1
Blast furnace gas, 4.1
Board of Trade, 3.1; 4.1.2
Bonuses, holiday 5.5
Breeze, 4.1.2
Breeze sales, coke and 4.2.2
British Electrical and Allied Industries Research Association, 14.1
British Gas Corporation Formation, 2.5
British Road Tar Association, 4.1.3
British Standards Institution, 3.3
British Sulphate of Ammonia Federation Limited, 4.1.3
British Tar Confederation, 4.1.3
British Tar Industry Association, 4.1.3
British Thermal Unit, 3.3.3
British Thermal Unit *see* Energy Review

Building and civil engineering craftsmen, 5.1
Business Statistics Office, 5.1

Calculation of bills, 3.3.1
Calorific value, 3.1; 3.3.1; 3.3.3; 4.1.1
Calorific value, declared 3.3.3
Calorific value of natural gas, 2.3
Calorific value *see* Energy Review
Canvey Island, 2.3; 9
Capital assets, 6.6
Capital expenditure, 6.6
Capital, working 6.6
Carbon monoxide, 10.2
Carburetted water-gas, 2.2
Causes of accidents, 5.3
Census of Distribution, 6.5; 12.2
Census of Employment, 5.1
Census of Population, 5.1
Census of Production, 3.1; 5.1; 5.4
Central heating, 4.2.3; 14.1
Chairman, emoluments to 5.4
Changes in holder stock, 4.1.1
Civil engineering craftsmen, building and 5.1
Co-partnership schemes, 5.4
Coal equivalent, 4.3
Coal equivalent *see* Energy Review
Coal gas, 2; 4.1.1
Coefficient *see* Energy Review, Energy
Coke and breeze sales, 4.2.2
Coke Associations, National Federation of Gas 4.1.2
Coke from coke ovens, hard 4.1.2; 4.2.2
Coke Marketing, Regional Associations in 4.1.2
Coke production, gas 2.5; 3.1; 4.1.2
Coke-oven gas, 2; 2.4; 4.1; 4.1.1
Colliery methane, 4.1
Commercial fuel market, total 4.2.1.2
Commercial market, 14.3
Commercial premises, split domestic 4.2.1.1
Commercial sales, 4.2.1.2
Commercial tariffs, 4.2.1.2
Communal heat schemes, 4.2.1.1
Comparability of fuels *see* Energy Review
Competition with oil, 4.2.1.2
Competitive fuel consumption, 4.2.1.3; 4.3
Computers, 15.1
Confederation of British Industry, 14.2
Confederation of British Industry *see* Energy Review

Consolidated trading and profit and loss account, 7
Consultative Council, Gas 2.5; 10.1
Consumer Association, 14.1
Consumers' Council, National Gas, 2.5; 10.1
Consumers' expenditure on gas, 11.1
Consumption, competitive fuel 4.2.1.3; 4.3
Consumption, level of 4.2.1.1
Consumption, pattern of domestic 4.2.1.1
Conversion factors see Energy Review
Conversion of appliances for natural gas, 2.3; 9.2; 14.1
Converters, gas 5.2
Cookers, 4.2.3; 14.1
Corporate planning, 15.1
Cost of living index, 5.4
Craftsmen, building and civil engineering 5.1
Creosote, 4.1.3
Crisis see Energy Review, Oil
Crude tar, 3.1; 4.1.3
Customer satisfaction, 10.1

Daily demand 3.3.4; 4.1.1
Daily information, 4.1.1
Data collection methods, 3.2
Days lost, 5.3
Deaths caused by gas, accidental 10.2
Declared calorific value, 3.3.3
Degree day, 3.3.5
Demand, daily 3.3.4; 4.1.1
Demand, hourly 4.1.1
Demand, maximum 3.1
Demand, temperature effect on gas 3.3.2; 3.3.5; 15.1
Department of Employment, 5.1; 5.4
Department of Energy see Energy Review
Development centre, Westfield 8
Development for fuel and power see Energy Review, Research and
Development, research and 8
Development see Energy Review, National Energy Research and
Direct sales, 4.2.1.3
Disconnections, 6.3; 15.2
Disputes, trade 5.3
Distribution load factor, 3.1
Diurnal variations, 6.2
Doctors' waiting rooms, 4.2.1.1; 14.3
Domestic appliances, hire of 4.2.1.1; 4.2.3
Domestic commercial premises, split 4.2.1.1
Domestic consumption, pattern of 4.2.1.1
Domestic sales, 4.2.1.1
Domestic water supply, 14.1
Drilling licences, 9.1
Drilling, rigs for 9.1

Earnings of gas workers, 5.4; 11.7
Economist Intelligence Unit, British Market Research Bureau, 14.1
Education and training, 5.8
Emoluments to chairman, 5.4

Energy balances see Energy Review
Energy coefficient see Energy Review
Energy crisis, 14.2
Energy Model Group see Energy Review
Energy modelling see Energy Review
Energy papers see Energy Review
Energy sector see Energy Review
Estimation of un-read gas, 3.3.2; 4.2.1
European Economic Commission, 5.5; 13
European Energy Data see Energy Review
Excluded employees, 5.1
Expenditure, capital 6.6
Expenditure on fuel and energy see Energy Review
Expenditure on gas, consumers' 11.1
Explosions caused by gas, 10.2
Extraction of benzole, 4.1.1; 4.1.3; 4.2.1; 4.2.1.5

Factories, HM Inspectors of 5.3
Family expenditure survey, 11.3
Feedstock to gas manufacturing plant, 4.2.1.5
Feedstock to petro-chemical plants, 4.2.1.3
Feedstock to power stations, 4.2.1.3
Financial targets, 7
Fire Research Station, 10.2
Fish and chip shops, 4.2.1.1
Fitters, gas 5.1; 5.4
Forecasting, 15.1
Forecasts see Energy Review
France, 15.2
Frigg Field, 9.1
Fuel market, total commercial 4.2.1.2
Fuel programming, 4.2.2
Fuel used by gas industry, price of 11.6

Gas Act 1948, 2.4; 2.5; 3.1; 7; 10.1
Gas Act 1965, 2.5
Gas Act 1972, 2.5
Gas bills, 7.1
Gas coke production, 2.5; 3.1; 4.1.2
Gas Consultative Council, 2.5; 10.1
Gas converters, 5.2
Gas Council, 2.5
Gas equivalent of benzole, 4.1.1; 4.2.1.5
Gas fitters, 5.1; 5.4
Gas Industry Training Board, 5.1
Gas Regulation Act 1920, 3.1
Gas supply area, 4.2.1.1
Gas trend, 4.2.3
Gas Undertakings Act 1934, 3.1
Government fuel policy see Energy Review
Government intervention see Energy Review
Government sales, 4.2.1.2
Grid control, 3.2
Grid, natural gas 9
Gross domestic product see Energy Review

Hard coke from coke ovens, 4.1.2; 4.2.2
Health Education Council, 10.2
Heat schemes, communal 4.2.1.1
Heat supplied, 4.3

Heat supplied *see* Energy Review
Heaters, greenhouse 4.2.3
Heaters, space 4.2.1.1; 4.2.3; 14.1
Heaters, water 4.2.3; 14.1
Heating, central 4.2.3; 14.1
Heating of working-class dwellings, 14.1
Heyworth Committee, 2.4
High-paid workers, 5.4
High-pressure slagging gasifier, 8
High-pressure transmission, 6.3
Hire of domestic appliances, 4.2.1.1; 4.2.3
Hire purchase of appliances, 4.2.3
Historical data, 3.1; 12.1
HM Inspector of Factories, 5.3
Holder capacity, 15.2
Holder stock, changes in 4.1.1
Holders, 6.2
Holding companies, 2.4; 3.1
Holiday bonuses, 5.5
Hourly demand, 4.1.1
Hours of work, 5.4
Hydro-electric power *see* Energy Review

ICI gas reformers, 6.1
ICI sales, 4.2.1.3
Illuminating power, 3.1
Image of gas, 14.1
IMSSOC, 5.1
Incentive payments, 5.4; 5.5
Incinerators, 4.2.3
Income from sales, 7
Income Statistics, National 11.1
Incomes, National Board for Prices and 5.1; 5.5; 5.6; 7; 9.2
Index of labour costs, 11.7
Industrial fuel use, 14.2
Industrial market research, 14.2
Industrial revenue, 11.4
Industrial sales, 4.2.1.3
Injury payments, sickness and 5.5
Input output tables *see* Energy Review
Inspectors of Factories, HM 5.3
Institute of Manpower Studies System of Occupational Classification, 5.1
Institution of Gas Engineers, 1; 2.1; 3.2.2; 6.3; 10.2; 15.1
International Colloquium on Marketing Gas, 4.2.1.1; 4.2.3; 13
International data, 13
International Gas Union, 13
Investment in energy *see* Energy Review

Labour costs, 5.5; 11.7
Labour costs, index of 11.7
Labour turnover, 5.2
Labour wastage, 5.2
Leaks of gas, 6.3
Level of consumption, 4.2.1.1
Lighting, railway station 4.2.1.2
Lighting, street 2.1; 3.1; 4.2.1.4

Liquefied petroleum gas, 4.1
Load factor, 3.3.4; 6.1
Load factor, distribution 3.1
Load factor, manufacturing 3.1
Load factor, system 3.3.4; 15.2
Load research, 14.1
London Gas Light and Coke Company, 2.1; 2.4; 4.2.1.2; 14.1; 14.3
Losses in reforming, 4.2.1.5
Losses in transmission, 4.2.1; 6.3
Lurgi process, 2.2; 4.1.1; 6.1

Mains, 6.3
Manufacturing load factor, 3.1
Mark-sensing documents, 3.2
Market research, 3.2; 4.2.3; 14
Market research, industrial 14.2
Marketing, appliance 7
Marketing Gas, International Colloquium on 4.2.1.1; 4.2.3; 13
Maximum day, 3.3.4
Maximum demand, 3.1
Maximum hour, 3.3.4
Maximum output, 3.3.4
Maximum output, week of 4.1.1
Maximum overall week, 4.1.1
Measurement, units of 3.3
Merrett Cyriax, 14.2
Meter accuracy, 3.3.1; 4.1.1
Meter readers, 5.1; 5.6
Meter reading, 3.3.2; 4.2.1
Meters, 3.3.1; 4.2.1.1; 4.2.1.2; 4.2.1.3; 6.4
Methane, colliery 4.1
Methods, data collection 3.2
Methods of gas production, 2.2; 6.1
Micro-Simplex, 6.1
Mines Department, 4.1.1
Modelling *see* Energy Review
Morecambe Field, 9.1
Municipal gas companies, 2.4; 2.5
Murdoch, William, 2.1

Naphthalene, 4.1.3
National Benzole Association, 4.1.3
National Board for Prices and Incomes, 5.1; 5.5; 5.6; 7; 9.2
National Economic Development Office, 4.3
National Energy Research and Development *see* Energy Review
National Federation of Gas Coke Associations, 4.1.2
National fuel policy, 15.2
National Gas Consumers Council, 2.5; 10.1
National Income statistics, 11.1
National insurance contributions, 5.5
National Joint Council, 5.4
Nationalisation, 2.5; 3.2
Natural gas, 2.3; 4.1.1; 4.2.1.3; 9
Natural gas, conversion of appliances for 2.3; 9.2; 14.1

Natural gas grid, 9
Natural gas transmission system, 4.1.1
Natural gas wells, 9.1
Non-statutory undertakers, 3.1; 4.1.1
North Sea natural gas, 2.3; 2.5; 4.2.1.3; 9
Northern Ireland Administration, 2.6

OECD *see* Energy Review
Oil, competition with 4.2.1.2
Oil crisis *see* Energy Review
Oil equivalent, 4.3
Oil equivalent *see* Energy Review
Oil gasification, 2.2; 4.1.1; 6.1
Onia Gegi, 6.1
Output, 7
Output, average 3.3.4
Output, maximum 3.3.4
Output, week of maximum 4.1.1
Overtime payment, 5.4
Own use by gas industry, 4.2.1; 4.2.1.5
Oxidation process, Shell partial 6.1
Oxide, spent 4.1.3

Part-time workers, 5.1
Partial oxidation process, Shell 6.1
Pattern of domestic consumption, 4.2.1.1
Payments, incentive 5.4; 5.5
Payments, sickness and injury 5.5
Performance indicators, 5.6
Petro-chemical plants, feedstock to 4.2.1.3
Petroleum (Production) Act 1918, 9
Petroleum (Production) Regulations 1934, 9
Petroleum industry *see* Energy Review
Phenol, 4.1.3
Pipe breakages, 6.3
Pitch, 4.1.3
Planning, corporate 15.1
Plant capacity, 6.1
Plant register, 6.1
Plant utilization, 3.3.4
Plumbers, 5.1
Postal questionnaires, 3.2
Power gas, 6.1
Power stations, feedstock to 4.2.1.3
Prepayment meters, 4.2.1.1
Pressure, standard temperature and 4.1.1
Pressure variations, temperature and 4.2.1
Price of fuel used by gas industry, 11.6
Price of gas, 11
Prices and Incomes, National Board for 5.1; 5.5; 5.6; 7; 9.2
Primary fuels *see* Energy Review
Production, methods of gas 2.2; 6.1
Productivity, 5.6
Profit and loss account, consolidated trading and 7
Profit-sharing schemes, 5.4
PROJECT MAC, 3.2; 4.2.3; 6.5; 7
Public administration, 4.2.1.2; 4.2.1.4
Public Services, 4.2.1.2

Quality control in appliances, 4.2.3

Railway station lighting, 4.2.1.2
Recruitment, 5.2
Recruitment and wastage of university graduates, 5.2
Reformers, ICI gas 6.1
Reforming, losses in 4.2.1.5
Refrigerators, 4.2.3; 14.1
Regional Association in Coke Marketing, 4.1.2
Regional data, 5.2; 12
Regions, standard 12.2
Research and development, 8
Research and development for fuel and power *see* Energy Review
Response rate, 3.2
Retail Price Index, 11.1; 11.2; 11.3
Retort house workers, 5.1
Revenue, 7
Rigs for drilling, 9.1
Road tar, 4.1.3
Road Tar Association, British 4.1.3

Safety of gas, 10.2
Sales, coke and breeze 4.2.2
Sales, commercial 4.2.1.2
Sales, direct 4.2.1.3
Sales, domestic 4.2.1.1
Sales, government 4.2.1.2
Sales, income from 7
Sales, industrial 4.2.1.3
Sales of appliances, 4.2.3; 14.1
Sales of gas, 4.2.1
Secondary fuels *see* Energy Review
Select Committee on Gas 1961, 5.8; 9
Service layers, 5.1
Service workload investigation model, 5.7
Services, 6.3
Shell partial oxidation process, 6.1
Shift allowances, 5.4
Shift workers, 5.1
Showrooms, 6.5
SI units, 3.3
Sickness, 5.3
Sickness and injury payments, 5.5
Society of British Gas Industries, 4.2.3
Space heaters, 4.2.1.1; 4.2.3; 14.1
Spent oxide, 4.1.3
Split domestic commercial premises, 4.2.1.1
Standard industrial classification, 4.2.1.2; 4.2.1.3
Standard regions, 12.2
Standard temperature and pressure, 4.1.1
Statutory gas companies, 2.4; 3.1
Stock, changes in holder 4.1.1
Storage of gas, 6.2
Street lighting, 2.1; 3.1; 4.2.1.4
Substitutability of fuels *see* Energy Review

SUBJECT INDEX

Sulphate of Ammonia Federation Limited, British 4.1.3
Sulphate of ammonia production, 3.1; 4.1.3
System load factor, 3.3.4; 15.2

Tar Association, British Road 4.1.3
Tar Confederation, British 4.1.3
Tar, crude 3.1; 4.1.3
Tar Industry Association, British 4.1.3
Tar, road 4.1.3
Telemetry, 3.2; 3.3.2
Teleprinters, 3.2
Temperature and pressure, standard 4.1.1
Temperature and pressure variations, 4.2.1
Temperature effect on gas demand, 3.3.2; 3.3.5; 15.1
Temporary staff, 5.2
Thermal content, 4.3
Thermal content *see* Energy Review
Thermal equivalent, 4.1.1
Therms, 3.3.3
Total commercial fuel market, 4.2.1.2
Trade disputes, 5.3
Trading and profit and loss account, consolidated 7
Training Board, Gas Industry 5.1
Training, education and 5.8
Transmission, high pressure 6.3
Transmission, losses in 4.2.1; 6.3
Transmission system, natural gas 4.1.1
Transport workers, 5.1
Trench yards per man-day, 5.6
Tumbler dryers, 4.2.3

Un-read gas, estimation of 3.3.2; 4.2.1
Unaccounted for gas, 4.2.1; 6.3
Unbilled gas, 4.2.1.2
United Nations, 13
United States, 13
Units of measurement, 3.3
Units of measurement *see* Energy Review
University graduates, recruitment and wastage of 5.2
Useful energy *see* Energy Review
Useful heat, 4.3

Visual display units, 3.2

War-time data, 4.1.1; 4.1.2
Warm air units, 4.2.3
Wash boilers, 4.2.3; 14.1
Washing machines, 4.2.3; 14.1
Water gas, 4.1.1
Water-gas, carburetted 2.2
Water heaters, 4.2.3; 14.1
Water supply, domestic 14.1
Week of maximum output, 4.1.1
Weekly statement on fuel, 4.1.1
Weir Committee, 5.6
Wells, natural gas 9.1
West Sole Field, 9.1
Westfield Development Centre, 8
Winsor, Frederick Albert 2.1
Working capital, 6.6
Workload, 5.7; 15.1

21: ELECTRICITY

David Nuttall

REFERENCE DATE OF SOURCES REVIEWED

This review is believed to represent the position, broadly speaking, as it obtained in 1977. The Addendum (p. 204) has been added at proof reading stage, May 1979, taking account as far as possible of any major changes in the situation.

INDEX TO INITIALS USED IN THE TEXT OR IN QUOTED REFERENCES

AGB	Audits of Great Britain
AMDEA	Association of Manufacturers of Domestic Electrical Appliances
BEAMA	British Electrical Appliance Manufacturers' Association
BS	British Standards Institution
CEGB	Central Electricity Generating Board
D of E	Department of Energy
E & W	England and Wales
EC	Electricity Council
ECRC	Electricity Council Research Centre
EEB	Eastern Electricity Board
EEC	European Economic Community
EMEB	East Midlands Electricity Board
GJ	Gigajoule
GVA	Gigavolt-ampere
GW	Gigawatt
GWh	Gigawatt hour
HMSO	Her Majesty's Stationery Office
IEE	Institute of Electrical Engineers
km	Kilometer
kVA	Kilovolt-ampere
kVAh	Kilovolt-ampere hour
kW	Kilowatt

kWh	Kilowatt hour
LEB	London Electricity Board
LF	Load Factor
MANWEB	Merseyside & North Wales Electricity Board
MD	Maximum Demand
MEB	Midlands Electricity Board
MJ	Megajoule
MVA	Megavolt-ampere
MW	Megawatt
MWh	Megawatt hour
NCB	National Coal Board
NEEB	North Eastern Electricity Board
NIES	Northern Ireland Electricity Service
NSHEB	North of Scotland Hydro-Electric Board
NWEB	North Western Electricity Board
QRL	Quick Reference List
SEB	Southern Electricity Board
SEEB	South Eastern Electricity Board
SMD	Simultaneous Maximum Demand
SSEB	South of Scotland Electricity Board
SWaEB	South Wales Electricity Board
SWEB	South Western Electricity Board
TWH	Terawatt hour
UK	United Kingdom
UN	United Nations
YEB	Yorkshire Electricity Board

ACKNOWLEDGEMENTS

A work such as this, aiming to cover the output from so many undertakings and activities, requires the help of very many people—all of them busy coping with the demands of modern management for data which will help them in the constant drive for more efficient control. I hope I do not forget anyone but apologise in advance if I do.

Primarily, for the provision of facilities for digging out much of the information I must thank the Chairman, Mr E. Booth, and Chief Commercial Officer, Mr N. Osborn, of the Yorkshire Electricity Board.

For the never failing, patient and efficient response to my request for more and more information about sources, thanks to Mr H. Forshaw, Mr W. Sewell, Mr A. Matthews, Mr R. Robinson, Mrs D. Webley, Mrs H. Burnett, and Mrs J. Lee—all of the Commercial Department of the YEB, and to Mr H. Hammersley, Mr A. Bridge, Mr B. Brown, Mr A. Barker, and Mr N. Jackson of the Engineering, Accountancy, and Secretarial Departments.

The Commercial Adviser to the Electricity Council, Mr R. Forman, allowed me the run of his department, within which I must pick out Mr T. A. Boley, Mr G. G. Petersen, Dr J. M. W. Rhys, and Mr J. G. Boggis for particular mention.

Mr R. G. Hancock, Head of the Intelligence Section of the Electricity Council, was particularly good in giving me the benefit of his very wide experience of information gathering over many years and allowing me the use of the superb collection of statistics in the Electricity Council's Library.

Mr P. E. Watts of the CEGB not only gave me lots of information but was typically trenchant in his comments on the use I made of it.

I owe more generalised thanks for the essential source data supplied by the South of Scotland Electricity Board, the North of Scotland Hydro-Electric Board, and the Northern Ireland Electricity Service.

At, and following a critical symposium dealing with an early draft of this work I received much constructive criticism, particularly from Dr S. Rosenbaum, Mr W. N. T. Roberts, and Mr W. A. Hawkins.

Before undertaking this project I had never realised the invaluable part which could be played by an editor. Professor W. E. Maunder, and Mrs J. Horwood of his department, have put their impress on this work and without them I have no doubt it would never have materialised at all, let alone in the relatively tight and tidy version now published.

Notwithstanding all these acknowledgements I of course accept responsibility for any errors or omissions.

Finally I must not only acknowledge the forbearance of my wife in not complaining about a house littered with papers for months on end, but in giving practical help in proof reading, and not being above the odd comment on my occasional diversions from a truly objective approach to some of the economic statistics.

CONTENTS OF REVIEW 21

	Addendum	204
1.	**Introduction**	205
2.	**Before Nationalisation**	206
3.	**After Nationalisation**	209
3.1.	*1948–1959*	209
3.2.	*From 1958*	209
	3.2.1. The Grid and Supergrid Systems	210
3.3.	*Scotland*	211
3.4.	*Great Britain*	211
3.5.	*Northern Ireland*	212
4.	**Statistics in the Modern Electricity Industry**	213
4.1.	*General*	213
	4.1.1. Layout	214
4.2.	*Energy Production, Use and Measurement*	214
	4.2.1. Power	215
	4.2.2. Quantity	215
	4.2.3. Load Factor	215
	4.2.4. Pressure	216
	4.2.5. Meters	216
	4.2.6. Periodicity of Meter Reading	216
4.3.	*Plant and Efficiency*	217
	4.3.1. England and Wales	217
	4.3.1.1. Generating Plant	217
	4.3.1.2. Transmission and Distribution Plant	219
	4.3.2. South Scotland	221
	4.3.2.1. Generating Plant	221
	4.3.2.2. Transmission and Distribution Plant	221
	4.3.3. North Scotland	221
	4.3.3.1. Generating Plant	221
	4.3.3.2. Transmission and Distribution Plant	222
	4.3.4. Scotland as a Whole	222

	4.3.5. Northern Ireland	222
	4.3.5.1. Generating Plant	222
	4.3.5.2. Transmission and Distribution Plant	222
	4.3.6. Great Britain/United Kingdom	223
	4.3.7. Standby Plant in Industry	223
4.4.	*Power*	224
	4.4.1. England and Wales	224
	4.4.1.1. CEGB	224
	4.4.1.2. Area Boards	225
	4.4.2. South Scotland	226
	4.4.3. North Scotland	226
	4.4.4. Scotland	226
	4.4.5. Northern Ireland	226
	4.4.6. Great Britain	226
4.5.	*Electricity Produced and Consumed*	226
	4.5.1. England and Wales	226
	4.5.1.1. Small Administrative Entities	229
	4.5.2. South Scotland	229
	4.5.3. North Scotland	330
	4.5.4. Northern Ireland	230
	4.5.5. Great Britain/United Kingdom	231
	4.5.6. Weather Effect	233
	4.5.7. Private Generation	233
	4.5.8. Abroad	233
4.6.	*Consumer Classification*	234
	4.6.1. England and Wales	234
	4.6.1.1. Small Administrative Entities	234
	4.6.2. Scotland	234
	4.6.3. Northern Ireland	235
4.7.	*Revenue and Prices*	235
	4.7.1. England and Wales	235
	4.7.2. Scotland	235
	4.7.3. Northern Ireland	235
	4.7.4. Great Britain/United Kingdom	236
	4.7.5. Electricity Price Indices	236
5.	**Financial Statistics**	237
5.1.	*General*	237
	5.2.1. England and Wales	237
	5.2.2. Scotland	238
	5.2.3. Northern Ireland	238
5.3.	*Revenue*	238
	5.3.1. England and Wales	238
	5.3.2. Scotland	240
	5.3.3. Northern Ireland	240
	5.3.4. Great Britain	240

5.4.	*Capital*	240
	5.4.1. England and Wales	240
	5.4.2. Scotland	241
	5.4.3. Northern Ireland	242
	5.4.4. Great Britain	242
5.5.	*Financing Capital Expenditure*	242
	5.5.1. England and Wales	242
	5.5.2. Scotland	243
	5.5.3. Northern Ireland	243
6.	**Statistics of Other Commercial Services**	244
6.1.	*General*	244
	6.2.1. England and Wales	244
	6.2.2. Scotland	245
	6.2.3. Northern Ireland	245
	6.2.4. Great Britain/United Kingdom	245
7.	**Employee Statistics**	247
7.1.	*England and Wales*	247
7.2.	*Scotland*	248
7.3.	*Northern Ireland*	248
7.4.	*Great Britain*	248
8.	**Research**	249
8.1.	*Organisation*	249
8.2.	*Research Results*	250
8.3.	*Use of Resources*	250
	8.3.1. England and Wales	250
	8.3.2. South Scotland	251
	8.3.3. North Scotland	251
9.	**Conclusion**	252
Quick Reference List		
	Key to Publications	283
Bibliography		285
Appendices		287
Subject Index		293

ADDENDUM

The main body of this review represents the position in 1977. The following notes account for differences up to mid-1979 in the statistics for England and Wales.

1. The Electricity Council *Annual Report* [QRL 3] for 1977/78 included for the first time a section on performance indicators. Three diagrams were included, showing:
   (i) the trend in delivered costs of fuel alongside the trend in the retail price index and in the average price per kWh;
   (ii) the trend in the number of employees in the industry alongside employees per unit sold; and
   (iii) the trend in thermal efficiency of fossil fuel steam stations alongside the trend in load factor in ACS conditions.

These diagrams are appearing in the 1978/79 *Report*, together with an additional diagram showing the trend in industrial electricity prices alongside the wholesale price index.

2. The financial statements in the 1977/78 *Annual Report* [QRL 3] continued on an historic cost basis, but as a first move towards inflation accounting 40% supplementary depreciation was added to the normal provision for depreciation at historic cost. The supplementary depreciation was itemised in the Consolidated Accounts.

In the 1978/79 *Annual Report* 40% supplementary depreciation is again being charged and in addition an inflation accounting statement is included to demonstrate the possible effects of inflation accounting on the industry. It must be emphasized that this statement is only a demonstration; the industry has not yet moved away from historic cost accounting.

3. The 1978 *Handbook of Electricity Supply Statistics* [QRL 23] contained four new tables:
   (i) CEGB Bulk Supply Tariff—analysis of revenue. This table gave figures already provided in the CEGB *Annual Report* [QRL 4].
   (ii) A table showing the development of the electricity industry in Northern Ireland. This was derived from figures published by the Northern Ireland Electricity Service.
   (iii) An analysis of sales of electricity to industrial consumers and transport undertakings in Great Britain, taken from the *Digest of UK Energy Statistics* [QRL 13].
   (iv) A comparison of average prices of fuels used by the gas and electricity supply industries in Great Britain, taken from the *Digest of UK Energy Statistics*.

4. The table on ownership levels of electrical appliances in selected European countries was omitted from the 1978 *Handbook* [QRL 23] because up-to-date figures were not available. It was not re-introduced in 1979.

CHAPTER 1

INTRODUCTION

This review is primarily concerned with statistical sources for the electricity supply industry as it has evolved since nationalisation. It covers the generation, main transmission, and retail distribution of electrical energy, the other commercial activities of the industry such as the retailing of domestic and commercial electrical appliances, the contracting service which it sells to the public, and the research activities of the industry.

Before nationalisation the supply industry had relatively minor connections with the manufacture of equipment, both industrial and domestic, but this no longer applies and the manufacture of generation and transmission plant is not covered below.

Nationalisation gave rise to a radical change in the output and standardisation of statistics and accordingly the main emphasis is on the statistical sources as they developed from 1948 onwards.

However, the electricity industry has always had a tradition of providing good statistical coverage of its activities and Section 2 below deals with pre-nationalisation statistical sources. Section 3 covers the organisation of the industry after nationalisation and Section 4 then initiates the survey of post-nationalisation statistics, leading to a concentration on those statistics currently published.

Workers wanting a quick lead to sources of statistics of a particular facet of the electricity supply industry should first read Section 4.1.

CHAPTER 2

BEFORE NATIONALISATION

Those interested in the early history of the electricity supply industry, insofar as that history can be revealed by statistics, are recommended to consult the original paper in the field—G. H. Daniel's *Electricity and Gas Statistics* [B 1]. This publication, originally available in 1950, is important for cover to 1948 or so and is summarised in the remainder of this section as an indication of its content for those who may have difficulty in gaining access to a copy. (Researchers interested in historical information should see the 'References to Statistical Sources' appended to [B 1].)

The supply of electricity only became recognisable as an industry in the early 1880s, when the first private companies were floated and local authorities began to take powers to supply electricity to the public. At first there was little technical case for integrating or co-ordinating the growing number of small undertakings. As a consequence, no official national statistics were issued. However, at this early stage the *Journal of the IEE* [B 13], the *Electrical Review* [QRL 17], the *Electrical Times* [QRL 18], and the *Electrician* [B 6] did give useful quantitative information, largely drawn from the published accounts of individual undertakings.

A major step forward came in 1897 with the publication of the first edition of Garcke's *Manual of Electrical Undertakings* [B 3] covering the year 1896. Based on published accounts, this gave for each co-operating authorised undertaking particulars of its financial position, and also of the amounts of electricity generated and sold, the numbers of lamps and customers served, the prices authorised and charged, the horse-power of the engines installed, and the nature of the distribution system. From around 1913 virtually all undertakings were covered. Subsequently, annual editions included national summaries, extending over a series of years, of the more important of the figures given for the separate undertakings.

Statistically, the next important advance followed from the Electricity (Supply) Act of 1919, providing for the appointment of Electricity Commissioners, responsible for promoting, regulating and supervising the supply of electricity. Section 27 of the Act made it the duty of the undertakers to furnish the Commissioners with such accounts, statistics and returns as they might require. These powers, the Commissioners' appreciation of the importance of reliable information, and the wide-spread recognition of the need for re-organising the industry go a long way to explain the comprehensive nature of the annual statistics which the Commissioners proceeded to build up—statistics which at the time were among the most comprehensive ever published for a British industry.

As from 1920 the Commissioners produced annual reports on *Generation of Electricity in Great Britain* [B 12]. These gave, on a calendar year basis for each separate station, its type, units generated and sent out, fuel consumption per unit, thermal efficiency, maximum load and load factor. (For definitions of these last three terms see Sections 4.3.1.1, 4.2.1, and 4.2.3.)

The main statistical effort of the Commissioners was based on their annual statistical return. Section A gave administrative details, such as the extent of the area of supply, numbers of premises and consumers, the staffs employed and their salaries and wages. Section B dealt systematically with the undertakers' finances, the capital or loans raised and expended, operations on revenue account, the appropriation of the surpluses on this account, and the changes in depreciation, reserve and other balances. It also dealt with particulars of the tariffs for electricity charges in force at the end of each year. Section C covered systems of supply, generators, boilers, condensing facilities, transmission lines, amounts of electricity generated, purchased, used, and sold, analyses of sales according to types of consumer, and details of maximum loads, load factors, and fuel consumed in generation. Initially, the coverage was anything but complete, and it was not until May 1925 that the Commissioners were able to publish their first *Return of Engineering and Financial Statistics* [B 10] covering the three yearly financial returns ending with 1922/23. This publication was then issued annually until the 1939–45 war and came to an end with the issue for 1947/48.

The first substantial changes made during the life of these Returns were those introduced in the volume for 1932/33, mainly as a result of the Electricity (Supply) Act of 1926. This Act set up the Central Electricity Board, whose principal function was to construct main transmission lines (known as the Grid), to standardise frequency, and consequently to ensure that national requirements were generated in the most economical way by

(*a*) purchasing the total output of the country's main stations (the 'selected' stations) and
(*b*) selling supplies in bulk to authorised undertakers (including the owners of the 'selected' stations).

The new arrangements made it necessary to change the presentation of the statistics for the industry. These changes, together with those which experience had suggested to be desirable were introduced in the 1932/33 volume.

There was a reduction in the amount of detail collected and published after the outbreak of the 1939–45 war.

As for short-period statistics, the Commissioners began in 1930 to release to the technical press monthly figures of electricity generated and electricity sent out. From January 1946, monthly statistics, covering fuel consumption, electricity generated, electricity sent out, generating capacity installed, and simultaneous maximum demand have been published in the *Monthly Digest of Statistics* [QRL 25].

In accordance with the Electricity Act of 1947 nationalising the industry (dealt with more fully in Section 3 below) the Electricity Commission was dissolved on 31 July 1948. At that date their annual return had not been issued for 1946/47 and 1947/48 and the then responsible Government Department, the Ministry of Fuel and Power, accordingly arranged to complete the series by issuing the volumes for those years.

After the dissolution of the Electricity Commission, to provide for the continued supply of the detailed information required about the whole industry, the Ministry drew up new forms of return for the year 1948 and subsequent years. These forms were designed to ensure, as far as possible, continuity with the Commissioners' statistics and, at the same time, comparability with the statistics for the other fuel and power industries and with the requirements of the Census of Production. They asked for enough details about persons employed, wages and salaries, materials purchased, capital expenditure, and the value of output and other work done to meet the requirements of this Census, and to make it unnecessary for overlapping returns to be rendered both to it and to the Ministry. The information was called for on a calendar year basis and has been published in the Ministry's *Statistical Digest* [QRL 13] alongside similar information for the other fuel and power industries.

Mr Daniel's paper goes on to

(*a*) define the pre-nationalisation field of electricity generation and distribution undertakers

(*b*) define the periods of time covered in the statistics in use at the time of nationalisation

(*c*) give the various definitions of plant capacity; electricity generated, sent out, purchased, sold, and lost; maximum load, maximum demand and load factor; fuel consumption and thermal efficiency in use at the time of nationalisation

(*d*) cover the labour statistics, financial statistics, and analyses of sales available up to the time of nationalisation.

CHAPTER 3

AFTER NATIONALISATION

3.1. 1948–1958

The British Electricity Authority and fourteen Area Electricity Boards were established under the Electricity Act 1947. On 1 April 1948 they took over the electricity supply industry throughout Great Britain, except

(*a*) in the District (extended by the 1947 Act) of the North of Scotland Hydro-Electric Board, which was established in 1943 under the Hydro-Electric Development (Scotland) Act, 1943 and
(*b*) some small electricity supplies provided by undertakings outside the scope of the previous Electricity Supply legislation and amounting to a fraction of one per cent of the supplies to the public.

The Authority divided their system into fourteen Generating Divisions, but from 1 April 1954 the Merseyside and North Wales Division and the North Western Division were amalgamated to form the North West, Merseyside and North Wales Division.

On 1 April 1955, under the Electricity Reorganisation (Scotland) Act, 1954, the Authority's generation and transmission undertakings in Scotland (the South East Scotland and South West Scotland Divisions) and the distribution undertakings of the two Scottish Area Boards (South East Scotland and South West Scotland) vested in a new public authority called the South of Scotland Electricity Board, and the title of the Authority was changed to the 'Central Electricity Authority'. There were thus reductions from 14 to 12 in the number of Area Boards and from 13 to 11 in the number of the Authority's Generating Divisions. It was agreed with the South of Scotland Board that the main transmission facilities taken over by that Board should continue to run interconnected with the rest of the network of main transmission lines (the Grid).

3.2. From 1958

The Electricity Act, 1957, dissolved the Central Electricity Authority, and established the Central Electricity Generating Board (CEGB) and the Electricity Council.

The CEGB took over the Authority's functions of generation and main transmission.

The Electricity Council comprises a chairman, two deputy chairmen, and up to three other members, all appointed directly by the Minister; the chairman and two other members of the Generating Board; and the chairmen of the twelve Area Boards.

From 1 January 1958, the Council has had the duties of

(*a*) advising the Minister on questions affecting the supply industry, and
(*b*) promoting and assisting the maintenance and development by the Generating Board and the Area Boards of an efficient, co-ordinated and economic system of electricity supply.

Thus the Council constitutes the machinery for consultation on, and formulation of, general policy for the industry as a whole, and in addition has specific functions relating to borrowing for capital development and other requirements of the industry, the settling and carrying out of programmes of research, the constitution of the industrial relations machinery for negotiation and joint consultation, and the publication of consolidated accounts and an annual report reviewing the activities and progress of the industry as a whole.

Individual Boards (including the CEGB) must consult the Council before settling their capital programmes requiring the Minister's approval, and before settling their tariffs for the supply of electricity.

Thus the electricity supply system in England and Wales in 1978 comprises:

(*a*) the power stations and the interconnecting network of main transmission lines (the Super-Grid), owned and operated by the CEGB, who supply electricity to the Area Boards, to railway haulage or traction consumers, and to other consumers (known as direct consumers) where specifically authorised by the Minister;
(*b*) the distribution networks owned and operated by the twelve Area Electricity Boards since April 1948, together with the lower voltage parts of the Grid taken over from the CEGB in 1969 (see 3.2.1 below). The Area Boards plan and carry out the distribution and sale of electricity to consumers. Apart from very small purchases from outside sources, 440 M units in 1975/76 out of a total usage of 196,000 M units, and minimal generation by the South Western Board, they buy their supplies of electricity from the CEGB and these are delivered to the distribution networks direct from the power stations or from points in the Grid.

3.2.1. *The Grid and Supergrid Systems*

Although in the 1890s suggestions had been made that pit-head generation and three-phase alternating current distribution were the probable future trends, electricity supply continued to expand for 20 years with mixed networks of direct current and alternating current.

In 1918 the pressures of the 1914–18 war and the growing use of electricity for power made clear both the need for the interconnection of power stations and for a national controlling body.

Following the Act of 1926 and the formation of the Central Electricity Board, the 132,000 volt grid was created for selected power station interconnection. For about ten years the UK grid developed in this form and was operated in seven self-contained zones, with normally-open emergency interconnection between zones, because of the difficulties envisaged in stable operation of several hundred generators with different characteristics connected to a single system.

In 1938 a trial operation with the seven zones connected to form a single system was so successful that it became apparent that the technical difficulties of operating a national network had been exaggerated, and from that time the grid has been operated as a single system.

In the early part of the 1939–45 war the interconnected grid proved to be valuable in enabling supplies of electricity to be maintained or rapidly restored when the normal local sources of supply were cut off by enemy action and in permitting the strategic siting of war factories, even in localities where sufficient local generation did not exist. Experience in the successful bulk transmission of power indicated that new generating stations need not be sited in, and matched to, the developed load centres, but could be located near coalfields and designed for the maximum economic size. This approach to the siting of large new generating stations, coupled with the ever increasing demand for electricity, led to the need for superimposing a higher transmission voltage on the 132,000 volt grid.

In 1947, at the time of nationalisation of the electricity supply industry, there had been experience with an experimental 275,000 volt line, but plans to establish a supergrid system utilising this voltage had not been finalised. The first section of the supergrid system was brought into service in 1953. Ten years later the first experimental 400,000 volt line was energised.

The progressive development of 275,000 and 400,000 volt supergrid systems led to a re-consideration of the role of the 132,000 volt system. In general its function changed from that of transmitting power over long distances to that of distributing supplies in local areas. Because of this change in role, responsibility for most of the 132,000 volt system was transferred from the CEGB to the twelve Area Boards in April 1969. The transfer involved assets valued at about £350 M with depreciation provisions of around £90 M per annum.

3.3. Scotland

In Scotland, the electricity supply industry is owned and operated by

(*a*) the North of Scotland Hydro-Electric Board (NSHEB), and
(*b*) the South of Scotland Electricity Board (SSEB).

Each of these Boards is responsible for generation, transmission and distribution in its own area.

3.4. Great Britain

Principal events in the history of the Electricity Supply Industry in Great Britain up to 1973 are recorded in some detail in *Electricity Supply in Great Britain—A Chronology* published by the Electricity Council in 1973 [B 8].

The organisation of the industry, as at the end of 1975, is dealt with in some detail in *Electricity Supply in Great Britain—Organisation and Development, 31 March 1975*, published by the Electricity Council in 1975 [B 9].

3.5. Northern Ireland

In Northern Ireland, the Electricity Supply (Northern Ireland) Order 1972 created a new structure for the electricity supply industry and established the Northern Ireland Electricity Service (NIES).

Under the terms of the Electricity (Transfer of Functions and Dissolution) Order (Northern Ireland) 1973 all the functions exercisable immediately before 1 April 1973 by the Northern Ireland Joint Electricity Authority, the Electricity Board for Northern Ireland, and the Electricity Departments of the Belfast Corporation and of the Londonderry Development Commission were transferred to the Service as from 1 April 1973. As in Scotland, the NIES is responsible for generation, transmission and distribution in its area.

CHAPTER 4

STATISTICS IN THE MODERN ELECTRICITY INDUSTRY

4.1. General

The *Annual Reports and Accounts* of the CEGB [QRL 4], of the Area Boards of England and Wales [QRL 5], of the South of Scotland Board [QRL 7], and the North of Scotland Hydro-Electric Board [QRL 6], with their associated Statements and Appendices, the *Annual Report* of the Northern Ireland Electricity Service [QRL 8], and the *CEGB Statistical Yearbook* [QRL 32], are the primary sources of statistics about the supply industry in the UK. However, the *Electricity Council Statement of Accounts and Statistics* [QRL 31] is not just a useful source of consolidated or summated statistics for the industry in England and Wales. It contains a summary in standardised form of many of the most useful statistics for individual Boards and some statistics not found in the Area Board reports. Indeed the research worker interested in supply statistics for England and Wales would be well advised almost always to go first to this publication.

From 1972/73 both the Council and the CEGB have published volumes separate from their annual reports, dealing with statistics. However, several useful statistics remain in the annual report volumes, and thus workers in the electricity statistics field cannot afford to concentrate on the separate Electricity Council and CEGB statistical volumes only. Thus, in consulting the reports of the electricity Council, CEGB, Area Boards, and Scottish Boards, it may be necessary to refer to their text, Statements, and Appendices.

The *Electricity Council Handbook of Electricity Supply Statistics* (referred to below as *ESS Handbook*) [QRL 23] is particularly valuable. Published annually, it gives some original statistics, and is of great value for long period statistics dating back in some cases to the early 1920s.

The annual *Digest of UK Energy Statistics* [QRL 13] (the *Energy Digest*), published annually by the Department of Energy, is another source of information about the electricity supply industry, useful in that electricity can here be seen as one element in the totality of sources of energy available in the UK. Many of the figures are available earlier from other sources but the summation of its information into Great Britain or United Kingdom totals can save effort. A feature of its figures is that some are available for calendar years, as opposed to the more usual fuel industry financial year periods and indeed some of its tables give statistics for both calendar and financial year periods. This publication is not least valuable for its explanatory notes on energy in general, and electricity production, distribution, and prices in particular.

A valuable source of 'occasional' statistics is the series of Parliamentary Select Committee publications. Their varied nature precludes listing here but examples from two of them will indicate the sort of specialist information available:—

House of Commons Paper 117 of the 1972–73 Session [QRL 27] deals with *Nuclear Power Policy*, and Appendix 4 (dated July 1972) gives 'Comparative Costs of Electricity Generation'. In this paper the CEGB provided information—then the most up-to-date for the calendar year 1971—on actual electricity sent out, cost, and cost per unit sent out (p/kWh) (see 4.2.2) for the seven Magnox nuclear generation stations then in operation, for eight recent coal-fired stations, and three recent oil-fired stations. Detailed notes are given on the calculation of the figures. Since the stations operated at different load factors (see 4.2.3) a further table shows the generating costs for average Magnox, coal and oil stations at January 1972 money values and assuming a common load factor of 75%. Separate calculations are made assuming interest rates of 8% and 10% respectively.

A second paper, HC 145 73 i–vii of the 1973–74 Session—*Choice of a Reactor System* [QRL 11]—provides up-to-date information, not available elsewhere, on capital costs, production costs, and operating experience for various sorts of nuclear plants, in the United Kingdom and abroad. The information is provided by the SSEB and the CEGB.

It may be thought that searching for information from the complex mass of House of Commons Papers could be akin to searching for a needle in a haystack but the Electricity Council Intelligence Section keeps a good index of such papers and is always prepared to help the serious research worker.

4.1.1. *Layout*

Section 4.2 below explains the units employed in relation to the production, use, and measurement of electrical energy. Sections 4.3 to 4.7 deal with the associated statistics.

Consequent upon energy production and distribution are the ancillary functions of finance, appliance sales, repairs and maintenance, personnel, and research, the statistics of which are dealt with in Sections 5 to 8 below.

In each of the Sections 4.3 to 7, the analysis begins with the various Board and Electricity Council Reports, and concludes with comments on other significant sources.

There is bound to be some repetition of source description below. For instance, in dealing with 'Equipment and Efficiency Factors' in 4.3 it is necessary, in order to cover measures of equipment efficiency, to mention statistics of energy supplied by that equipment. Such statistics are mentioned again in dealing with energy production as such.

4.2. Energy Production, Use, and Measurement

The principal measurements when there is a flow of electrical energy are concerned with power, quantity, and pressure.

4.2.1. *Power*

This aspect of energy flow is concerned, ideally, with the instantaneous energy demand where electricity is supplied. In practice it is measured by finding the average quantity of energy flowing over a short period, typically 15, 30, or 60 minutes. It is measured in kilowatts (kW) or kilovolt-amperes (kVA). These two quantities, identical for a direct current supply, are in general different from each other for an alternating current supply. An electricity text book should be consulted by anyone to whom the difference between these entities may be significant.

Where larger supplies are concerned, multiples of kW or kVA are used for convenience. The megawatt (MW) and megavolt-ampere (MVA) are respectively equal to 1000 kW and 1000 kVA. Occasionally the further multiples by 1000, gigawatt (GW) or gigavolt-ampere (GVA), are found.

The highest value of this power occurring during, say, a day, a week, a month, or a year is known as the maximum demand (MD) in the period. The concept of MD in the supply industry is of the highest importance, physically and economically, since it determines the physical capacity of the equipment required to cope safely with the supply at maximum power, and hence the cost of the capital equipment required.

4.2.2. *Quantity*

This aspect of energy flow is concerned with the amount of electrical energy used over a given period. It is generally measured in terms of the kilowatt-hour (kWh), a quantity of energy equivalent to the use of one kW for one hour or, say, 2 kW for half an hour, etc. So important is this unit of quantity, the kWh (originally a Board of Trade unit), that the general word 'unit' is often used synonymously with it. Thus '100 units' is synonymous with '100 kWh'.

The analogous unit to kVA, the kVAh, is also used in the literature, but to nothing like the extent of the kWh.

As in 4.2.1 above, multiples by 1000 and 1000 000 are often used. For kWh these are the MWh and GWh respectively. Occasionally a multiple by 10^9, the terawatt hour (TWh), is found.

There is an increasing use of an alternative unit of quantity—the joule. This unit is very small and in this system quantity is most often expressed as MJ and GJ. One kWh = 3.6 MJ.

4.2.3. *Load Factor*

Load factor is an important entity, linking power and quantity. It can be defined by the formula

$$LF\,(\%) = \frac{U \times 100}{T \times MD}$$

where U is the number of kWh used on a system in a given period (year, month, day, etc.)

MD is the maximum demand on the system during the period, in kW

T in the number of hours in the period

An analogous entity used by the CEGB is the average load on a system expressed as a percentage of the average maximum output capacity of the system. This can be regarded as a utilisation load factor, as opposed to the system load factor defined above.

4.2.4. *Pressure*

This characteristic of energy flow is measured in volts (V), or its usual multiple by 1000, the kilo-volt (kV). Transmission of electrical energy always involves some loss of energy and pressure. This loss in pressure can be reduced by increasing the size of the conductor in order to reduce its resistance. (The study of change in pressure in the transmission of alternating current involves another entity, impedance, and anyone interested in this aspect is recommended to consult an electricity transmission reference book). The loss of useful energy can be reduced by operating at an increased voltage and it is a matter of economics to determine the proper balance between the expense of providing high voltage equipment on the one hand and the expense of sustaining high losses on the other. In the UK the largest bulk supplies are transmitted at 400,000 V, whereas the normal pressure for use by the vast majority of consumers is 240 V.

4.2.5. *Meters*

The instruments used for measuring power and quantity vary from the expensive, sophisticated meters used at Grid Supply Points to the inexpensive instruments used for measuring the 240 V supplies typically found in houses, shops, and offices.

All meters are designed and maintained to operate within set limits of accuracy and all, except a few of the meters for dealing with the very highest voltages, are subject to *British Standard 37 (BS 37)* (see [B 7].)

The smaller meters operate under statutory requirements of accuracy (see the Electricity Supply (Meters) Act of 1936) and are periodically removed from their installations to be tested. Comparable requirements do not apply legally to many of the large supplies given under special agreement but generally the Area Boards operate such meters under the requirements at least as strict as the statutes require for the smaller supplies.

The design, operation, and maintenance of the meters required for the measurement of bulk supplies given to the Area Boards by the CEGB are subject to an agreement between those bodies, known as the *Metering Memorandum* [B 55].

4.2.6. *Periodicity of Meter Reading*

The periodicity of meter readings varies enormously. At the generating stations and Grid Supply Points half hourly readings are recorded, whilst at the other end of the scale the vast majority of low voltage (240 V) consumers have their meters read quarterly.

Any investigation into the 'use' or 'output' of electrical energy must take into account the stage at which the energy flow is measured. The difference between energy produced at the generator terminals and energy used at the terminals of the ultimate consumers' supply points is due to

(*a*) the energy used by ancillary equipment in the generating station
(*b*) the energy dispersed as heat in the mains, cables, transformers, and switchgear of the distribution systems used in transferring the energy to its ultimate consumers
(*c*) the energy used in the meters themselves.

Other complications militating against a direct comparison between 'energy produced' and 'energy sold' are:

(i) At least 90% of consumers' meters are read quarterly, over a cycle giving continuous use of meter readers and continuous calculation and distribution of consumers' bills. Thus the precise amount of electricity consumed by users in a given calendar period is impossible to measure and can only be estimated.
(ii) Certain supplies are too small to be measured economically. They are charged on a basis independent of actual usage.
(iii) Some un-metered supplies are used in the Board's works and offices.

Until 1968/69 sales of units were on a 'billed' basis, i.e. they were aggregates of bills rendered during a given period. From that year onward they are on a 'sold' basis, i.e. billed units adjusted for the unbilled units to give an estimate of the true units consumed during the period.

The estimate of unbilled units is derived by considering two independent approaches:

(*a*) the way in which the purchase of units from the CEGB and other sources has varied from month to month during the last quarter of the financial year is used to derive the theoretical effect on the consumers' use during the quarter and hence the consumers' use of electricity between the dates of their meter readings and the end of the financial year (i.e. unbilled units)
(*b*) the thermal losses in the Area Board transformers, high voltage transmission, low voltage distribution, and meters is estimated in great detail. The relationship Units purchase − units lost = units billed + unbilled units (end year) − unbilled units (beginning year) is then used to derive the required estimate of unbilled units at the end of the year.

Providing the two estimates are reasonably near together they lead to an agreed estimate of unbilled units.

4.3. Plant and Efficiency

4.3.1. *England and Wales*

4.3.1.1. *Generating Plant*

Statistics relating to generating stations appear in different groupings in the CEGB annual report [QRL 4] and in their statistical yearbook [QRL 32]. Total numbers of stations at the 'latest' March 31, together with class declared net capabilities (formerly known as maximum output capacities), subdivided into coal-fired, oil-fired, coal/oil-fired, coal/gas-fired, nuclear, diesel, gas turbine, hydro, and pumped storage stations, and ancillary gas-turbine plant appear in [QRL 4]. The increase in generating capacity in the financial year is also given.

A less detailed type-grading is available in [QRL 32] but with a subdivision by the five geographical regions into which the CEGB is organised for the day to day operation of its activities. This gives the installed capacities (gross capabilities) of the generators and of the boilers, together with the maximum output capacity (declared net capability), electricity supplied, utilisation load factor (see 4.2.3 above), and thermal efficiency (i.e. the calorific value of the electricity supplied expressed as a percentage of the calorific value of the fuel consumed). (The difference between installed capacity and maximum output capacity is accounted for by the normal power consumption attributable to the auxiliary equipment in the station.)

[QRL 32] also gives a detailed description of each power station in each region, with numbers and capacities of individual generators, steam pressures and capacities of boilers, maximum output capacities, electricity supplied, average loads, and thermal efficiencies.

Further tables of age and capacity of steam driven generating sets and boilers (excluding those in nuclear stations) are given in [QRL 32] together with equipment details of the twenty power stations with highest thermal efficiencies in the 'latest' financial year.

Historical information on fuel usage, costs of generation, and numbers of 'generation employees' is given for coal, gas, and oil fired power stations, covering the 'last' ten years. In an attempt to examine operational efficiencies, independent of money values, two entities are derived:

(a) The number of generation employees per megawatt sent out and
(b) The total units supplied per generation employee.

The movement of these two measures over the 'latest' decade gives some indication of the change in labour productivity in generation over the period.

Similar information is given for nuclear power stations.

Information on fuel usage is summarised in four tables, with the figures for the previous year for comparison.

The first two tables show the average works costs in pence per kWh (p/kWh) of generation for coal- and oil-fired stations and for nuclear stations. The sub-divisions of these costs indicate that 'work costs' cover the costs of purchasing and handling the fuel, and operating, repairing and maintaining the stations.

The third table uses the concept of 'coal-equivalent' to give a breakdown of the coal equivalence of the coal, oil, gas, and nuclear fuels actually used. In this, unit masses of oil and gas are respectively equal to 1.74 and 2.10 unit masses of coal respectively in thermal value. The coal equivalent of nuclear fuel is more complicated. In 1975/76 the CEGB used a formula to convert nuclear kWh sent out into the equivalent use of coal in a modern conventional power station. Coal is assumed to have a calorific value of 25 gigajoules per tonne, and a standard thermal efficiency of 35% is applied to the output of the CEGB nuclear stations in commission in 1975/76. It follows that the conversion factor varies from year to year according to the variation in these two factors.

The fourth table shows the sources of coal delivered to the CEGB from the various National Coal Board regions, and from abroad.

Investigators in the field of generation requiring historical information in some detail, but not quite to the degree available in the CEGB reports, should consult the Council annual accounts and statistics report [QRL 31]. There they will find information for each of the 'last' ten years on number of power stations in commission, installed and maximum output capacities, and electricity supplied, by type (steam, etc.), plant commissioned, under construction, or planned year by year, fuels burned, with their average calorific values and thermal efficiency, and works costs of generation.

The *ESS Handbook* [QRL 23] shows total installed generation capacity (gross capability) from 1922/23 and ouput capacity (net capability) from 1947/48, with breakdowns of this latter figure into coal, oil, coal/oil, coal/gas, nuclear, diesel, gas turbine, hydro, and pumped storage from 1955. The output capacity of plant commissioned each year from 1935 is also given. Fuel costs, calorific values of fuel, works costs per kWh, and thermal efficiencies are shown from 1932 for conventional steam stations. Works costs and thermal efficiencies of nuclear stations are shown from 1962/63.

The *Monthly Digest of Statistics* [QRL 25] is useful for up to date information on the amount of generating equipment commissioned month by month, in England and Wales and in the United Kingdom as a whole.

The *Digest of Welsh Statistics* [QRL 14] shows the maximum output capacity of generation plant in Wales for 1938, 1949, 1959, and for the 'latest' six or seven years.

4.3.1.2. *Transmission and Distribution Plant*

This term covers both lines (often subdivided into 'overhead lines' and 'underground cables') and transformers. These are owned by the CEGB and the Area Boards.

Some care is necessary in considering the historical statistics of transmission lines and transformers operating at 132 kV, 66 kV, and 22 kV, owing to the transfer of ownership from the CEGB to Area Boards mentioned in 3.2.1 above. Perhaps the best guide to the transition is given in the Council annual accounts and statistical report [QRL 31] (Appendix VIII in the report for 1975/76). There is a distinction between 'ownership' and 'operation'. Although ownership of (i.e. financial responsibility for) much transmission plant operating at 132 kV, 66 kV, and 22 kV passed from the CEGB to the Area Boards in April 1969, the CEGB continued on an interim basis to operate and maintain (as agent) much of the plant, and indeed to build and commission new plant on behalf of the Area Boards.

The terms 'extra high voltage', 'high voltage', 'medium voltage', and 'low voltage' are not invariably used with consistency as general terms, but references within tables are usually unambiguous.

Lengths of transmission lines are normally expressed in 'circuit km' but sometimes in 'route km'. One route km of single circuit is equivalent to one circuit km, whereas one route km of double circuit is equivalent to two circuit km.

In considering transformation it is necessary to take careful note of whether a specified voltage is primary or secondary. For instance, a secondary voltage at a point of supply from the CEGB can be a primary voltage to the Area Board. Further caution is needed when dealing with transformer capacity. This can vary with ambient temperature and with hours of continuous operation. Where precise comparisons between figures from different sources are required, it may well be necessary to refer to the compilers of the statistical information.

With all these cautions in mind we may now examine the statistical sources in this field.

[QRL 32] shows the regional distribution at the financial year end of

(a) route km and circuit km of Grid lines, subdivided by operational voltages ranging from 400 kV to 66 kV or lower, with a sub-division of the total figures into overhead and underground and

(b) transformer capacities, subdivided by voltage, together with the numbers of transformers and substations.

There is also a table giving technical details of the major transmission work carried out during the year under review.

A table of particular interest (no. 19 in the report for 1974/75 but not continued into the 1975/76 report) is an example of a defensive response by the CEGB to objections to overhead lines in what the objectors see as areas of natural beauty. This table shows the comparative costs of overhead lines and underground cables of equal capacity.

As with generation, [QRL 31] gives useful summary tables of annual information for the latest decade, covering circuit km of transmission lines owned by the CEGB, subdivided by design voltage. These tables use ownership as a type determinant, whereas the comparable tables in [QRL 32] use operational voltage. Notes to the tables in [QRL 31] make clear this distinction.

When describing Area Board systems, the nomenclature 'transmission' is generally replaced by 'distribution', and 'lines' are more often referred to as 'mains'.

Most Area Boards devote a table in one of their annual report appendices to showing the subdivision by 'voltage' and 'overhead/underground' of circuit km of mains at the beginning and end of the financial year under review, with a sub-analysis of the mains commissioned and taken out of commission during the year. For the Area Boards, of course, the range of voltages is different from that for the CEGB, with an upper voltage of 132 kV and a lower one of the lowest supply voltage, 240 V. The table gives similar beginning- and end-year figures for the number of transforming points and the transformer capacities, both subdivided into 'over 650 V' and '650 V and under'. These latter classifications refer to secondary voltage, whereas the CEGB transformer classifications refer to primary voltage.

Again, [QRL 31] is useful in giving ten-year summaries relating to transmission lines and transformers owned by the Area Boards in total and two-year summaries of key figures relating to transmission lines and transformers, sub-classified by Area Board.

4.3.2. South Scotland

In terms of capacity and output the SSEB system is one-tenth of that for England and Wales. The SSEB annual report [QRL 7] covers generation, transmission, and distribution.

4.3.2.1. Generating Plant

[QRL 7] shows the installed capacity and maximum available output capacity for each individual power station operated by the Board, indicating the type—conventional thermal, hydro-electric, nuclear and gas turbine.

Historical information on electricity generated and supplied, load factor, thermal efficiency, and coal and oil consumed is given for each of the 'latest' ten years.

The *ESS Handbook* [QRL 23] gives particulars of output capacity and power station output from 1948 to date.

4.3.2.2. Transmission and Distribution Plant

A table in [QRL 7] shows the size of the transmission and distribution system at the year end, and the equipment commissioned and taken out of commission during the year. Pressure levels ranging from 400,000 V to '11,000 V and under' are used in classifying numbers of substations, and capacity of transformers. The circuit km of overhead lines and underground cables at nine levels of pressure from 400,000 V to 240 V are shown. The relationship between circuit km and route km at various voltages is shown in a further table.

4.3.3. North Scotland

In terms of capacity and output the NSHEB system is between 35% and 40% of the size of the SSEB system. The NSHEB annual report [QRL 6] covers generation, transmission, and distribution.

4.3.3.1. Generating Plant

Hydro-electric schemes, both conventional and pumped storage, predominate in the NSHEB system, although the Board also operates steam and diesel stations. Accordingly, production of electricity varies with the area-wide and local incidence of rainfall. The Board takes account of this variation by producing in [QRL 6] statistics of water availability not found in the reports of the other UK authorities.

In giving the characteristics of the conventional hydro-electric generation for each station, the gross head of water is given, together with the installed capacity. In addition the units actually sent out in the year from each station are compared with the average annual output, the latter being a reflection of performance with average water availability. The variation of water in store is illustrated in a chart showing the actual water in store each month as a percentage of maximum possible in the year of the report, as compared with the range of this percentage month by month for a period of over 20 years.

For pumped storage stations, the gross head of water is given, together with the installed pumping and generating capacities. The units sent out and the units used on pumping are given. The units sent out include generation from the catchment area flow.

The installed capacity and output of each steam and diesel generating station are given.

The *ESS Handbook* [QRL 23] gives particulars of installed capacity and power station output from 1948 to date.

4.3.3.2. *Transmission and Distribution Plant*
Transmission statistics are limited to the circuit km of high voltage lines and cables and their associated transformer capacity, the circuit capacities of high and low voltage lines and cables used in distribution, and their associated transformer capacity.

The length of submarine cable in service is also given.

4.3.4. *Scotland as a Whole*

The *Scottish Abstract of Statistics* [QRL 30] publishes some consolidated information for Scotland, dating back to 1951 and derived from the SSEB and NSHEB annual reports.

As far as equipment is concerned, consolidated figures of generation installed capacity are given. This Abstract is chiefly valuable for bringing together long historical series of figures for which it would otherwise be necessary to refer to many copies of the annual reports of the Scottish Boards.

4.3.5. *Northern Ireland*

The maximum demand on the NIES system is around 75% of that on the NSHEB system, but the installed generation capacity is some 90% of that of the NSHEB. This smaller utilisation of capacity reflects the ability of the NSHEB system to use its interconnection with the SSEB system.

4.3.5.1. *Generating Plant*
In the NIES annual report [QRL 8] figures are given for the 'latest' two years, showing for each power station the installed capacity, maximum demand met, plant load factor, efficiency, units generated, used in the station, and sent out.

The *Digest of Statistics for N. Ireland* [QRL 15] gives, for 1939, 1949, 1959, and for each year from 1963 to date, the maximum capacity of generating plant.

4.3.5.2. *Transmission and Distribution Plant*
[QRL 8] gives considerable detail in a table showing the route km of 275 kV and 110 kV lines, subdivided into single and double circuit, overhead lines and underground cables. Numbers of high-voltage substations and transformers, together with capacities of associated transformers, are given.

For the lower voltage distribution systems, the circuit km, overhead and underground, are shown, subdivided between operation voltages of 33 kV, 11 and 6.6 kV, and 400 and 240 V.

4.3.6. *Great Britain/United Kingdom*

The *Energy Digest* [QRL 13] gives numbers of generating stations in Great Britain, plant capacity, and plant commissioned, for calendar years and financial years, covering the latest 10 calendar years and 6 financial years.

This Digest also provides particularly interesting information on the usage of generating stations in the latest year. A principal aim of any interconnected generating supply system is to use its most economic stations for the maximum time and conversely to bring in its least efficient stations for only the minimum possible time. A table covering the public system in Great Britain shows the number of stations, their output capacity, electricity supplied and average plant load factor, analysed within 5% bands of plant load factor—from over 85% to under 5%. The figures are also summarised in a cumulative distribution. There is no attempt in this table to give average thermal efficiencies within load factor bands. A quite separate table shows, for the 'latest' three years, the output capacity and electricity supplied by stations in given bands of thermal efficiency.

Yet another analysis of the generation output of the public system in Great Britain shows output capacity, electricity supplied, plant load factor, works cost per kWh, and average thermal efficiency within bands indicative of size of station, varying from under 5 MW to over 1000 MW. This information excludes nuclear stations, for which only overall information is given.

Related figures indicating efficiencies in financial terms are published for the latest year for the public system in Great Britain. The table shows output capacity, electricity supplied and average load, within bands of pence per kWh of fuel cost.

An indication of variation of generation works costs in Great Britain is given by another table covering the latest 11 years. This shows costs per ton and per kWh of coal and coke, oil and other fuels (excluding nuclear) and per kWh of repairs and maintenance, and other operating costs. The information is rather out of date (over 18 months) by the time it is published.

Business Monitor PQ 602 [QRL 10] (i.e. Production, Quarterly, SIC class 602—Public Supply Electricity) shows the output capacity of the public supply system of Great Britain, and the new plant commissioned during the period, for the preceding calendar year and for the 'latest' five quarters.

4.3.7. *Standby Plant in Industry*

Some industrial firms install standby generation plant—in general only brought into use when there is an interruption to their supply from the public system. The results of a survey in 1975 of 42,000 firms employing 20 or more persons, investigating the extent of standby plant are published in *Business Monitor M 11* [QRL 10]. There was an 80% response to the survey.

The survey covered the following points:

(*a*) the peak electricity demand from the public supply in the last year
(*b*) whether the firm had standby plant for use only during restriction or interruption of the public electricity supply

224   ELECTRICITY

  (c) the year of installation and nominal capacity of such plant, and the fuel used
  (d) whether orders had been placed for standby plant
  (e) the capacity of any other generation plant and whether the electricity produced in a year normally exceeded 1 million kWh.

4.4. Power

The idea of 'maximum demand' (MD) has been referred to in 4.2.1 and it is now perhaps the time to illustrate the concept of 'Simultaneous Maximum Demand' (SMD).

Let two Area Boards, X and Y, make demands on the CEGB exemplified by the following table, where the figures refer to MW taken per half hour, the most common time unit used in such measurements:

Half Hour Ended	Maximum Demand (MW)		
	X	Y	X + Y
0800	3000	3600	6600
0830	3100	3800	6900
0900	3200	4000	7200
0930	3400	4200	7600
1000	3600	4100	7700
1030	3500	4000	7500
1100	3400	3900	7300

It will be seen that the MD of X is 3600 MW in the half hour ended 1000, the MD of Y is 4200 in the half hour ended 0930, and the MD of the common demand on the CEGB is 7700 MW in the half hour ended 1000. This last figure is known as the SMD of X and Y on the CEGB. The same principle applies, of course, when considering the summated demands of all the 12 Area Boards of England and Wales on the CEGB. The SMD of the 12 Area Boards cannot be greater than the sums of their individual maximum demands, and in general will be less than this sum. This so called 'diversity' effect of the summation of demands varying in time is very important throughout the field of electricity distribution, being greatest at the lowest voltage in the system, where the SMD of a group of houses is very much less than the sum of their individual MDs.

4.4.1. *England and Wales*

4.4.1.1. *CEGB*
Only a minute fraction of the available information on the way the demand on the CEGB varies from half hour to half hour is published outside the industry. Apart from the measurement of power outputs at each generator, mainly of internal

interest to the CEGB, demands are measured throughout the year at every point where electricity is transferred to its customers, i.e. the Area Boards, various 'direct' consumers, including British Rail, the SSEB and France. These measurements are required for the complex method of charging its customers. The figures are also summated for operational purposes, to give the SMD on each of the seven 'Grid Control Areas' of the CEGB.

Each year the CEGB publishes in its annual report [QRL 4] graphs (known as load curves) of the variation of demand on the system through the 24 hours of its 'high peak' and 'low peak' days. The former is the day (normally a mid-winter weekday) when the simultaneous half-hourly demand on its system reached its maximum value in the financial year, and the latter is the day when the daily peak was at its lowest figure of the year (normally a summer Sunday).

Quantitatively, the only figure given in the report is that for the peak half hour of the year. However, there is a tremendous amount of information available within the industry on demand variation at hundreds of points within the CEGB system and requests to them for such information from serious workers outside the industry are considered sympathetically.

Up to date information on the MD in England and Wales, and in the United Kingdom is given monthly in [QRL 25].

The *ESS Handbook* [QRL 23] gives particularly useful information on the variations of MD on the national grid system annually from 1947/48. The MD actually supplied is shown together with the estimated potential MD and the estimated MD in average cold spell (acs) conditions. ('Potential' demand is that demand which would have been met if adequate resources had been available to meet all requirements at normal frequency and voltage. Estimated MD in acs conditions is determined by calculating the yearly peak that would correspond to the range of weather likely to be experienced in a span of 100 years and selecting the median.) Load factors, actual and adjusted to take account of departure from normal conditions, are given in the table for each year.

4.4.1.2. *Area Boards*

Publication in annual reports [QRL 5] of information about patterns of demand varies from Board to Board, but common to them all is a tabular analysis of the maximum half-hourly demand on its system during the financial year. Specifying the actual half-hour, the figures show how much of this demand was met from the CEGB, from other Boards, from outside sources, from its own generation in the case of the South Western Board, and the extent of demand supplied to other Area Boards.

Here again useful information is available in [QRL 31].

A comparison is given for the last two available years of the make-up of the SMD of each Area Board in terms of purchases from the CEGB and interchange with other Area Boards.

[QRL 23] gives information about MDs of each Area Board at intervals from 1920 to date. There is a change of basis in 1950/51 but the provision of figures on both bases for this year enables some degree of continuity to be maintained on an estimated basis.

4.4.2. South Scotland

The SSEB annual report [QRL 7] gives for each of the latest ten years the make-up of the SSEB generation at the peak half-hour of each year. This illustrates vividly the flexible variation from year to year in the method of satisfying the peak electricity requirements of South Scotland. The contributions of nuclear, conventional thermal, gas turbine, and hydro-electric power stations, the interchanges with the NSHEB and the CEGB, and purchases from British Nuclear Fuels Ltd at Chapelcross are given.

4.4.3. North Scotland

The NSHEB annual report [QRL 6] gives the system MD and its date of occurrence. The variation of demand throughout the day of occurrence of this peak demand is shown in a chart, which also shows the variation in demand during a typical summer day.

4.4.4. Scotland

Within both Scottish Boards records are maintained of demand variation throughout the year. Research workers with a serious need for such information should approach the Boards directly.

4.4.5. Northern Ireland

The annual report of the NIES [QRL 8] shows in its text the date, time, and amount of the MD sent out to the system.

4.4.6. Great Britain

Business Monitor [QRL 10] shows the MD met in Great Britain by the public supply system in the preceding calendar year and the 'latest' five quarters.

The *Energy Digest* [QRL 13] gives, for 10 or 11 years in total, and for 4 years with subdivision between England and Wales, and Scotland, MDs met by the public system in Great Britain, with estimates of the potential demsnds, i.e. including an allowance for load shed by voltage reduction or disconnection, or load reduced by frequency reduction. Although in the earlier years the MD is shown against a calendar year the figure quoted is in fact a financial year one. The whole series is thus on a financial year basis.

Load factors and average thermal efficiencies are given for the same periods.

4.5. Electricity Produced and Consumed

4.5.1. England and Wales

A very useful table in the CEGB statistical report [QRL 32] (Table 2 in the report for 1975/76) shows the flow of electrical energy from generation to bulk consumer. Figures are given back to 1920, with some element of estimation for the years

4.5.1 STATISTICS IN THE MODERN ELECTRICITY INDUSTRY

before 1948/49. A valuable facet of this table is its illustration of the nomenclature applied to energy consumption at various stages of its progress.

For each year there is shown, in GWh (see 4.2.2 above):

(a) Units generated in CEGB power stations
(b) Units used within the stations ('on-works')
(c) Units supplied by power stations = (a) − (b) (This figure can occur as units sent out (uso))
(d) Units taken in bulk from the SSEB
(e) Units taken in bulk from France
(f) Units purchased in bulk from non-public sources in England and Wales
(g) Units 'available' = (c) + (d) + (e) + (f)
(h) Units used ('lost') in transmission to points of supply
(j) Units sold ('supplied') = (g) − (h)
There follows an analysis of (j):
(k) Units supplied in bulk to SSEB
(l) Units supplied in bulk to France
(m) Units sold in bulk to Area Boards
(n) Units sold in bulk to direct Consumers

From this table, comparisons between (d) and (k) and between (e) and (l) give the net flow to or from South Scotland and France respectively.

A separate analysis of (c) above for the year of report is given, subdivided into generating regions, and further subdivided into types of generation—steam, nuclear, diesel, gas turbine, and hydro. Still more detailed information is given for the current year by a breakdown of the (c)-type information between individual generating stations in each region.

An analysis of (m) shows for the current year the sales to each Area Board, virtually giving for each Board the number of units sold in the CEGB Bulk Supply Tariff categories Standard, Night, and Peak.

Energy Trends [QRL 20], followed at an interval of a few weeks by the *Monthly Digest* [QRL 25], show for each month the amount of each primary fuel used in generation, the amount of electricity generated by conventional and nuclear steam plant, and the total electricity made available to the public systems in England and Wales.

The *ESS Handbook* [QRL 23] shows the electricity generated and supplied from 1920, and by type of plant (coal and oil, natural gas, nuclear, diesel, gas turbine, hydro, and pumped storage) from 1960, together with the coal equivalent of the fuels consumed from 1962/63. An analysis of the use of fossil fuel in power stations is given in detail from 1947/48, with some figures for occasional years between 1920/21 and 1946/47.

Possibly the earliest indication to workers outside the industry of the movement of electricity sales is provided every four or five weeks by tables in the *Electrical Review* [QRL 17] and the *Electrical Times* [QRL 18]. These tables show, with a lag of about seven weeks, the electricity sold to individual Area Boards by the CEGB in 'standard review periods' of four or five weeks.

When examining statistics of energy consumed at Area Board level, care must be taken with nomenclature. Energy 'sold' or 'supplied' by the CEGB becomes energy 'purchased' by Area Boards, and after transfer through a distribution chain, energy 'sold' to the ultimate customers. Comparisons between these various quantities are particularly subject to the considerations outlined in 4.2.6 above.

Standard to all Area Board annual reports [QRL 5] are tables showing, for current and preceding years, the numbers of units purchased from their main suppliers (the CEGB), from other Area Boards, and from other sources. (The South Western Board shows the number of units supplied by its own generators.) The numbers of units sold to other Area Boards is also given, and thus the nett totals of units purchased in bulk are arrived at.

The division of unit sales into the usual Area Board classes of customer (domestic, farms, commercial, combined domestic and commercial (e.g. combined house and shop), industrial, public lighting and traction) is sometimes given two or three times—in Appendices, Statements and in the main text. Caution is needed if comparisons are required between figures for various Area Boards for the class 'combined premises'. The position is relatively straightforward where, say, a combined house and shop has only one meter. However, if the domestic and shop premises are separately metered and charged, the practice of allocating units between domestic, commercial and combined premises can vary from Board to Board, without indication in the statistical tables. This can also apply to farms.

Tables of sales of off-peak units are given in certain of the Area Board annual reports but the practice in dealing with these sales is not consistent between Boards. This arises from the existence of day/night or two-rate tariffs (also known, for domestic customers, as White Meter tariffs) with electricity consumed at different times of the twenty four hours being measured separately on different registers of the same meter. In looking at statistics of 'off-peak units' it is necessary to determine whether or not the figures include the 'night period' units taken on a two-rate tariff, which are not properly off-peak tariff units.

It is also as well to note that there is no straightforward relationship between the categories Unrestricted, Off-peak, Day, and Night units used by the Area Boards, and the categories Standard, Night, and Peak employed by the CEGB.

The Council annual accounts and statistics report [QRL 31] is again of considerable interest in giving historical and comparative information. In a first analysis, figures are given, for the current and preceding years, of units sold to the usual Area Board customer classes, for each Area Board in England and Wales, together with the sales by the CEGB to its own direct consumers.

A second analysis shows for each of the latest ten years the flow of electrical energy from generation at the power stations to its final use on the customers' premises.

A third analysis shows the sales of energy to the usual Area Board customer classes in each of the latest ten years.

Fourth and fifth analyses show, respectively for restricted hour (off-peak) tariffs and two rate (day/night) tariffs, the sales to the usual Area Board customer classes, in the current and preceding years. Care must be taken in using the figures in this last analysis, since they include the units used both by day and by night, and are thus in no way related to the sales on off-peak tariffs. These two analyses and are thus is no way related to the sales on off-peak tariffs. These two analyses are particularly important since not all Boards show the figures in their individual reports.

An interesting table in [QRL 31], not available by summing information in the Area Board reports, gives an analysis of sales to the various industrial categories (broad SIC categories): gas, water, etc., coal mining and quarrying, etc. Not only is an analysis given for the current year, but changes in the breakdown over the last four years are also given.

For historical data on retail electricity sales the *ESS Handbook* [QRL 23] is particularly valuable. After a stab at total sales in 1900, the handbook is on safer ground with analyses of sales to the usual Area Board customer categories at five year intervals from 1920 to 1945 and annual figures thereafter. There is a similar breakdown of off-peak sales from 1963/64, with total off-peak sales from 1957/58 to 1962/63.

Further tables give separate Area Board sales at intervals from 1920 to date, and sales to the usual Area Board customer categories in 1920, 1938, and the latest year.

Figures from the above tables are used to derive average consumptions of electricity per head of population, per domestic customer, and per overall customer at five year intervals from 1920 to 1945 and each year thereafter.

[QRL 14] shows for 1949, 1959, and for the latest seven years the flow of electricity generated in Wales. This shows the amounts of electricity used in the generating plant itself, transferred to England, lost in transmission, etc., and finally the sales to customers in Wales.

4.5.1.1. *Small Administrative Entities*

Generally speaking, the only source of statistics relating to the smallest entities in Area Boards (i.e. Areas and Districts) is the *Electrical Times Electricity Supply Handbook* [QRL 19]. Information is given, varying from Area Board to Area Board, on consumption of electricity (total, and sometimes domestic) in each Area and District.

In addition this publication provides a limited amount of statistical information relating to Alderney, Guernsey, Jersey, and two undertakings in the Isle of Man.

4.5.2. *South Scotland*

As a proportion of total electrical usage, the interchanges between the CEGB and its electrical neighbours, Scotland and France, are very small. However, for the SSEB, its interchanges with the CEGB and the NSHEB, together with its purchases from British Nuclear Fuels Ltd (BNFL) have varied between $+22\%$ and -5% of its requirements in the last ten years. As with 'Power' (4.4.2) a table in the annual report [QRL 7] illustrates the make-up of the electricity delivered each year to the SSEB system, showing the flexible variation from year to year in the method of satisfying the energy requirements of South Scotland.

After making allowance for the losses of units in transmission, distribution, etc., a further table shows the division of unit sales into classes of consumer (domestic, farm, commercial, industrial, public lighting, and traction).

Sales of off-peak electricity have always been relatively higher in South Scotland than in England and Wales. The number of off-peak units sold to each of the classes—domestic, farm, commercial and industrial—is given in [QRL 7] for each of the latest ten years.

The *ESS Handbook* [QRL 23] shows the electricity output of the power stations and the electricity sold in the Board's area from 1948 to date.

[QRL 30] gives an interesting breakdown of the sales of units by the SSEB to its industrial customers in 1961, and in each of the latest ten years. The breakdown categories are coal mining; iron and steel; engineering and electrical; shipbuilding and vehicles; other metal goods; chemicals; textiles, leather and clothing; food, drink and tobacco; construction; and gas and water.

An early indication of the movement of electricity sales is provided every four or five weeks by tables in the *Electrical Review* [QRL 17] and *Electrical Times* [QRL 18]. These tables show, with a lag of about seven weeks, electricity sales in 'standard review periods' of four or five weeks in the SSEB and NSHEB.

Information on electricity sales, total consumers, and domestic consumers relating to small administrative entities (Areas and Districts) in the SSEB and the NSHEB is published in [QRL 19].

4.5.3. *North Scotland*

A table in the NSHEB annual report [QRL 6] shows the units supplied to the system subdivided into mainland and isolated systems. The former are further subdivided into hydro, pumped storage, steam, and diesel stations belonging to the NSHEB, and purchases from the United Kingdom Atomic Energy Authority and from the SSEB. After allowing for unit losses in transmission, distribution, etc., the sales of electricity are then analysed by consumer classes—domestic, farms, commercial, industrial, public lighting, and the Invergordon smelter. This last consumer's usage is shown separately because of its size and special character. It uses about 50% more electricity than all the other NSHEB industrial consumers taken together.

The *ESS Handbook* [QRL 23] shows the electricity output of the power stations and the electricity sold in the Board's area from 1948 to date.

For early indicators of sales, and sales in Areas and Districts, see 4.5.2 above.

4.5.4. *Northern Ireland*

The NIES report [QRL 8] gives a fairly detailed analysis of the way in which energy flows to the distribution system. Numbers of units generated, used in the power stations, imported from, and exported to, Eire, and lost in high voltage transmission are given for the year of the report. Historical information on units sent out from generating stations is shown for the past 10 years or so with a break from calendar to financial year between 1967 and 1968/69. The numbers of units provided from each of the board's generating stations are given for the current and preceding years.

On the retail side there is no analysis of sales to the various consumer classes. The total units sold in each of the latest ten years are shown.

[QRL 15] shows, for 1939, 1949, 1959, and 1963 to date, the electricity sent out from power stations and the retail sales to customers, subdivided into domestic and farms, public lighting, and 'other'.

Information on electricity sales, total consumers, and domestic consumers in the Areas within N. Ireland is published in the *Electrical Times Electricity Handbook* [QRL 19].

4.5.5. *Great Britain/United Kingdom*

The *Monthly Digest* [QRL 25], with a lag of some 10 weeks, shows for each month the amount of each primary fuel used in generation, the amount of electricity generated by conventional and nuclear steam plant, and the total electricity available to the public systems in the UK.

This Digest also gives information, with a lag of 4 or 5 months, on the quarterly sales of electricity within the UK, subdivided into sales to the iron and steel industry, to other industries, and to the domestic customers.

Business Monitor [QRL 10] shows primary fuels used (coal, oil, gas, nuclear, hydro) and electricity generated (conventional steam, nuclear, and 'other') on the public supply system in Great Britain for the preceding calendar year and the 'latest' five quarters.

For the UK the *Energy Digest* [QRL 13] shows, for between 8 and 10 years, the total electricity supplied by thermal, hydro, and nuclear stations, and purchased from industrial producers, together with the various fuels used in the production.

On the retail sales side the *Digest* gives figures for annual sales of electricity for some 8 years within the UK, with a unique sub-division into sales to collieries, fuel conversion industries, agriculture, the iron and steel industry, other industries, railways, road transport, domestic customers, and public services. (Further information is given of private generation for some of these customer classes.)

For Great Britain the *Digest* [QRL 13] gives calendar year information, for 11 years and financial year information, subdivided into England and Wales, and Scotland for 6 years, on electricity generated in the public system, used on works, purchased from outside sources, and sold to customers.

The fuels used and types of generation in the public system are brought out separately, with summer/winter analyses, and splits between England and Wales, and Scotland for the latest three years.

Separate analyses using the Department of Energy returns for Great Britain show for the latest ten years or so the unit sales from the public supply system, the numbers of customers, total revenues, and the derived prices and sales per customer for the domestic, farms, public lighting, and traction classes, and for a more detailed classification of customers on the commercial and industrial sides. The commercial classes are combined premises, shops, offices, public buildings, hotels, and HM forces. The industrial classes are water works, gas works, drainage and pumping stations, iron and steel, engineering, food drink and tobacco, coal mining, chemical and allied trades, textiles leather and clothing, paper printing and stationery. Similar figures are given for transport undertakings.

A separate analysis in the *Energy Digest* [QRL 13] into the usual Area Board customer classifications is useful in bringing together in one table for each undertaking in the UK the sales, prices, and numbers of customers for the 'latest' two years.

Business Monitor [QRL 10] shows for the public supply system in Great Britain, for the preceding calendar year and the latest five quarters:

(a) unit sales and revenue subdivided over the usual Area Board categories.
(b) unit sales to the following industrial categories: gas, water, etc.; coal mining; other mining; bricks, pottery, etc.; iron and steel; non-ferrous metal manufacture; chemicals; shipbuilding; other non-electrical engineering; electrical engineering; vehicles; miscellaneous metals; textiles; leather; clothing; food, drink and tobacco; timber, furniture; paper, printing, publishing; construction; other industries.

Regional Statistics [QRL 29] gave in 1975 estimates of electricity, solid fuel, gas, and liquid fuel consumption by final users—'industrial', 'domestic', and 'all'—for 1974 for each of the English standard regions and for Wales, Scotland, and N. Ireland. The figures were provided in therms, on a heat supplied basis. Comparisons between fuels, which these figures suggest, can be misleading in that a major use of electricity is in motive power and the energising of sophisticated electrical and electronic equipment and not for the production of heat as such. The expression of energy in terms of any one accounting unit is only valid for the purpose of inter-fuel comparisons provided the basis of the conversions and the nature of the unit are made clear. A regular table shows the regional analysis of electricity sales in kWh for the latest six years, subdivided over the domestic, farm, public lighting, traction, commercial, and industrial classes.

Most production of electricity is secondary, in that it is derived by conversion of primary sources of energy such as coal or oil. However, the production of electricity from nuclear energy or from hydro-electric power is regarded as 'primary'. *Energy Trends* [QRL 20] shows, with a two month delay, both the coal equivalent and oil equivalent of the nuclear and hydro electricity produced in the UK for each of the latest three months, with comparative figures for the previous year, together with calendar year figures for the previous five years or so.

This publication goes on to show the final consumption in the UK by the user groups—iron and steel, other industries, transport, domestic sector, and 'other' final users—in therms of heat supplied. (The caution about the 'heat supplied' basis mentioned above also applies here.) The figures are given for the 'latest' nine quarters or so.

A further table shows the coal equivalence of the coal, oil, gas, nuclear energy, and hydro-electric power put into the generation of electricity on the public system, and the consequential output of electricity. Separate figures for the UK and for England and Wales are given for each of the latest three months and for the previous six calendar years.

Units of electricity sold by the UK public system to the categories iron and steel, other industry, domestic, and 'other' are given for the latest nine quarters or so and for the previous five calendar years.

4.5.6. Weather Effect

The weather has a significant effect on the usage of electricity with particular concern to (a) the day to day operation of the generation side of the industry and (b) the appreciation of underlying longer term trends of development.

The Electricity Council and the CEGB have investigated the effects of various elements of the weather (of which the most significant are temperature, cooling power of the wind, and illumination).

The Council compiles but does not publish monthly estimates of electricity consumption by each Area Board in England and Wales, and by the SSEB and NSHEB, adjusted to normal weather conditions (see [B 2]).

The *Energy Digest* [QRL 13] publishes figures annually for seasonal, and weather, corrected electricity produced.

4.5.7. Private Generation

Energy Trends [QRL 20] publishes quarterly statistics of electricity generated privately by industrial producers in the UK, subdivided within broad industrial groupings. The figures are given for each of the nine latest quarters and for each of the six latest calendar years.

The *Energy Digest* [QRL 13] publishes statistics of electricity generated privately by industrial producers in the UK. There is subdivision by type of equipment (thermal, hydro, nuclear) and annual figures are shown for a 10 year period.

The *ESS Handbook* [QRL 23] shows the amount of electricity generated privately in Great Britain within broad industrial groupings, from 1955 to date.

4.5.8. Abroad

Although the present volume is primarily concerned with UK statistics, a lead into the statistics of the electricity supply industry abroad can be found in the *ESS Handbook* [QRL 23].

The Handbook gives the following information, derived from the *Annual Bulletin of Electric Energy Statistics for Europe* [QRL 2], the *Eurostat Energy Statistics Yearbook* [QRL 21], and the *Eurostat Quarterly Bulletin of Energy Statistics* [QRL 22]:

(a) The output capacity of public and private generation in each EEC country, the electricity produced by public and private conventional, nuclear, and hydro stations, and by public and private generation separately, together with imports and exports of electricity, and the average consumption per head of population.
(b) The consumption of coal, lignite, oil, natural gas, and derived gas in EEC public supply power stations.
(c) The final consumption of electricity from all sources by various industries in each EEC country. The industries, which exclude the energy sector, are iron and steel, non-ferrous metals, chemicals, glass and pottery, etc., ore extraction, food drink and tobacco, textiles leather and clothing, paper printing and publicity, engineering and other metal trades, and 'other'.

(d) The electricity generated (GWh) privately in each EEC country, classified according to the industrial category of the producer. The categories are hard coal mines, brown coal mines, refineries, iron and steel, chemicals, non-ferrous metals, paper, textile, 'other', railways, and 'common', i.e. owned by companies operating in more than one industry.

Further information is available in the UN publication *World Energy Supplies* [QRL 34].

4.6. Consumer Classification

4.6.1. *England and Wales*

Since 1965 or so there has been a significant change in the nomenclature applied to electricity consumers in England and Wales. Years ago it was general practice to refer to the final users of electricity as consumers, arising from the use of this word in the various Acts regulating the use of electricity. However, a more aggressive marketing policy brought about the use of the term 'customer' and the variation can be seen occurring over the years in the Area Board literature in general, and annual reports in particular. The practice is not as prevalent in Scotland and N. Ireland as in England and Wales.

Generally speaking, statistics on numbers of customers in each of the usual Area Board classes (domestic, farms, etc.) can be found associated with one of the sources of statistics of retail unit sales to each class, guidance to which is given in the references in 4.5.1 to Area Board and Electricity Council sources.

The *ESS Handbook* [QRL 23] shows the numbers of 'all' customers in 1920, 1925, and 1930, the numbers of 'all', domestic/farm, commercial, industrial, and public lighting customers in 1932, 1935, 1938, 1940 and 1945, and the numbers in the usual Area Board customer categories annually from 1947/48 to date. Further tables show for each Area Board

(a) the area, population, and numbers of domestic customers at various intervals from 1932 to date and
(b) the total number of customers at intervals from 1920 to date.

[QRL 14] shows for 1949, 1959, and the 'latest' seven years or so the classification of customers in Wales into the usual Area Board classes.

4.6.1.1. *Small Administrative Entities*
See [QRL 19] for information relating to numbers of consumers in the smallest administrative entities (Areas and Districts) within the UK Boards, and in the island undertakings of Alderney, Guernsey, Jersey, and Isle of Man.

4.6.2. *Scotland*

For the Scottish Boards the analyses of numbers of consumers by class accompany one of the annual report sources of unit sales by consumer class (see 4.5.2.1 and 4.5.2.2).

The *ESS Handbook* [QRL 23] shows the number of consumers in each Board from 1948 to date.

4.6.3. *Northern Ireland*

Although the NIES annual report [QRL 8] does not give an analysis of unit sales by consumer class, the number of consumers is shown, broken down into domestic, farming, commercial and industrial (up to 20 kVA demand), and commercial and industrial (over 20 kVA demand). The total number of off-peak consumers is also given.

[QRL 15] shows a subdivision of the number of consumers into domestic, farm, public lighting and 'other' classes, for 1950, 1955, 1960, and 1964 to date.

4.7. Revenue and Prices

4.7.1. *England and Wales*

Roughly 97% of CEGB electricity sales is taken by the 12 Area Boards—the remainder going to the railways and other 'direct' consumers. The amounts of money charged to each Area Board, broken down into the service, capacity, and running charges as defined in the CEGB Bulk Supply Tarriff are shown in the CEGB annual report [QRL 4], together with the figures for the preceding year.

At the retail level revenues per consumer class and the derived figures of pence per unit for each class can be found associated with the statistics of retail unit sales to each class, guidance to which is given in the references in 4.5.1 to Area Board and Electricity Council sources.

The *ESS Handbook* [QRL 23] shows revenue per unit sold in 1935/36—1937/38, and 1947/48 to date, for each of the usual Area Board categories of customer (domestic, farm, etc.). For each Area Board overall revenue per unit is given at intervals from 1948/49 to date, and for each customer category for 1950/51, 1960/61, and the latest available year.

[QRL 14] shows for 1949, 1959, and the 'latest' seven years or so, the average revenue per unit sold in Wales to customers in various customer classes.

4.7.2. *Scotland*

For the Scottish Boards the analyses of revenue per consumer class accompany one of the annual report analyses of unit sales by consumer class. (See 4.5.2.1 and 4.5.2.2.)

The *ESS Handbook* [QRL 23] shows the average revenue per unit sold from 1948 to date for each Board.

4.7.3. *Northern Ireland*

There is no analysis of revenue by consumer class in the NIES annual report [QRL 8]. The total revenue from retail sales of energy is shown for each of the latest ten years.

4.7.4. Great Britain/United Kingdom

The *Energy Digest* [QRL 13] uses information compiled by the Dept of Employment in its derivation of retail price indices for the UK to show the variation in price of electricity, coal and coke, gas, and fuel and light to domestic users. The information is given as monthly averages for each year from 1962, and separate monthly figures are given for the 'latest' two years. The up to date monthly figures are published in the *Monthly Digest* [QRL 25], enabling the monthly variation to be found during the yearly interval between productions of the *Energy Digest* [QRL 13].

A separate table in [QRL 13] covering the three latest Decembers shows typical prices to domestic customers of electricity, solid fuels, liquid fuels and natural gas in 14 large towns in Great Britain. The electricity information is particularly interesting in giving prices at five different levels of consumption—750, 2500, 5000, 10000 and 30000 units per annum.

To complement the above information on retail prices, [QRL 13] shows estimated consumers' domestic expenditure in the UK on fuel and light for the latest 11 years subdivided into electricity, coal, coke, gas, and oil. This gives slightly more detail than the *National Income and Expenditure Blue Book* figures [QRL 26]. Note that they are expenditures by consumers defined in the 'National Income' sense. For quarterly figures on fuel and light see *Economic Trends* [QRL 16].

Information is also given on the prices of fuels used by industry in Great Britain. The fuels are electricity, coal, heavy fuel oil, gas oil, and gas. A complementary table shows the average prices of fuels used by the electricity and gas industries.

For quarterly revenues from retail sales in the public supply system of Great Britain to the usual Area Board classes of customer, see the *Business Monitor* reference in 4.5.5 [QRL 10].

This publication also shows revenues from meter rents, from sales of appliances, steam, and scrap, and from contracting work.

4.7.5. Electricity Price Indices

There is a widespread practice of displaying price indices (particularly domestic) in tables and charts. The form of electricity tariffs means that such derived statistics can be misleading. Electricity tariffs for domestic customers generally take the form of a fixed component (e.g. a standing charge or a higher priced initial block of consumption) and a running rate. The overall price paid by a customer will thus vary according to his consumption. Price indices can therefore be of two forms. Firstly an index of average price paid (more normally referred to as average revenue) where the index varies not only with the level of the tariff but also the level of consumption. Secondly an index where consumption is held constant. There are significant differences between the trends and magnitudes of the two indices but each has its use and place.

CHAPTER 5

FINANCIAL STATISTICS

5.1. General

In the field of financial and economic statistics there is now a wealth of information available in the published reports of the nationalised Boards in general, and in those of the Electricity Boards in particular.

5.2.1. *England and Wales*

The finances of the electricity supply industry are broadly based on principles laid down in the Electricity Act of 1947, and modified in detailed application to the Area Boards by the Electricity Act of 1957. In accordance with these statutes each Board should arrange for its outgoings over a period to be covered by its income, for its tariffs to be at once as simple as possible and yet to avoid giving undue preference to individual persons or classes of person. For some years the industry interpreted this last requirement to mean that the average costs of affording supply to a given group of consumers should be determined, and that a tariff structure to reflect these costs should then be designed. The pattern of financial statistics was originally designed in part to enable these requirements to be fulfilled. (The use of marginal costing has modified the use of these figures for tariff design purposes.)

However, Government intervention in the financial arrangements of the industry has modified the above mentioned rather simple scheme of financial objectives. In 1961 a White Paper [B 11] was used to justify asking the electricity supply industry to agree to earn larger returns than the minimum required by the 1947 and 1957 Acts. Later, however, the Government stepped in to revoke this policy in favour of keeping prices down, even when it was known that large deficits would result. Compensation payments were made to the Boards to balance these 'forced' deficits. Most Boards have taken care that their published figures should enable them to demonstrate this Government intervention. In any case this practice complies with the modern idea of maximising the information disclosed by the accounts.

The principal sources of information on the broad financial performance of the Boards are the standardised Revenue Accounts and Balance Sheets published as Statements in the annual reports [QRL 5] together with Statements supporting these principal accounts. For each Area Board annual report these Statements are very similar in form but differ in numbering scheme.

There are necessarily differences of detail in the make-up of the Statements of the CEGB and Area Boards, reflecting their differences in function.

5.2.2. *Scotland*

The finances of the Scottish Boards are broadly subject to the same principles as those of the electricity supply industry in England and Wales. At one time they were expected to increase their prices to increase their return on capital, but in the early seventies they were required to restrict their price increases in the interests of national counter-inflation policies.

5.2.3. *Northern Ireland*

The NIES has only been in operation since April 1973 and thus initially this Service operated under conditions of Government imposed price restraint. These restraints and consequential compensations have been comparable with those in England and Wales.

5.3. Revenue

5.3.1. *England and Wales*

The income figures of the CEGB in its annual report [QRL 4] are broken down into 'sales of electricity' (over 99% of the total) and three other categories. The expenditure figures are divided over ten broad headings, of which generation, depreciation, and rents rates and insurances account for some 95% of the total.

The income figures of the Area Boards in their annual reports [QRL 5] are subdivided into 'sales of electricity' (again, over 99% of the total) and two other categories. The broad headings of expenditure categories reflect the Area Board main costs—purchase of electricity, depreciation, distribution, and rates covering some 95% of the total, the remainder being covered by seven other categories. The operating profit on the contracting and sale of appliance activities is shown in this account.

For CEGB and Area Boards, taking account of the interest paid in the year then enables the figure of profit or loss for the year's operation to be shown. From 1970 until 1976 the Government compensated the Boards for any losses they incurred in conforming to Government policies on price restraint. The amounts of compensation are published in the accounts.

The Electricity Council annual accounts and statistics report [QRL 31] is particularly valuable for financial statistics. One Statement gives a consolidation of the revenue accounts of the CEGB, the Area Boards, and the relatively small revenue expenditure of the Electricity Council itself.

Apart from this there is a summary, Area Board by Area Board, for the current and preceding years, of the 'broad heading' information referred to above.

Within Boards, a principal use of allocations of expenditure over various headings is for budgetary control. However, the above-mentioned broad heading allocations are not sufficiently detailed for this purpose. More valuable are the analyses of these allocations given in separate tables.

For the CEGB, the Revenue Expenditure Statement in [QRL 4] analyses the revenue expenditure into really detailed sub-allocations. For instance, the revenue heading 'generation' has 14 sub-allocations, with seven of them—fuel cost, depreciation, interest, repairs and maintenance, operation, and fuel handling—representing some 97% of the total. 'Transmission' has 12 sub-allocations, of which six—interest, depreciation, repairs and maintenance, rates, salaries and general charges—represent some 93% of the total. Similar sub-allocations are available for administration, training safety and welfare, and research.

The Revenue Expenditure Statement of each [QRL 5] analyses Area Board revenue expenditure into considerable detail. For instance, 'distribution' is analysed into seven sub-allocations, including salaries and superannuation, repairs and maintenance of mains and services, etc. Revenue expenditure under the other 'broad headings' are similarly broken down.

[QRL 31] is again a valuable source of information about the details of Area Boards revenue accounts. The standardisation of revenue expenditure sub-allocations has meant that the Council can bring together these details for each Area Board, for the current and preceding years. It is thus possible to draw comparisons of these very detailed figures between Area Boards in a given year, and also to examine change over a period of time in measures of performance arrived at in a relatively standard manner.

Difference in function between CEGB and Area Boards makes economic comparison difficult but in any case an attempt to use their respective Revenue Expenditure Statements would be negatived by the practice of the CEGB in allocating depreciation and interest over their sub-allocations, whereas the Area Boards do not so allocate their depreciation and interest figures.

The *ESS Handbook* [QRL 23] gives the combined trading results of the supply industry since 1948/49. The figures cover England and Wales from 1955/56, but also include the South of Scotland from 1948/49 to 1954/55.

A further table brings out information from 1952/53 not readily obtainable elsewhere. This is an analysis of revenue expenditure under the headings fuel, salaries, depreciation, interest, rates and other costs.

The CEGB, in its statistical yearbook [QRL 32] shows figures over ten years illustrating 'Works cost per kWh of electricity supplied by power stations', 'Cost per tonne of fuel burnt', and 'Cost per gigajoule (GJ) consumed' (there are 3600 kJ in a kWh of electricity). These figures lose much of their force as financial efficiency indicators over time by the effect of inflation—currently in fuel cost primarily, and wage and interest rates to a lesser degree.

Similarly although the costs in the Area Board Revenue Expenditure Statements of [QRL 5] attempt to remove scale from the cost allocations by deriving figures of 'pence per unit sold', any comparisons over middling periods of time are bedevilled by the increasing pressure of inflation. Comparisons between Area Boards are hindered by, amongst other things, the effect on Boards' finances of the differing proportions of industrial electricity consumption, with its relatively low cost of distribution.

[QRL 23] shows works cost per kWh for conventional steam stations from 1932, and for nuclear stations from 1962/63.

[QRL 14] shows for 1949, 1959, and the 'latest' seven years or so, the values of purchased materials and fuels used in the electricity supply industry in Wales, together with the values of output and other work done analysed in some detail, the principal items being sales of electricity, and sales of appliances. There is a change of basis for the analysis from 1973/74 onwards compared with previous years. The figures are used to arrive at values of net output from the supply industry in Wales.

5.3.2. *Scotland*

Since the Scottish Boards are responsible for generation, transmission, and distribution within their areas, their accounts combine many of the features of the CEGB and Area Board accounts. Both Boards in their annual reports [QRL 6] and [QRL 7] show separately their generation, transmission and distribution revenue expenditures and give the same sort of detailed sub-analyses as the CEGB and Area Boards. Both Boards choose to make allocations of depreciation figures over their detailed sub-allocations in the manner of the CEGB. In this they differ from the Area Boards in England and Wales.

[QRL 23] shows for each Scottish Board the net profit (balance of revenue) from 1948 to date.

5.3.3. *Northern Ireland*

The NIES accounts [QRL 8] are similar to those of the Scottish Boards in that they separate their generation, transmission, and distribution revenue expenditures. Some detailed sub-analyses are published.

[QRL 15] gives breakdowns of revenue costs (generation, main transmission, distribution, and 'other'). Volume 45 gives the figures for the NIES for 1973/74 and 1974/75, and for the former constituent undertakings for 1971/72 and 1972/73.

5.3.4. *Great Britain*

Until 1975 the *Energy Digest* [QRL 13] provided a useful summary for the 'latest' four years of the values in Great Britain of gross output and work done, and the costs of purchased material, fuels, and merchanted goods in the electricity, coal, gas, petroleum refining, and petroleum and natural gas production industries. This enables figures of net output to be derived for each energy industry.

Similar, but not identical, figures are now being published in the *Business Monitor* series [QRL 10].

5.4. Capital

To an economist/statistician, balance sheets, prepared in a standard way over the years, are useful in measuring past capital performance and assessing future capital requirements.

5.4.1. *England and Wales*

The CEGB balance sheet, found in [QRL 4], with its broad subdivision into fixed and current assets, and current liabilities is relatively straightforward. The appearance of 'initial' nuclear fuel as a fixed asset is an interesting item, giving a slightly exotic flavour to the accounts.

The dominant figures in the balance sheet of March 1976 are the initial capital expenditure on property, plant, and equipment, and the depreciation and other capital provisions. Subsequent Statements analyse each of these figures in considerable detail. In the first of these Statements, under the heading 'generation', separate figures are given for conventional and nuclear stations. Amongst the detail of actual capital spending during the year four figures, the expenditure on land and buildings, and on plant and machinery, relating to conventional and nuclear generation respectively, dominate the current capital expenditure, representing some £363M of the £367M expenditure in 1975/76.

The second explanatory Statement allocates the annual depreciation and allied provisions between the generation, transmission, research and general categories.

Incidentally, the CEGB has such a large investment in research that the Board finds it worthwhile to bring out an analysis of assets devoted to this subject.

The Area Board balance sheets in their annual reports [QRL 5] are compiled on a standard basis with the same broad headings as the CEGB. Differences of detail reflect the difference in functions between the CEGB and Area Boards. Thus, whilst there is no mention of fuel in the Area Board balance sheets, the latter do need to show figures for electricity accounts outstanding, estimated electricity used but 'unread' (see 4.2.6) and the hire purchase business of the Area Boards.

The dominant figures in the balance sheets are the capital expenditure on fixed assets at original costs and the associated depreciation provisions. These two figures are analysed into further detail in other Statements. The Statement of Fixed Assets analyses the initial capital expenditures as at the beginning and end of the year, with the expenditure and writing-off during the year, divided into 13 categories of fixed assets (with three additional categories for generation in the South Western Board). The dominant figures are those for plant and machinery, mains—underground and overhead, and services (i.e. the connections between the distribution mains and the customers' installations). On average, historically, expenditure over these categories covers some 85% of the total.

As with the revenue accounts, the standardisation of Area Board balance sheets and sub-analyses means that [QRL 31] can display this information for all Area Boards, together with that for the CEGB.

[QRL 23] gives combined balance sheets for the supply industry since 1948/49. The figures cover England and Wales from 1955/56, but also include the South of Scotland from 1948/49 to 1954/55. In addition there is a detailed analysis of the variations of the working capital of the supply industry in England and Wales from 1956.

5.4.2. *Scotland*

The balance sheets and their sub-analyses for the Scottish Boards in [QRL 6] and [QRL 7] give information broadly in line with that given in the CEGB and Area Board Accounts.

[QRL 23] shows for each Scottish Board the capital expenditure from 1948 to date.

5.4.3. *Northern Ireland*

Whereas the balance sheet of the NIES in [QRL 8] is similar in make-up to those of the other UK undertakings less detail is published in sub-analyses. For example, it is understandable in view of the size of the undertaking that in the analysis of fixed assets, the initial cost, capital expenditure, and amount written off during the year, and asset value at the end of the year are shown for the broad heading distribution, and not subdivided into land, equipment, lines and cables, etc.—information which is published in the accounts of the other UK undertakings.

[QRL 15] gives some breakdown of capital expenditure over the last few years. Volume 45 gives a break-down (different from year to year) across generation, main transmission, distribution, and 'other' headings—covering the NIES in 1973/74 and 1974/75 and the former constituent undertakings in 1971/72 and 1972/73.

5.4.4. *Great Britain*

The *Energy Digest* [QRL 13] gave figures for Great Britain of capital expenditure up to 1973 for the electricity, coal, gas, petroleum refining, and petroleum and natural gas production industries. Longer period figures with sub-analyses for more detailed capital expenditure are given for the electricity, coal and gas industries.

5.5. Financing Capital Expenditure

5.5.1. *England and Wales*

Emphasis on the financial return on the public money invested in the electricity supply industry has led Boards over the years to demonstrate the disposition of their funds. Formerly, tables within the texts of CEGB and Area Board annual reports showed this information with varying amounts of detail. Now, however, standard Statements in [QRL 4] and [QRL 5] show the 'Source and Application of Funds'. These valuable Statements, a meeting place for the revenue and capital accounts, amongst other things allow checks to be kept on self-financing, i.e. the extent to which each Board relies on its own resources to finance its capital development. Incidentally, the use of 'own resources' in this statement can appear rather paradoxical since fairness, or just compatibility with past practice, requires Government compensation for the Board revenue lost in the interests of the counter-inflation policy to be regarded as 'own resources'!

The *ESS Handbook* [QRL 23] gives an analysis, for each year from 1948/49, of the capital expenditure of the supply industry and the methods of financing this expenditure. A principal purpose of this table is to derive a self-financing ratio for each year. Notes to the table indicate the way that Government compensation for price restraint has been treated in deriving these ratios.

Between 1962/63 and 1973/74 the financial objectives of the industry were variously expressed in terms of 'gross return' or 'net return' on net assets. Values of these two factors are given in a table covering the period 1948/49 to date.

5.5.2. *Scotland*

[QRL 6] and [QRL 7] give tables demonstrating the methods of financing the capital requirements of the Scottish Boards.

[QRL 23] shows for each of the Scottish Boards their financial objectives from 1962/63, together with the gross and net returns on assets, and the self-financing ratios from 1967/68 to date.

5.5.3. *Northern Ireland*

The NIES annual report [QRL 8] does not tabulate the method of financing the Board's capital requirements. A note to the accounts shows the proportion of new capital provided from internal resources and if funding details were required comparable to those of the other UK undertakings it would be necessary to extract the figures from the accounts.

CHAPTER 6

STATISTICS OF OTHER COMMERCIAL SERVICES

6.1. General

All undertakings in the United Kingdom (excluding the CEGB) sell electrical appliances and provide contracting services. However, they have no monopoly in these activities as they do in selling electricity and this has affected the way in which they prepare their accounts for the activities.

6.2.1. *England and Wales*

Each Area Board annual report [QRL 5] has a standardised form of accounts for Contracting and Sales of Appliances (the CSA accounts). This gives a two by two split of income showing contracting, and sales of appliances on one hand, and cash/credit and hire purchase on the other. Expenditure is subdivided to show direct costs (materials, salaries, hire purchase interest) and various indirect costs proper to the activity. This account also shows the derivation of the 'operating profit' which is included in the overall Board revenue account.

The CSA figures are collected together in detail in the Council annual accounts and statistics report [QRL 31]—Statement A7 (a) and (b) in the volume for 1975–76. Thus comparisons between Area Boards can be drawn relatively easily for a particular year.

Comparison over a period of years is more difficult in that:

(a) the CSA accounts varied in content when VAT was introduced and Purchase Tax abolished in 1973.
(b) the treatment of hire purchase, etc. interest charges was changed from 1973/74.
(c) the make-up of indirect costs was changed in 1973/74.
(d) the onset of increased rates of inflation has meant that it is almost impossible to estimate sales volume variation from sales income variation.

The inclusion of specific appliance volume statistics in Area Board reports varies between Boards and from year to year. Some Boards indicate their sales of some major appliances by number or graphically and others indicate the load in kW connected on off-peak tariffs, subdivided between various types of appliance.

The *ESS Handbook* [QRL 23] shows:

(a) the number of shops in each Area Board
(b) Ownership levels of around 45 types of electrical appliance in England and Wales, varying from air conditioning units to water heaters. The figures

are derived from sample surveys and give information for 1933, 1946, 1955, 1961, 1966, 1972 and 1975.

The highest number of appliance categories covered in one year is 41 in 1972, the lowest, 12, in 1955 and 1975.

The Electricity Council Report [QRL 3] shows sales of ten different major appliances in the latest year.

6.2.2. *Scotland*

The Scottish Boards each publish separate accounts for their CSA activities in [QRL 6] and [QRL 7]. These are similar in layout to those of the Area Boards in England and Wales but there is one significant difference in treatment. In the Scottish Board accounts the financing costs of hire purchase debt are carried into the CSA Accounts whereas in the Board accounts for England and Wales the operating profit makes no allowance for the financing costs.

The SSEB annual report [QRL 7] shows the numbers of cookers, water heaters, washing machines, refrigerators, storage radiators and direct heaters sold in each of the latest ten years.

The NSHEB annual report [QRL 6] does not show any statistics of sales of numbers of appliances.

6.2.3. *Northern Ireland*

There is no separate published account covering the contracting and sale of appliance activities of the NIES but their annual report [QRL 8] shows the numbers of cookers, refrigerators, freezers, vacuum cleaners, washing machines, storage radiators, direct heaters, spin dryers, tumbler dryers and water heaters sold in the two most recent years.

6.2.4. *Great Britain/United Kingdom*

The *ESS Handbook* [QRL 23] shows the numerical sales by Electricity and Gas Boards of cookers, water heaters, washing machines, refrigerators, storage radiators, and gas heaters. Some of the figures are available from 1955/56 onwards, and cover England and Wales up to 1959/60, and Great Britain after this.

Indications of changes in the levels of electrical appliance sales can be found in monthly statistics published in the *Monthly Digest* [QRL 25]. Index numbers are given for values of sales in Great Britain by radio and electrical goods shops, sales by radio and television rental specialists, and electricity showrooms (i.e. shops).

Business Monitor [QRL 10] publishes quarterly numbers of electrical appliances sold by the public supply industry in Great Britain. The appliance categories are cookers, immersion heaters, self-contained heaters, washing machines, refrigerators, food freezers, non-storage space heaters, and storage space heaters. The figures cover the preceding year and the 'latest' five quarters.

The Association of Manufacturers of Domestic Electrical Appliances (AMDEA) publish very detailed statistics on volume and value of domestic electrical appliance output in the UK, covering some 40 appliance categories. The figures are available monthly, quarterly and annually [QRL 33]. The quarterly and annual figures also cover in varying degrees UK imports and foreign production. These figures are continuations of figures formerly supplied by the British Electrical Appliance Manufacturers' Association (BEAMA).

Market research information is available on the domestic appliance market collected by Audits of Great Britain (AGB) [QRL 24] and sold to subscribing organisations. The AGB Home Audit is a quarterly survey of 35,000 homes in Great Britain, chosen as a random sample. These homes provide detailed information about their appliance acquisitions during the preceding three months. The Audit concerns itself with private households and thus appliances sold to, say, commercial customers are not included. Figures are given for each fuel where appropriate. Thus for example the ownership of central heating systems covers gas, electric, solid fuel, and oil appliances, together with systems of communal supply.

AGB will consider assisting serious research workers with relevant information from their survey.

CHAPTER 7

EMPLOYEE STATISTICS

Terms and conditions of employment in the electricity supply industry in Great Britain are settled by national agreement between the management and trade unions and a single negotiating system has been established, covering around 200,000 employees. The system is based on five national negotiating bodies to meet the needs of the various classes of worker, namely:

National Joint Industrial Council (NJIC) for the industrial staff,
National Joint Board (NJB) for technical engineering staff,
National Joint Council (NJC) for administrative and clerical staff,
National Joint (Building and Civil Engineering) Committee (NJ(B&C)C) for building and civil engineering workers, and
National Joint Managerial and Higher Executive Grades Committee (NJMC).

Each national body is composed of representatives of the employers and the appropriate trade unions.

7.1. England and Wales

The Area Board annual reports [QRL 5] publish year end numbers of employees using classifications loosely based on the above structure, i.e. managerial and higher executive; technical; executive, clerical, accountancy, sales, etc.; industrial; and technical staff trainees and apprentices.

The CEGB uses a similar classification in [QRL 4] to give the numbers of its employees in its individual Regions, and at Headquarters and Divisions.

The Electricity Council in [QRL 31] summarises the above figures and in addition gives figures for the latest decade of employees in the industry, subdivided into the above classes.

Some individual Area Boards show the aggregate remuneration of their employees in their annual reports [QRL 5].

The *ESS Handbook* [QRL 23] gives:

(a) numbers of employees in the supply industry subdivided into the above classes, for CEGB and each Area Board, for the latest four to six years
(b) total employees in the supply industry from 1949 to date, with a sub-division into managerial, etc. from 1952 to date
(c) the salaries and wages paid to employees in England and Wales, from 1955/56

(d) average hourly earnings and weekly hours worked by manual wage earners in electricity supply, all manufacturing industries, and all industries, in 1938, 1948 and annually thereafter, derived from Ministry of Labour earnings and hours enquiries.

[QRL 14] shows, for 1949, 1959 and the latest six years or so, the average number of employees in the supply industry in Wales—sub-divided into the two main categories 'operative' and 'administrative, technical and clerical', together with the wages and salaries paid to each category.

7.2. Scotland

In their annual reports, [QRL 6] and [QRL 7], the Scottish Boards publish the numbers of their employees using similar, but not identical classifications to those used by the Boards in England and Wales.

The SSEB report shows in a table, and the NSHEB report in a graph, the variation in total numbers of employees over the 'latest' ten years.

[QRL 30] shows numbers of employees of each of the Scottish Boards for the latest six years, together with their salaries and wages.

7.3. Northern Ireland

The NIES annual report [QRL 8] shows for the latest two years the total numbers of its employees, together with the numbers of those employees working in power stations.

[QRL 15] shows numbers of total employees. Volume 45 is of particular interest in giving the figures for March 1974 and March 1975 for the NIES, and the numbers in the former constituent undertakings for the two previous years.

7.4. Great Britain

The *Annual Abstract* [QRL 1] shows for June in each of the latest three years the numbers of electricity staff employees and unemployed in the UK and in Great Britain.

The *Energy Digest* [QRL 13] provides a useful summary for the latest four years of the average numbers of employed and net output per employee in each of the UK fuel industries, i.e. electricity, coal, gas, petroleum refining, and petroleum and natural gas production. This information is not provided in subsequent editions but is now being published in the *Business Monitor* series [QRL 10].

Data on manpower in Electricity Industry are also given in the national statistics produced by the Department of Employment. Figures are published in the monthly *Department of Employment Gazette* [QRL 12] and the annual *British Labour Statistics Yearbook* [QRL 9]. A full description of employment statistics is given in *British Employment Statistics* [B 4].

Details of data on *Wages and Earnings* and *Strikes*, by Andrew Dean and Jim Durcan, are given in this series of Reviews of UK Statistical Sources.

CHAPTER 8

RESEARCH

8.1. Organisation

The following extract from a section on 'Research' in an Electricity Council publication *Electricity Supply in Great Britain—Organisation and Development* [B 9] summarises the research activities of the supply industry in Great Britain.

The Electricity Act, 1957, requires the Electricity Council to settle from time to time, in consultation with the Secretary of State, a general programme of research into matters affecting the supply of electricity and other functions of the Council and the Electricity Boards in England and Wales. In practice these general programmes are settled each year and much of the work is carried out in collaboration with the two Scottish Boards, who contribute to research costs.

Research falls into two broad categories—technological on one hand and commercial and economic on the other.

Technological research comes under four main headings:

(*a*) generation, including converting energy from fuel into electricity, and the disposal of the by-products,
(*b*) main transmission of electricity,
(*c*) distribution of electricity from grid tapping points to consumers' terminals, and
(*d*) utilisation research, with the object of developing new and more efficient ways of using electricity.

Commercial and economic research aims to predict how much electricity will be required in the future, where and for what purpose; to assess load characteristics and the cost of supplying various kinds of load; and to provide information about consumers' buying habits. Research in these fields provides important data for forecasting the country's electricity needs and planning to meet them and also for developing the industry's policies with regard to tariffs, selective load building and marketing.

Technological research on generation and main transmission is undertaken primarily at the Generating Board's laboratories; research into Area Board problems, both technological and economic, is undertaken by the Boards and by the Electricity Council, and in the field of technological research this is largely the function of the Electricity Council Research Centre (ECRC) at Capenhurst, established in 1966 for intensive research in the distribution of electricity and its utilisation. ECRC works closely with Area Board staffs and with the Marketing Department of the Council, to promote and develop the results of research.

At the centre of the supply industry's research planning are the Electricity Council's Research Committee, concerned with technological research, and the Commercial Policy Committee, with commercial and economic research. These committees examine research proposals and exercise a general watch over the research programmes. There is in addition, to advise over the whole field of research, the Electricity Supply Research Council which includes a number of eminent scientists from outside the industry as well as experts from within the industry.

The Electricity Council considers and settles a final programme of research for the supply industry as a whole, for submission to the Secretary of State each year. The programme comprises direct research carried out by the Electricity Boards themselves, sponsored research undertaken for the Industry, and co-operative research with other organisations.

In 1966, the supply industry and certain large manufacturers set up a Steering Committee (the Power Engineering Research Steering Committee) to develop and co-ordinate collaboration on research within the electrical industry. This Committee includes representatives of the Electricity Council and Electricity Boards and senior executives of electrical manufacturers, cable-makers, and boiler-makers. Observers from the Department of Energy also attend.

8.2. Research Results

A list of those research publications which have significant statistical content and which are available to workers outside the industry is included as a supplement to the Bibliography. In addition a wealth of material exists about consumer behaviour which could be made available to serious research workers.

8.3. Use of Resources

8.3.1. *England and Wales*

The CEGB is responsible for between 80% and 90% of the revenue expenditure on research in the electricity supply industry in England and Wales. Its *Annual Report and Accounts* [QRL 4] gives breakdowns of the research expenditure

  (*a*) which is allocated to the 'Research' item of its annual accounts—subdivided into six headings, of which salaries, materials and services, and 'proportion of general charges' account for some 96% and
  (*b*) which occurs elsewhere in its annual accounts. The two principal items are depreciation and interest, accounting for some 93% of this sub-analysis.

An item 'Research' appears in the accounts of each Area Board [QRL 5]. In fact, the Electricity Council undertakes financial responsibility for the vast majority of expenditure on research other than that carried out by the CEGB and this expenditure is then allocated amongst Area Boards. The expenditure is shown under six headings [QRL 31] but two items—salaries and related costs, and materials, services—account for some 95% of the total.

There is no direct indication of the manpower involved in research but some indication could be derived from year to year by using the salaries allocation in the CEGB and Electricity Council figures referred to above.

No account is given by the Electricity Council of the capital expenditure on items for Research, since this is very small for the distribution and utilisation side of research. However, the assets used for generation and transmission research by the CEGB are considerable (over £50M at 'initial cost') and an analysis is given under four headings (of which land, buildings and civil works, and plant and machinery account for some 95% of the total) [QRL 4].

The *ESS Handbook* [QRL 23] shows the annual capital expenditure on fixed assets by the CEGB, covering the figures year by year for the last 14 years or so.

8.3.2. *South Scotland*

The SSEB report [QRL 7] gives a breakdown of its research and development revenue expenditure, which shows that around 70% of this expenditure is accounted for by its contributions to CEGB and Electricity Council research.

8.3.3. *North Scotland*

The NSHEB report [QRL 6] gives a minimal sub-analysis of its research revenue expenditure, divided into salaries and materials, goods and services.

CHAPTER 9

CONCLUSION

Reviewing the statistics of England and Wales, Scotland (North and South), and Northern Ireland in one volume naturally gives rise to the question of compatibility between the statistics of the various undertakings. There are, of course, differences of approach, but none of them appears to me to be misleading. There is no very good reason why the arrangements of the statistics of these autonomous bodies should be identical and it seems to me that such differences as there are result mainly from the difference in size between the undertakings.

The electricity supply industry has a long tradition of serious treatment of its statistical information and significant comparisons between the management statistics of the various undertakings are relatively simple to draw from the mass of information provided.

Incidentally, the surprising thing to this reviewer is the scant use of this information in the published works of economic researchers.

QUICK REFERENCE LIST—TABLE OF CONTENTS

Generation Equipment	256
Power stations and operating results	256
Plant capacity and output	257
Plant efficiency	258
Fuel and other generation costs	259
Load factor distribution of generation plant	260
Sources of coal	260
Variation of water in store	260
Standby generating plant in industry	260
Transmission and Distribution Equipment	261
Major transmission works	261
Transmission lines	261
Transmission plant costs	262
Main transformers and substations	262
Transformers	262
Power (Maximum Demand)	263
Maximum demand and load factor	263
Maximum demand	264
Load curves	265
Electricity Produced and Consumed	265
Production and disposal of electricity	265
Bulk sales and purchases of electricity	265
Electricity produced and consumed	266
Electricity produced	267
Supply of electricity	267
Fuels used and electricity produced	268
Electricity sales to customers/consumers	269
Electricity consumed	271
Electricity sales to industrial consumers	271
Electricity sales on off-peak and two-rate tariffs	271
Average consumption of electricity	272
Electricity sales (weather adjusted)	272

ELECTRICITY

Customer/Consumer Classification — 272
  Number of customers/consumers — 272
  Domestic customers, areas, and population — 273
  Number of off-peak and day/night customers — 273

Revenue and Prices — 273
  Bulk sales of electricity — 273
  Revenue from customers/consumers — 273
  Retail prices — 274
  Consumers' expenditure on electricity — 274
  Electricity used in industry — 274
  Fuel used by electricity industry — 274

Financial Statistics — 275
  Balance sheets — 275
  Revenue accounts — 275
  Capital expenditure — 275
  Working capital — 276
  Revenue expenditure — 277
  Source and application of funds/self-financing ratios — 277
  Net profit — 278
  Expenditure and output — 278
  Works costs — 278
  Operational costs — 278
  Output — 279

Contracting and Sales of Appliances — 279
  Revenue accounts — 279
  Numbers of shops — 279
  Sales of appliances — 280
  Production of appliances — 280
  Ownership levels of appliances — 280
  Acquisition and ownership of appliances — 280

Employees — 280
  Numbers of employees — 280
  Salaries, wages, and related costs — 281
  Average earnings and hours worked — 282

Research — 282
  Finance of research — 282
  Revenue expenditure on research — 282
  Capital expenditure on research — 282

QUICK REFERENCE LIST

Type of Data	Breakdown/Detail of Analysis	Area	Frequency	Publication (see QRL Key)	Text Reference and Remarks
GENERATION EQUIPMENT					
Power stations	Number of stations and declared net capability* by type of station and change in capability in year	E & W	Annual	[QRL 4]	4.3.1.1. *Formerly maximum output capacity
Power stations and operating results	Total number of stations, declared gross and net capability, and electricity supplied by type of plant: latest 10 years	E & W	Annual	[QRL 31]	4.3.1.1
Power stations and operating results in each of the 5 CEGB regions	Number of stations, declared gross capability of generators and boilers, declared net capability, electricity supplied, average load and thermal efficiency—all by type of station: latest year	E & W	Annual	[QRL 32]	4.3.1.1
Individual power stations and operating results in each region	Name and type of station, declared gross and net capabilities, number of generators, steam pressure and temperature, steam capacity, firing and cooling methods, electricity supplied, average load and thermal capacity: latest year	E & W	Annual	[QRL 32]	4.3.1.1
Details of generators and boilers*	Numbers by age and capacity (MW and kg/s): latest year	E & W	Annual	[QRL 32]	4.3.1.1. *Excludes boilers in nuclear stations

QUICK REFERENCE LIST 257

Total generating plant capacity	Gross capability at intervals from 1922/23 to 1946/47. Gross and net capabilities yearly from 1947/48 to date	E & W	Annual	[QRL 23]	4.3.1.1
Generating plant capacity by type of plant	Net capability by type of station at intervals from 1955/56 to 1965/66 and yearly from 1970/71 to date	E & W	Annual	[QRL 23]	4.3.1.1
Plant commissioned	New plant commissioned in each of last 15 months or so	E & W and UK	Monthly	[QRL 25]	4.3.1.1
Plant capacity	At 1938, 1949, 1959, 1969 and yearly for the latest 7 years or so	Wales	Annual	[QRL 14]	4.3.1.1
Plant capacity	Installed and maximum available output capacity of individual power stations by type of station: latest year	South Scotland	Annual	[QRL 7]	4.3.2.1
Plant capacity	For individual power stations: (a) Hydro—gross head of water, installed capacity, average annual output, actual output: latest year (b) Steam and diesel—installed capacity and output: latest year	North Scotland	Annual	[QRL 6]	4.3.3.1
Conventional steam stations and operating results	Number and capacity of stations, electricity output, fuels consumed, costs of fuels, and works costs: yearly for latest 10 years	South Scotland	Annual	[QRL 7]	4.3.2.1
Plant capacity and output	Output capacity and electricity supplied: 1948/49 to date	South Scotland	Annual	[QRL 23]	4.3.2.1
Plant capacity and output	Output capacity and electricity supplied: 1948/49 to date	North Scotland	Annual	[QRL 23]	4.3.3.1

Type of Data	Breakdown/Detail of Analysis	Area	Frequency	Publication (see QRL Key)	Text Reference and Remarks
GENERATION EQUIPMENT (*contd.*)					
Plant capacity and output	Installed capacity, electricity generated and sent out: 1951, 1961, and yearly from 1966/67	Scotland	Annual	[QRL 30]	4.3.4
Plant capacity and output	For individual power stations—installed capacity, maximum demand met, plant load factor, efficiency, units generated, used in the station, and sent out: latest year	Northern Ireland	Annual	[QRL 8]	4.3.5.1
Plant capacity and output	Output capacity and electricity sent out: at intervals from 1939, and yearly from 1963 to date	Northern Ireland	Annual	[QRL 15]	4.3.5.1
Plant capacity and output	Number and capacity of stations, capacity of plant commissioned, and electricity generated and supplied: latest 10 years	GB	Annual	[QRL 13]	4.3.6
Plant capacity, output, and efficiency	Numbers of stations, output capacity, electricity supplied, load factor, works cost, and thermal efficiency: totals for types of station: by bands of output capacity: latest 2 years	GB	Annual	[QRL 13]	4.3.6
Plant capacity and new plant	Output capacity and new plant commissioned in each of the latest 5 quarters, and in the latest complete calendar year	GB	Quarterly	[QRL 10]	4.3.6
Plant commissioned and under construction or planned during year	Generating sets, boilers, and reactors: latest 10 years	E & W	Annual	[QRL 31]	4.3.1.1

QUICK REFERENCE LIST

Generating plant commissioned	Net capability yearly: 1935 to date	E & W	Annual	[QRL 23]	4.3.1.1
Data for the 20 coal and oil fired stations with highest thermal efficiency	Steam pressure and temperature, declared net capability, electricity supplied, average load, calorific value of fuel, thermal efficiency and age of station: latest year	E & W	Annual	[QRL 32]	4.3.1.1
Fuel, generation costs, and efficiency	Amount and type of fuel burnt, calorific value of fuel, average thermal efficiency, works cost per kWh, fuel costs, numbers of generation employees, employees per MW, and electricity output per employee: latest 8 years	E & W	Annual	[QRL 32]	4.3.1.1
Fuel and generation costs at steam power stations (excluding nuclear)	Total electricity supplied, fuel burnt by type, average calorific value of coal and 'all fuels', average thermal efficiency, cost of fuel, fuel cost per unit supplied, total works cost, cost of heat: latest 10 years	E & W	Annual	[QRL 31]	4.3.1.1
Cost and calorific value of fuel burnt in steam power stations	Cost per gigajoule and calorific value for coal and all fossil fuel: at intervals from 1932 to 1942, and yearly from 1947/48 to date. Costs for nuclear fuel: 1962/63 to date	E & W	Annual	[QRL 23]	4.3.1.1
Generation costs	Works cost and overall thermal efficiency—for conventional steam stations at intervals from 1932—for nuclear stations yearly from 1962/63	E & W	Annual	[QRL 23]	4.3.1.1

ELECTRICITY

Type of Data	Breakdown/Detail of Analysis	Area	Frequency	Publication (see QRL Key)	Text Reference and Remarks
GENERATION EQUIPMENT *(contd.)*					
Plant thermal efficiency	Numbers of stations, their output capacity, and electricity supplied, by bands of thermal efficiency: latest 3 years	GB	Annual	[QRL 13]	4.3.6
Works costs (excluding nuclear stations)	Number of stations, output capacity, electricity supplied, and works costs: by total or bands of fuel cost: latest year	GB	Annual	[QRL 13]	4.3.6
Works costs (excluding nuclear stations)	Fuel and works costs: yearly for latest 11 years	GB	Annual	[QRL 13]	4.3.6
Load factor distribution of generation plant	Numbers of stations and their output capacity by bands of load factor, with electricity supplied by plant in each band, by interval, and by cumulative distribution: latest year	GB	Annual	[QRL 13]	4.3.6
Sources of coal	Amount from each NCB region, other UK sources, and from foreign sources: latest 2 years	E & W	Annual	[QRL 32]	4.3.1.1
Variation of water in store	Actual water in store each month of latest year as percentage of maximum possible—compared with the range of such monthly percentages over the past 25 years (Chart)	North Scotland	Annual	[QRL 6]	4.3.3.1
Standby generating plant in industry	Rate of commissioning, number of installations and fuels used, maximum demand, by SIC class, by standard region: 1975	GB	Occasional	[QRL 10]	4.3.7

TRANSMISSION AND DISTRIBUTION EQUIPMENT

Major transmission works	Regional distribution of individual major transmission works completed, by voltage, overhead/underground length, or transformer and switchgear capacity: latest year	E & W	Annual	[QRL 32] 4.3.1.2
Main transmission lines	Route km and circuit km of high voltage transmission lines by region and transmission voltage, with subdivision by overhead and underground: latest year	E & W	Annual	[QRL 32] 4.3.1.2
Transmission lines	Circuit length of CEGB lines, existing, and commissioned during year, by voltage: latest 10 years	E & W	Annual	[QRL 31] 4.3.1.2
Transmission lines	Total circuit length of Area Board, lines existing, and commissioned during year, by voltage: latest 10 years	E & W	Annual	[QRL 31] 4.3.1.2
Transmission lines	For each Area Board, circuit length existing, and commissioned during year, by voltage: latest 2 years	E & W	Annual	[QRL 31] 4.3.1.2
Transmission lines	Circuit length existing, and commissioned during year, by voltage, by overhead lines and underground cables: latest year	South Scotland	Annual	[QRL 7] 4.3.2.2
Transmission lines	Relationship between circuit length and route length for 2 bands of voltage by underground/overhead: latest year	South Scotland	Annual	[QRL 7] 4.3.2.2

Type of Data	Breakdown/Detail of Analysis	Area	Frequency	Publication (see QRL Key)	Text Reference and Remarks
TRANSMISSION AND DISTRIBUTION EQUIPMENT (contd.)					
Transmission lines	Circuit lengths by voltage: latest 2 years. Length of submarine cable: latest year	North Scotland	Annual	[QRL 6]	4.3.3.2
Transmission lines	Route length, by voltage, by overhead/underground, by single and double circuit. Circuit length, by voltage, and by overhead/underground: latest year	Northern Ireland	Annual	[QRL 8]	4.3.5.2
Transmission and distribution mains	Area Board circuit km existing and commissioned during year, by voltage, and by overhead/underground: latest year	E & W	Annual	[QRL 5]	4.3.1.2
Transmission plant costs	Costs per km for 2 circuits of (a) overhead lines and (b) underground cables of equivalent capacity—at 132 kV, 275 kV, and 400 kV: latest at July 1975	E & W	Annual to 1975	[QRL 32]	4.3.1.2
Main transformers and substations	Capacities of main transformers by voltage, and numbers of transformers and 400 kV and 275 kV substations by regions: latest year	E & W	Annual	[QRL 32]	4.3.1.2
Transformers	Capacities of CEGB transformers existing, and commissioned during year, by voltage: latest 10 years	E & W	Annual	[QRL 31]	4.3.1.2

Transformers	Number and capacities of Area Board transforming points existing and commissioned during the year, by bands of secondary voltage: latest year	E & W	Annual	[QRL 5]	4.3.1.2
Transformers	Total capacity of Area Board transformers existing, and commissioned during the year, by voltage: latest 10 years	E & W	Annual	[QRL 31]	4.3.1.2
Transformers	For each Area Board, capacities existing, and commissioned during the year, by voltage: latest 2 years	E & W	Annual	[QRL 31]	4.3.1.2
Transformers	Number of substations and capacity, existing, and commissioned during the year, by voltage: latest year	South Scotland	Annual	[QRL 7]	4.3.2.2
Transformers	Capacity, by voltage: latest 2 years	North Scotland	Annual	[QRL 6]	4.3.3.2
Transformers	Number and capacity, by voltage; number with secondary voltage less than 110 kV: latest year	Northern Ireland	Annual	[QRL 8]	4.3.5.2
POWER (MAXIMUM DEMAND)					
Maximum demand and load factor	MD supplied, estimated maximum potential demand, estimated MD in 'average cold spell' conditions, system load factor (actual and adjusted to 'standard' weather): 1947/48 and yearly to date	E & W	Annual	[QRL 23]	4.4.1.1

ELECTRICITY

Type of Data	Breakdown/Detail of Analysis	Area	Frequency	Publication (see QRL Key)	Text Reference and Remarks
POWER (MAXIMUM DEMAND) *(contd.)*					
Maximum demand and load factor	MD supplied and time of occurrence for individual Area Boards. Analysis into MD supplied by CEGB, other Area Boards, and other sources; load factors: latest 2 years	E & W	Annual	[QRL 5] and [QRL 31]	4.4.1.2
Maximum demand and load factor	MDs met by, and load factors of, each Area Board: at intervals from 1920 to date	E & W	Annual	[QRL 23]	4.4.1.2
Maximum demand and load factor	MD met, estimated maximum potential demand, and load factor: latest 10 or 11 years. Sub-division of plant load factor by type of station: latest 4 years	GB	Annual	[QRL 13]	4.4.6
Maximum demand	MD in each of the last 15 months or so	E & W and UK	Monthly	[QRL 25]	4.4.1.1
Maximum demand	Time of occurrence, and make-up, of MD, by type of station, interchange with North Scotland Hydro-Electric Board and CEGB, purchase from British Nuclear Fuels Ltd, and other sources: latest 10 years	South Scotland	Annual	[QRL 7]	4.4.2
Maximum demand	Date of occurrence and size of MD met during latest year. Variation in demand for electricity during the day of highest MD in year and also during a typical summer day (Chart)	North Scotland	Annual	[QRL 6]	4.4.3

QUICK REFERENCE LIST 265

Maximum demand	Size and time of occurrence of MD: latest year	Northern Ireland	Annual	[QRL 8]	4.4.5
Maximum demand	MD met in preceding calendar year, and in the latest 5 quarters	GB	Quarterly	[QRL 10]	4.4.6
Load curves	Chart of variation in demand for electricity during 4 periods of 24 hours: days of (a) highest MD during latest year, (b) typical winter usage, (c) typical summer usage, and (d) lowest MD. Size and time of occurrence of MD: latest year	E & W	Annual	[QRL 4]	4.4.1.1

ELECTRICITY PRODUCED AND CONSUMED

Production and disposal of electricity	Electricity generated, used on works, supplied, interchanged with S. Scotland and France, and other sources, used in transmission, sold to Area Boards and direct consumers: at intervals 1920 to 1948, then yearly from 1951	E & W	Annual	[QRL 32]	4.5.1
Bulk sales of electricity	Sales by CEGB to each Area Board each month	E & W	Monthly	[QRL 17] and [QRL 18]	4.5.1
Bulk sales of electricity	Sales by CEGB to each Area Board, showing total sales and proportion which are 'night' and 'peak' within the definitions of the Bulk Supply Tariff: latest year	E & W	Annual	[QRL 32]	4.5.1
Production and supply of electricity	Electricity generated and supplied: at intervals from 1920 to 1940, then yearly from 1945	E & W	Annual	[QRL 23]	4.5.1

266　ELECTRICITY

Type of Data	Breakdown/Detail of Analysis	Area	Frequency	Publication (see QRL Key)	Text Reference and Remarks
ELECTRICITY PRODUCED AND CONSUMED (contd.)					
Bulk purchase of electricity	Electricity purchased by each Area Board from the CEGB, other Area Boards, and other sources; sales to other Area Boards: latest 2 years	E & W	Annual	[QRL 5] and [QRL 31]	4.5.1
Electricity produced and consumed	Electricity generated, by type of plant, sent out to distribution, interchanged with other sources, and sold to customers: 1938, 1949, 1959, and yearly from 1968	Wales	Annual	[QRL 14]	4.5.1
Production and disposal of electricity	Electricity produced, by type of station, interchanged with CEGB and North Scotland Hydro-Electric Board, purchased from British Nuclear Fuels Ltd, and others, sent out, and sold to consumers: latest 10 years	South Scotland	Annual	[QRL 7]	4.5.2
Electricity produced and consumed	Electricity supplied from power stations, and sold to consumers: each year from 1948/49	South Scotland	Annual	[QRL 23]	4.5.2
Electricity produced and consumed	Electricity supplied from power stations, and sold to consumers: each year from 1948/49	North Scotland	Annual	[QRL 23]	4.5.3
Electricity produced and consumed	Electricity sent out, and sales to consumers: latest 10 years	Northern Ireland	Annual	[QRL 8]	4.5.4

QUICK REFERENCE LIST 267

Electricity produced and consumed	Electricity sent out, and sales to 'domestic and farms', 'public lighting', and 'others': 1939, 1949, 1959, and the latest 13 years or so	Northern Ireland	Annual	[QRL 15]	4.5.4
Electricity produced	Electricity supplied from mainland stations, by type, interchanged with South Scotland Electricity Board and other sources, and supplied from isolated systems: latest 2 years	North Scotland	Annual	[QRL 6]	4.5.3
Electricity produced	Electricity produced by individual power stations: latest 2 years	Northern Ireland	Annual	[QRL 8]	4.5.4
Electricity produced	Electricity generated, sent out, interchanged with Eire, and transmission losses: latest year	Northern Ireland	Annual	[QRL 8]	4.5.4
Electricity produced	Electricity generated, by type of station, and interchanged with industrial producers: latest 10 years	UK	Annual	[QRL 13]	4.5.5
Electricity produced	Electricity generated, used on works, and purchased from outside sources: latest 10 years	GB	Annual	[QRL 13]	4.5.5
Electricity produced	Coal and oil equivalents of nuclear and hydro electricity production: latest 3 months, latest 6 years	UK	Monthly	[QRL 20]	4.5.5
Supply of electricity	Electricity supplied, by CEGB regions and type of station: latest year	E & W	Annual	[QRL 32]	4.5.1
Supply of electricity	Analysis of electricity supplied, by individual power stations: latest year	E & W	Annual	[QRL 32]	4.5.1
Supply of electricity	Electricity supplied, by type of plant: from 1960/61	E & W	Annual	[QRL 23]	4.5.1

268   ELECTRICITY

Type of Data	Breakdown/Detail of Analysis	Area	Frequency	Publication (see QRL Key)	Text Reference and Remarks
ELECTRICITY PRODUCED AND CONSUMED (contd.)					
Fuels used and electricity produced	Fuels used in generation, and electricity generated and supplied monthly (expressed as weekly averages): latest 12 to 15 months and latest 5 calendar years	E & W and UK	Monthly	[QRL 25]	4.5.5
Fuels used and electricity produced	Fuels used in generation, and electricity generated, supplied, and available: latest calendar year and of latest 5 quarters	GB	Quarterly	[QRL 10]	4.5.5
Fuels used and electricity produced	Amounts of fuels used, electricity generated by various methods, and electricity used adjusted for seasonal and weather effects: latest 10 years. (Summer/winter and England and Wales/Scotland sub-analyses for latest 3 years)	GB	Annual	[QRL 13]	4.5.5
Fuels used and electricity produced	Coal equivalents of fuels used in generation, and electricity generated and supplied: latest 3 months and latest 6 years	E & W and UK	Monthly	[QRL 20]	4.5.5
Fuel consumed in power stations	Coal equivalent of each fuel: from 1962/63	E & W	Annual	[QRL 23]	4.5.1
Fossil fuels consumed in power stations	Amounts of each fuel used: at intervals 1920/21 to 1938/39, yearly from 1945/46	E & W	Annual	[QRL 23]	4.5.1
Fossil fuels consumed in power stations	Amounts of each fuel used: latest 2 years	EEC	Annual	[QRL 23]	4.5.8
Fuels used	Amounts of fuels used, and their coal equivalents: latest 8 years	UK	Annual	[QRL 13]	4.5.5

QUICK REFERENCE LIST 269

Fuels consumption (all fuels)	Energy supplied (in therms) by each principal fuel in each standard region: latest year (in 1975) volume, not in 1976)	UK	Annual	[QRL 29]	4.5.5
Electricity produced	Plant capacity and output (public/private), by type of generation: latest year	EEC	Annual	[QRL 23]	4.5.8
Electricity produced (private generation)	Electricity generated outside public supply system, by type of generation: latest 10 years	UK	Annual	[QRL 13]	4.5.7
Electricity produced (private generation)	Electricity generated outside public supply system, by various industrial classes: latest 9 quarters and latest 6 years	GB	Quarterly	[QRL 20]	4.5.7
Electricity produced (private generation)	Electricity generated outside public supply system, by various industrial classes: from 1955	GB	Annual	[QRL 23]	4.5.7
Electricity produced (private generation)	Electricity generated outside public supply system: latest year	EEC	Annual	[QRL 23]	4.5.8
Electricity sales in EEC	Sales to broad industrial classes: latest year	EEC	Annual	[QRL 23]	4.5.8
Electricity sales to customers	Sales to each class of customer: latest 10 years	E & W	Annual	[QRL 31]	4.5.1
Electricity sales to customers	Sales by each Area Board to each class of customer: latest 2 years	E & W	Annual	[QRL 31]	4.5.1
Electricity sales to customers	Sales to each class of customer: at intervals from 1920 to 1947, then yearly (estimated total in 1900)	E & W	Annual	[QRL 23]	4.5.1
Electricity sales to customers	Sales by each Area Board: at intervals from 1920 to 1970/71 and yearly from 1973/74	E & W	Annual	[QRL 23]	4.5.1

270 ELECTRICITY

Type of Data	Breakdown/Detail of Analysis	Area	Frequency	Publication (see QRL Key)	Text Reference and Remarks
ELECTRICITY PRODUCED AND CONSUMED (contd.)					
Electricity sales to customers	Sales by each Area Board to each class of customer: 1920, 1938, and latest year	E & W	Annual	[QRL 23]	4.5.1
Electricity sales to customers	Sales in various administrative entities (Groups, Areas, Districts) in UK Boards, and in undertakings not subject to the UK Boards (e.g. Alderney Electricity Ltd): latest year	UK	Annual	[QRL 19]	4.5.1.1
Electricity sales to consumers	Sales in latest month	South Scotland	Monthly	[QRL 17] and [QRL 18]	4.5.2
Electricity sales to consumers	Sales to each class of consumer: latest 10 years	South Scotland	Annual	[QRL 7]	4.5.2
Electricity sales to consumers	Sales in latest month	North Scotland	Monthly	[QRL 17] and [QRL 18]	4.5.3
Electricity sales to consumers	Sales to each class of consumer: latest 2 years	North Scotland	Annual	[QRL 6]	4.5.3
Electricity sales to consumers	Sales in each administrative area: latest year	Northern Ireland	Annual	[QRL 19]	4.5.4
Electricity sales to customers	Sales to customer by broad class: UK quarterly during latest 2 or 3 years, and yearly for latest 7 years	UK	Quarterly	[QRL 25]	4.5.5
Electricity sales to customers	Sales to various classes of customer: latest 10 years	GB	Annual	[QRL 13]	4.5.5
Electricity sales to customers	Sales to various classes of customer: by Area Boards: latest 2 years	UK	Annual	[QRL 13]	4.5.5
Electricity sales to customers	Sales to each class of customer: latest calendar year and latest 5 quarters	GB	Quarterly	[QRL 10]	4.5.5
Electricity sales to customers	Sales to each class of customer in each standard region: latest 6 years	UK	Annual	[QRL 29]	4.5.5

QUICK REFERENCE LIST 271

Electricity sales to customers	Sales to broad categories: latest 9 quarters and latest 2 years	UK	Quarterly	[QRL 20]	4.5.5
Electricity consumed	Electricity sold to, and self-generated by, various industrial classes, together with sales to transport users, domestic, public administration and other 'commercial' users: latest 8 years	UK	Annual	[QRL 13]	4.5.5
Electricity consumed	Electricity used by 5 main classes (expressed in therms): latest 9 quarters and latest 2 years	UK	Quarterly	[QRL 20]	4.5.5
Electricity sales to industrial customers	Shares of sales between broad SIC classes of customer in latest year, with percentage growths for each of the classes year by year over the latest 5 years	E & W	Annual	[QRL 31]	4.5.1
Electricity sales to industrial consumers	Sales to certain broad SIC classes: 1961 and latest 10 years	South Scotland	Annual	[QRL 30]	4.5.2
Electricity sales to industrial customers	Sales to broad SIC classes: latest calendar year and latest 5 quarters	GB	Quarterly	[QRL 10]	4.5.5
Electricity sales to industrial and transport undertakings	Sales to broad SIC classes and transport undertakings: latest 11 years	GB	Annual	[QRL 13]	4.5.5
Electricity sales on off-peak tariffs	Sales by each Area Board to each class of customer: latest 2 years	E & W	Annual	[QRL 31]	4.5.1
Electricity sales on day/night (two rate) tariffs	Sales by each Area Board to each class of customer: latest 2 years	E & W	Annual	[QRL 31]	4.5.1
Electricity sales on off-peak tariffs	Totals 1957/58 to 1962/63 to each class of customer: 1963/64 to date	E & W	Annual	[QRL 23]	4.5.1
Electricity sales on off-peak tariffs	Sales to each class of consumer: latest 10 years	South Scotland	Annual	[QRL 7]	4.5.2

Type of Data	Breakdown/Detail of Analysis	Area	Frequency	Publication (see QRL Key)	Text Reference and Remarks
ELECTRICITY PRODUCED AND CONSUMED (*contd.*)					
Average consumption of electricity	Electricity sales per head of population, and per domestic, farm, and industrial customer: at intervals from 1920 to 1945, and yearly from 1947/48	E & W	Annual	[QRL 23]	4.5.1
Electricity sales (weather adjusted)	Sales adjusted for seasonal variations and weather effects: latest 10 years, subdivided winter/summer for latest 3 years	GB	Annual	[QRL 13]	4.5.6
CUSTOMER/CONSUMER CLASSIFICATION					
Number of customers	Numbers in various classes: at intervals from 1920	E & W	Annual	[QRL 23]	4.6.1
Number of customers	Totals in each Area Board: at intervals from 1920	E & W	Annual	[QRL 23]	4.6.1
Number of customers	Numbers in each class in each Area Board: latest 2 years	E & W	Annual	[QRL 31] and [QRL 5]	4.6.1
Number of customers	Numbers in various classes: at intervals from 1949 (total in 1938)	Wales	Annual	[QRL 14]	4.6.1
Numbers of consumers	Totals in SSEB area: 1948 to date	South Scotland	Annual	[QRL 23]	4.6.2
Number of consumers	Numbers in each class: 1967 to date	South Scotland	Annual	[QRL 7]	4.6.2
Number of consumers	Totals in NSHEB area: 1948 to date	North Scotland	Annual	[QRL 23]	4.6.2
Number of consumers	Numbers in each class: latest year	North Scotland	Annual	[QRL 6]	4.6.2
Number of consumers	Numbers in various classes: latest 2 years	Northern Ireland	Annual	[QRL 8]	4.6.3
Number of consumers	Numbers in various classes: at intervals from 1950	Northern Ireland	Annual	[QRL 15]	4.6.3

QUICK REFERENCE LIST 273

Number of customers	Numbers in various administrative entities (Groups, Areas, Districts) in UK Boards, and in undertakings not subject to the UK Boards (e.g. Alderney Electricity Ltd): latest year	UK	Annual	[QRL 19]	4.6.1
Domestic customers, areas, and population	Numbers in each Area Board: at intervals from 1932. Areas and populations: latest year	E & W	Annual	[QRL 23]	4.6.1
Number of off-peak customers	Numbers in each class in each Area Board: latest 2 years	E & W	Annual	[QRL 31] and [QRL 5]	4.6.1
Number of day/night customers	Number in each class in each Area Board: latest 2 years	E & W	Annual	[QRL 31] and [QRL 5]	4.6.1
REVENUE AND PRICES					
Bulk sales of electricity	Revenue obtained by CEGB from Area Board and other consumers, by service, capacity, and running charges: latest 2 years	E & W	Annual	[QRL 4]	4.7.1
Revenue from customers	Revenue in each Area Board from each class of customer: latest 2 years	E & W	Annual	[QRL 31] and [QRL 5]	4.7.1
Revenue from customers	Revenue per kWh sold, by each class: from 1935/36	E & W	Annual	[QRL 23]	4.7.1
Revenue from customers	Revenue (absolute and per kWh sold) in each Area Board: from 1948/49	E & W	Annual	[QRL 23]	4.7.1
Revenue from customers	Revenue per kWh sold in each Area Board from each class of customer: from 1950/51	E & W	Annual	[QRL 23]	4.7.1
Revenue from customers	Revenue per kWh sold from various classes of customer: from 1949	Wales	Annual	[QRL 14]	4.7.1

Type of Data	Breakdown/Detail of Analysis	Area	Frequency	Publication (see QRL Key)	Text Reference and Remarks
CUSTOMER/CONSUMER CLASSIFICATION (contd.)					
Revenue from consumers	Revenue (absolute and per kWh sold) from each class of consumer: latest 2 years	South Scotland	Annual	[QRL 7]	4.7.2
Revenue from consumers	Revenue (absolute and per kWh sold) from each class of consumer: latest 2 years	North Scotland	Annual	[QRL 6]	4.7.2
Revenue from consumers	Revenue per kWh sold: from 1948	South Scotland	Annual	[QRL 23]	4.7.2
Revenue from consumers	Revenue per kWh sold: from 1948	North Scotland	Annual	[QRL 23]	4.7.2
Revenue from consumers	Total revenue from retail sales: latest 10 years	Northern Ireland	Annual	[QRL 8]	4.7.3
Revenue from customers	Revenue from each class of customer: latest year and latest 5 quarters	GB	Quarterly	[QRL 10]	4.7.4
Retail prices	Indices of electricity prices: from 1962	UK	Annual	[QRL 13]	4.7.4
Retail prices	Indices of electricity prices: latest 7 months	UK	Monthly	[QRL 25]	4.7.4
Retail prices	Domestic electricity prices at 5 levels of consumption in 14 large towns: latest 3 years	UK	Annual	[QRL 13]	4.7.4
Consumers' expenditure on electricity	Indices at current and inflation adjusted prices: latest 11 years	UK	Annual	[QRL 13] and [QRL 26]	4.7.4
Electricity used in industry	Pence per kWh and pence per therm: latest 11 years (quarterly for latest year)	GB	Annual	[QRL 13]	4.7.4
Fuel used by electricity industry	Prices of various fuels: latest 12 years	GB	Annual	[QRL 13]	4.7.4

QUICK REFERENCE LIST 275

FINANCIAL STATISTICS

Balance sheets	CEGB assets, fixed and current, liabilities, borrowings, reserves: latest 2 years	E & W	Annual	[QRL 31] and [QRL 4]	5.4.1
Balance sheets	For each Area Board—assets, fixed and current, liabilities, borrowings, reserves: latest 2 years	E & W	Annual	[QRL 31] and [QRL 5]	5.4.1
Balance sheets	Analysis of assets and financing: from 1949 (includes some figures for Scotland in early years)	E & W	Annual	[QRL 23]	5.4.1
Balance sheets	Assets, fixed and current, liabilities, borrowings, reserves: latest 2 years	South Scotland	Annual	[QRL 7]	5.4.2
Balance sheets	Assets, fixed and current, liabilities, borrowings, reserves: latest 2 years	North Scotland	Annual	[QRL 6]	5.4.2
Balance sheets	Assets, fixed and current, liabilities, borrowings, reserves: latest 2 years	Northern Ireland	Annual	[QRL 8]	5.4.3
Revenue accounts	CEGB income (4 headings), expenditure (10 headings), interest, and compensation payments: latest 2 years	E & W	Annual	[QRL 31] and [QRL 4]	5.3.1
Revenue accounts	For each Area Board—income (4 headings), expenditure (10 headings), interest, and compensation payments, profit/loss on sales of appliances, etc.: latest 2 years	E & W	Annual	[QRL 31] and [QRL 5]	5.3.1
Revenue accounts	Consolidated details of income and expenditure for Electricity Council, CEGB, and Area Boards: latest 2 years	E & W	Annual	[QRL 31]	5.3.1

ELECTRICITY

Type of Data	Breakdown/Detail of Analysis	Area	Frequency	Publication (see QRL Key)	Text Reference and Remarks
FINANCIAL STATISTICS (contd.)					
Revenue accounts	Analysis of consolidated income, expenditure, and interest payments for Electricity Council, CEGB, and Area Boards (inc. South Scotland for first 7 years): from 1948/49	E & W	Annual	[QRL 23]	5.3.1
Revenue accounts	Income (2 headings), expenditure (9 headings), interest and compensation payments: latest 2 years	South Scotland	Annual	[QRL 7]	5.3.2
Revenue accounts	Income (2 headings), expenditure (9 headings), interest, and compensation payments: latest 2 years	North Scotland	Annual	[QRL 6]	5.3.2
Revenue accounts	Income (3 headings), expenditure (3 headings), interest, and compensation payments: latest 2 years	Northern Ireland	Annual	[QRL 8]	5.3.3
Capital expenditure	Detailed analysis of each CEGB heading: latest 2 years	E & W	Annual	[QRL 31] and [QRL 4]	5.4.1
Capital expenditure	Detailed analysis of each heading for each Area Board: latest 2 years	E & W	Annual	[QRL 31] and [QRL 5]	5.4.1
Capital expenditure	Detailed analysis of each heading: latest 2 years	South Scotland	Annual	[QRL 7]	5.4.2
Capital expenditure	Detailed analysis of each heading: latest 2 years	North Scotland	Annual	[QRL 6]	5.4.2
Capital expenditure	Detailed analysis of each heading: latest 2 years	Northern Ireland	Annual	[QRL 8]	5.4.3
Capital expenditure	From 1948	South Scotland	Annual	[QRL 23]	5.4.2

QUICK REFERENCE LIST

Capital expenditure	From 1948	North Scotland	Annual	[QRL 23]	5.4.2
Capital expenditure	Analysis before and after consolidation into NIES: from 1972	Northern Ireland	Annual	[QRL 15]	5.4.3
Capital expenditure	For electricity and the other fuel industries: to 1973	GB	Annual	[QRL 13]	5.4.4
Working capital	For electricity, gas, coal: from 1963 to date Analysis of current assets and liabilities: from 1956	UK E & W	Annual	[QRL 23]	5.4.1
Revenue expenditure	Detailed analysis of each heading of CEGB expenditure: latest 2 years	E & W	Annual	[QRL 31] and [QRL 4]	5.3.1
Revenue expenditure	Detailed analysis of each heading of expenditure for each Area Board: latest 2 years	E & W	Annual	[QRL 31] and [QRL 5]	5.3.1
Revenue expenditure	Analysis of expenditure over 6 detailed headings for the Electricity Council, CEGB, and Area Boards (inc. South Scotland for first 3 years): from 1952/53	E & W	Annual	[QRL 23]	5.3.1
Revenue expenditure	Detailed analysis of each heading of expenditure: latest 2 years	South Scotland	Annual	[QRL 7]	5.3.2
Revenue expenditure	Detailed analysis of each heading of expenditure: latest 2 years	North Scotland	Annual	[QRL 6]	5.3.2
Revenue expenditure	Detailed analysis of 2 headings: latest 2 years	Northern Ireland	Annual	[QRL 8]	5.3.3
Revenue expenditure	Analysis before and after consolidation into NIES: from 1972	Northern Ireland	Annual	[QRL 15]	5.3.3

ELECTRICITY

Type of Data	Breakdown/Detail of Analysis	Area	Frequency	Publication (see QRL Key)	Text Reference and Remarks
FINANCIAL STATISTICS *(contd.)*					
Source and application of funds	For CEGB and each Area Board—Analysis of funds raised from internal sources, borrowings, capital expenditure and other liabilities: latest 2 years	E & W	Annual	[QRL 4] and [QRL 5]	5.5.1
Source and application of funds	Analysis of funds raised from internal sources, borrowings, capital expenditure and other liabilities: latest 2 years	South Scotland	Annual	[QRL 7]	5.5.2
Source and application of funds	Analysis of funds raised from internal sources, borrowings, capital expenditure and other liabilities: latest 2 years	North Scotland	Annual	[QRL 6]	5.5.2
Source and application of funds, and self-financing ratios	Consolidated details for Electricity Council, CEGB, and Area Boards (including South Scotland to 1954/55): from 1948/49	E & W	Annual	[QRL 23]	5.5.1
Net profit	Balance of revenue: from 1948	South Scotland	Annual	[QRL 23]	5.3.2
Net profit	Balance of revenue: from 1948	North Scotland	Annual	[QRL 23]	5.3.2
Expenditure and output	Analysis of fuel and other costs, and value of output: from 1949	Wales	Annual	[QRL 14]	5.3.1
Works costs—CEGB	Fuel and other works costs per kWh, fuel costs per tonne, and per gigajoule: latest 10 years	E & W	Annual	[QRL 32]	5.3.1
Works costs	Fuel and other works costs per kWh: conventional stations from 1932, nuclear stations from 1962/63	E & W	Annual	[QRL 23]	5.3.1

QUICK REFERENCE LIST   279

Operational costs	Costs per kWh of energy purchases, distribution, customer service, etc. latest 2 years	E & W	Annual	[QRL 5]	5.3.1
Output	Analysis for electricity and the other fuel industries of gross and net output, wages and salaries, and employment: to 1973 in [QRL 11]: latest 6 years in [QRL 9]	GB UK	Annual	[QRL 13] and [QRL 10]	5.3.4

CONTRACTING AND SALES OF APPLIANCES

Revenue accounts	Sales, costs (direct and indirect), interest charges, and operating profit for each Area Board: latest 2 years	E & W	Annual	[QRL 31] and [QRL 5]	6.2.1
Revenue accounts	Sales, costs (direct and indirect), interest charges and operating profit: latest 2 years	South Scotland	Annual	[QRL 7]	6.2.2
Revenue accounts	Sales, costs (direct and indirect), interest charges and operating profit: latest 2 years	North Scotland	Annual	[QRL 6]	6.2.2
Numbers of shops	Numbers in each Area Board: latest year	E & W	Annual	[QRL 23]	6.2.1
Sales of appliances	Numbers of various appliances sold: latest year	E & W	Annual	[QRL 3]	6.2.1
Sales of appliances	Numbers of various appliances sold: latest 10 years	South Scotland	Annual	[QRL 7]	6.2.2
Sales of appliances	Numbers and value of various appliances sold: latest 2 years	Northern Ireland	Annual	[QRL 8]	6.2.3
Sales of appliances	Numbers of various electrical and gas appliances sold by Boards: from 1955	GB	Annual	[QRL 23]	6.2.4

280 ELECTRICITY

Type of Data	Breakdown/Detail of Analysis	Area	Frequency	Publication (see QRL Key)	Text Reference and Remarks
CONTRACTING AND SALES OF APPLIANCES (contd.)					
Sales of appliances	Indices of values of retail sales by radio and electrical goods shops, radio and television specialists and by electricity showrooms: latest 3 years or so	GB	Annual, quarterly, monthly	[QRL 25]	6.2.4
Sales of appliances	Numbers of various appliances sold by the electricity supply industry: latest 5 quarters	GB	Quarterly	[QRL 10]	6.2.4
Production of appliances	Numbers and values of production of domestic electrical appliances: latest month	UK	Annual, quarterly, monthly	[QRL 33]	6.2.4
Ownership levels of appliances	Details for around 45 types of appliance: from 1933	E & W	Annual	[QRL 23]	6.2.1
Acquisition and ownership of appliances	Numbers of domestic appliances acquired in period, ownership at a given time, market shares, by Area Board, source, method of payment, social class, age of housewife, new or existing house, initial/replacement/additional: latest quarter	GB	Quarterly	[QRL 24]	6.2.4
EMPLOYEES					
Numbers of employees	Numbers, by Electricity Council, CEGB, Area Boards, by class (managerial, etc.): latest year end	E & W	Annual	[QRL 31], [QRL 4] and [QRL 5]	7.1

QUICK REFERENCE LIST 281

Numbers of employees	Totals, by class (managerial, etc.): from 1949	E & W	Annual	[QRL 23]	7.1
Numbers of employees	Numbers, by Electricity Council, CEGB (Regions, Divisions, etc.), and Area Boards, by class: latest 4 to 6 years	E & W	Annual	[QRL 23]	7.1
Numbers of employees	Average numbers, by class: from 1949	Wales	Annual	[QRL 14]	7.1
Numbers of employees	Numbers, by class: latest 2 years. Totals: latest 10 years	South Scotland	Annual	[QRL 7]	7.2
Numbers of employees	Numbers, by class: latest 2 years. Totals: latest 10 years	North Scotland	Annual	[QRL 6]	7.2
Numbers of employees	Totals, for South Scotland and North Scotland: latest 6 years	Scotland	Annual	[QRL 30]	7.2
Numbers of employees	Totals, and numbers in power stations: latest 2 years	Northern Ireland	Annual	[QRL 8]	7.3
Numbers of employees	Totals: latest 4 years	Northern Ireland	Annual	[QRL 15]	7.3
Numbers employed and unemployed	Totals at June: latest 3 years	GB & UK	Annual	[QRL 1]	7.4
Numbers of employees and net output	Totals for electricity, coal, gas, petroleum refining, and petroleum and natural gas production: latest 4 years	GB	Annual to 1973 Annual from 1974	[QRL 13] [QRL 10]	7.4
Salaries and related costs	Salaries (industrial and non-industrial), national insurance, superannuation, etc.: from 1955	E & W	Annual	[QRL 23]	7.1
Salaries and wages	Totals, by class: from 1949	Wales	Annual	[QRL 14]	7.1
Salaries and wages	Totals, for South Scotland and North Scotland: latest 6 years	Scotland	Annual	[QRL 30]	7.2

282 ELECTRICITY

Type of Data	Breakdown/Detail of Analysis	Area	Frequency	Publication (see QRL Key)	Text Reference and Remarks
EMPLOYEES (*contd.*)					
Average earnings and hours worked	For male manual wage earners over 21 years of age in the electricity supply industry: from 1938	UK	Annual	[QRL 23]	7.1
RESEARCH					
Finance of research	CEGB revenue expenditure in year on, and value of assets used for, research: latest 2 years	E & W	Annual	[QRL 4]	8.3.1
Finance of research	Analysis of research expenditure into salaries, materials, etc.; depreciation on research assets of Electricity Council and CEGB—during year and cumulative: latest 2 years	E & W	Annual	[QRL 31]	8.3.1
Revenue expenditure on research	Proportion of Electricity Council research expenditure allocated to each Area Board: latest 2 years	E & W	Annual	[QRL 5]	8.3.1
Capital expenditure on research	Annual figures for CEGB: from 1962/63	E & W	Annual	[QRL 23]	8.3.1

Quick Reference List Key to Publications

Reference Number	Organisation Responsible	Title	Publisher	Frequency or Date	Remarks
[QRL 1]	Central Statistical Office	*Annual Abstract of Statistics*	HMSO, London	Annual	
[QRL 2]	United Nations	*Annual Bulletin of Electric Energy Statistics for Europe*	UN, New York	Annual	
[QRL 3]	Electricity Council	*Annual Report*	Electricity Council	Annual	
[QRL 4]	Central Electricity Generating Board	*Annual Reports and Accounts*	CEGB	Annual	
[QRL 5]	Area Boards of England and Wales	*Annual Report and Accounts*	Individual Area Boards: Eastern EB, East Midlands EB, London EB, Merseyside and North Wales EB, Midlands EB, North Eastern EB, North Western EB, South Eastern EB, Southern EB, South Wales EB, South Western EB, Yorkshire EB	Annual	
[QRL 6]	North Scotland Hydro-Electric Board	*Annual Report and Accounts*	NSHEB	Annual	
[QRL 7]	South Scotland Electricity Board	*Annual Report and Accounts*	SSEB	Annual	
[QRL 8]	Northern Ireland Electricity Service	*Annual Report and Accounts*	NIES	Annual	
[QRL 9]	Department of Employment	*British Labour Statistics Yearbook*	HMSO, London	Annual	
[QRL 10]	Department of Industry	*Business Monitors*	HMSO, London	Monthly, Quarterly, Annual, Occasional	
[QRL 11]	House of Commons	*Choice of a Reactor System* (HC 145)	HMSO, London	1973–74	
[QRL 12]	Department of Employment	*Department of Employment Gazette*	HMSO, London	Monthly	

Quick Reference List Key to Publications

Reference Number	Organisation Responsible	Title	Publisher	Frequency or Date	Remarks
[QRL 13]	Department of Energy	Digest of UK Energy Statistics	HMSO, London	Annual*	
[QRL 14]	Welsh Office	Digest of Welsh Statistics	HMSO, Cardiff	Annual	
[QRL 15]	N. Ireland Office	Digest of Statistics, N. Ireland	HMSO, Belfast	Annual	
[QRL 16]	Government Statistical Service	Economic Trends	HMSO, London	Monthly	
[QRL 17]	Electrical Review	Electrical Review	IPC Electrical/Electronic Press	Weekly	
[QRL 18]	Electrical Times	Electrical Times	IPC Business Press	Weekly	
[QRL 19]	Electrical Times	Electricity Supply Handbook	IPC Electrical/Electronic Press	Annual	
[QRL 20]	Department of Energy	Energy Trends	HMSO, London	Monthly	
[QRL 21]	EEC	Eurostat Energy Statistics Yearbook	Statistical Office of the European Community (Luxembourg)	Annual	
[QRL 22]	EEC	Eurostat Quarterly Bulletin of Energy Statistics	Statistical Office of the European Community (Luxembourg)	Quarterly	
[QRL 23]	Electricity Council	Handbook of Electricity Supply Statistics	Electricity Council	Annual	
[QRL 24]	Audits of Gt Britain Ltd (AGB)	Marketing Reports	AGB, Audit House, Eastcote, Ruislip	Annual, Quarterly	
[QRL 25]	Central Statistical Office	Monthly Digest of Statistics	HMSO, London	Monthly	
[QRL 26]	Government Statistical Service	National Income and Expenditure Blue Book	HMSO, London	Annual	
[QRL 27]	House of Commons	Nuclear Power Policy (HCP 117)	HMSO, London	1972–73	
[QRL 28]	Treasury	Public Expenditure White Paper	HMSO, London	Annual	
[QRL 29]	Central Statistical Office	Regional Statistics	HMSO, London	Annual	
[QRL 30]	Scottish Office	Scottish Abstract of Statistics	HMSO, Edinburgh	Annual	
[QRL 31]	Electricity Council	Statement of Accounts and Statistics	Electricity Council	Annual	
[QRL 32]	Central Electricity Generating Board	Statistical Yearbook	CEGB	Annual	
[QRL 33]	Association of Manufacturers of Domestic Electrical Appliances (AMDEA)	Statistics for the Domestic Electrical Appliance Industry	AMDEA	Annual, Quarterly, Monthly	
[QRL 34]	United Nations	World Energy Supplies	UN, New York	Annual	

* Previously published by Ministry of Fuel and Power 1946–1955; Ministry of Power 1956–1969; Ministry of Technology 1970; Department of Trade and Industry 1971–1972.

BIBLIOGRAPHY

[B 1] Daniel, G. H. The Sources and Nature of Statistical Information in Special Fields of Statistics—Electricity and Gas Statistics *Journal Royal Statistical Society* (series A) Vol 113 Pt 4 1950 pp 509–530 Reprinted in *Sources and Nature of the Statistics of the UK* Kendall, M. G. (Ed) Vol. 1 1952 London. Oliver and Boyd for Royal Statistical Society

[B 2] Davies, M. *The Relationship between Weather and Electricity Demand* Institute of Electrical Engineers, Monograph 3 145 1958

[B 3] Garcke *Manual of Electrical Undertakings* Electrical Press Ltd, London. Annually 1865 to 1948–49

[B 4] Mackay, D. I. and Buxton, N. K. *British Employment Statistics* Basil Blackwell, Oxford 1977

[B 5] Chief Engineers' Conference Plant Committee *Code of Practice for the Metering of Supplies from the CEGB* The Electricity Council, 30 Millbank, London SW1P 4RD, 1973

[B 6] The *Electrician*, London 1878–1952

[B 7] British Standards Institution *Electricity Meters* British Standards Institution, 2 Park St, London W1A 2BS

[B 8] Electricity Council *Electricity Supply in Great Britain—A Chronology* The Electricity Council, 30 Millbank, London SW1P 4RD, 1973

[B 9] Electricity Council *Electricity Supply in Great Britain—Organisation and Development* The Electricity Council, 30 Millbank, London SW1P 4RD, 1975

[B 10] Electricity Commission *Electricity Supply: Return of Engineering and Financial Statistics* HMSO London 1920–1945–46 (Issued by Ministry of Fuel and Power for 1946–47 and 1947–48)

[B 11] The Treasury *The Financial and Economic Obligations of the Nationalised Industries* Cmnd 1337 HMSO London, 1961

[B 12] Electricity Commission *Generation of Electricity in Great Britain* HMSO London. Annually 1920 to 1948

[B 13] *Institute of Electrical Engineers Journal* IEE London

APPENDICES

1. List of Papers Produced by the Economics and Forecasting Branch
   (Electricity Council)   288
2. Annual Return to Department of Energy on Electricity Supply Industry:
   Distribution   291

LIST OF PAPERS PRODUCED BY THE ECONOMICS AND FORECASTING BRANCH (ELECTRICITY COUNCIL)

Report Number	Title	Prepared by	Date of Report
EF 1	Forecasting Sales of Storage Radiators	M. R. Marshall	October 1971
EF 2	Refrigerators—Differences between Manufacturers' Delivery and AGB Acquisition Data	M. R. Marshall	November 1971
EF 3	Effect on Certain UK Industries of EEC Entry	G. R. Martin	October 1971
EF 4	An Examination of the Relationship between Connection Charges and Connected Load in New Housing	C. H. Bayly	June 1972
EF 5	An Analysis of Cooker Sales over the Period 1970/1–1972/1	T. A. Boley	June 1972
EF 6	Area Board of Domestic Storage Radiators—A Model Approach to Forecasting and Setting Advertising Levels	M. R. Marshall	October 1972
EF 7	Recent Trends in the Domestic Cooker Market	M. R. Marshall	November 1972
EF 8	Forecasts of Electricity Sales and Demand in AD 2000	T. A. Boley	March 1973
EF 9	An Analysis of Council's Adopted Load Estimates for the Period 1973/74–1980/81	T. A. Boley	March 1973
EF 10	Long Term Estimates of Appliances Sales through Area Board Shops	T. A. Boley	April 1973
EF 11	UK Economic Prospects 1972–1980	T. A. Boley	July 1973
EF 12	Housing Forecast for 1973/74–1979/80	R. P. Wilkins	August 1973
EF 13	Allocation of National Publicity Expenditure on Appliances	G. R. Martin	August 1973
EF 14	UK Economic Prospects 1972–1980	T. A. Boley	September 1973
EF 15	Load Forecasting Procedures in the Electricity Supply Industry in England and Wales	T. A. Boley	October 1973
EF 16	Forecasting Sales and Demand in the Domestic Sector	M. R. Marshall	October 1973
EF 17	Forecasts of Electricity Sales and Demand in AD 2000	T. A. Boley	October 1973
EF 18	Forecasting Sales and Demand in the Industrial Sector	T. A. Boley	October 1973
EF 19	UK Economic Prospects 1973–1980	G. R. Martin	February 1974
EF 20	Forecast of Housing Completions 1973/74–1975/76	D. J. Hatch	February 1974
EF 21	Changes in Methods of Heating New Homes	Mrs F. P. Thomas	February 1974
EF 22	The Use of an Industrial Production Function as the Basis for the Derivation of the Industrial Electricity Demand Function	J. Ford	March 1974
EF 23	Introducing Probability into Forecasts	M. R. Marshall	May 1974
EF 24	The Relationship between Electricity Use and Economic Growth in the Domestic Sector and Possible Domestic Use in the 1980s	M. R. Marshall	April 1974
EF 25	Polynomially Distributed Lag Structures	M. J. Bridge	May 1974
EF 26	Forecasting the Market for Washing Machines—A Review of Current Methodology	M. J. Bridge	March 1974
EF 27	Electricity Council Short-Term Economic Forecasting Model	Miss M. J. Verrall	April 1974
EF 28	Forecasting Electricity Sales and Demand in the Industrial Sector	M. Chouthi	April 1974
EF 29	A Review of the Efficiencies of Fuel Usage	G. G. Petersen / Miss M. Verrall	July 1974
EF 31	A Method of Breaking Down Quarterly Forecasts into Review Periods	L. Fletcher	May 1974
EF 32	The Possible Effects of Changes in Structure and Technology on Electricity Use in Industry and Commerce	M. Chouthi	January 1974
EF 33	The Accuracy of Appliance Forecasts	D. Hatch	October 1974
EF 34	Weekly Demand Weather Correction	L. Fletcher	June 1974

APPENDICES

Report Number	Title	Prepared by	Date of Report
EF 35	Analysis of Council's 1973/74 Adopted Estimates for Sales and SMD up to 1979/80	R. P. Wilkins	August 1974
EF 36	UK Fuel Use Since 1950 and Prospect for the 1980's	M. R. Marshall	July 1974
EF 37	A Short Review of Private Generation in Industry	M. Bridge	August 1974
EF 38	The Assessment of Forecast Probability in the Domestic Sector (Computing Procedure)	A. Bates	August 1974
EF 39	A Description of the Application of Probability Theory to the Industrial Force	M. Chouthi A. Bates	September 1974
EF 40	A Forecast of Housebuilding Over the Period 1974/75–1982/83	Mrs F. Thomas	August 1974
EF 41	UK Economics Prospects 1974–1984	G. R. Martin Miss M. Verrall G. F. Carter	August 1974
EF 42	An Analysis of Commercial Electricity Consumption by Sector	D. Hatch	October 1974
EF 43	Computing at Electricity Council Headquarters (An Analysis of Expenditure	R. A. Thompson	August 1974
EF 44	Forecast of Major Domestic Appliance Sales 1974/75–1975/76	T. A. Boley	October 1974
EF 45	Working Party Report on Forecasting Maximum Demand (In Draft Form)	M. Chouthi	October 1974
EF 46	An Analysis of Domestic Electricity Consumption Since the mid 1950's	S. Junankar	May 1975
EF 47	An Attempt to Estimate the Price Elasticity of Domestic Consumption on Area Board Basis	R. P. Wilkins	October 1974
EF 48	An Econometric Analysis of Area Board Sales to Industry	J. Ford	January 1975
EF 49	The Summation of Area Board Maximum Demand Probability Forecasts (A Description of Computing Procedure)	A. Bates	December 1974
EF 50	Patterns of Acquisition of Consumer Durables: A Review of an Article by J. J. Habden and J. F. Pickering, Oxford Bulletin of Economics and Statistics (May 1974)	S. Junankar	December 1974
EF 52	Forecasts of Unit Sales and CEGB Maximum Demand in 1981/82	M. R. Marshall	November 1974
EF 53	Forecast of Major Domestic Appliance Sales 1974/75 to 1976/77 (AMC 1258)	D. J. Hatch	
EF 54	A Review of UK Economic Prospects to 1984/85 (Updating the August 1974 Economic Forecast Paper, EF 41)	G. R. Martin	
EF 55	Interpretation of Council's 1974/75 Load Estimates	M. R. Marshall	April 1975
EF 56	Forecast of Major Domestic Appliance Sales 1975/76–1976/77 (AMC 1303)	D. J. Hatch	May 1975
EF 57	Forecasting the Market for Refrigerators—A Review of Current Methodology	M. R. Marshall	July 1975
EF 59	UK Economic Prospects 1975–1985	G. R. Martin M. Bridge Miss Verrall	August 1975
EF 60	Forecast of Housing Completions for the Period 1975/76 to 1982/83	S. Junankar	August 1975
EF 61	Breakdown of Domestic Electricity Consumption—1954/55 to 1974/75	D. J. Hatch	August 1975
EF 62	Indices of Domestic Fuel Prices 1955–1975	I. Landgrebe A. J. Anscomb	February 1976
EF 63	An Examination of Methods of Forecasting Industrial Sales of Electricity	J. S. Foreman-Peck	1972

ELECTRICITY

Report Number	Title	Prepared by	Date of Report
EF 64	The Effect of Prices and Economic Growth on Consumers' Energy Requirements	T. A. Boley D. L. Walker	1974
EF 65	Forecast of Major Domestic Appliance Sales 1976/77–1977/78	D. J. Hatch	November 1975
EF 66	Forecasts of Unit Sales and CEGB Maximum Demand in 1982/83	M. R. Marshall	December 1975
EF 67	Load Forecasting Methods and Procedures in the Electricity Supply Industry in England and Wales	T. A. Boley	September 1974
EF 68	A Review of the Market for Direct Acting Domestic Space Heaters	S. Junankar	
EF 69	An Analysis of Domestic Electricity Sales in the South Western Electricity Board Area 1963/64–1974/75	D. J. Hatch Miss L. Rumbelow	February 1976
EF 70	An Analysis of Domestic Electricity Sales in the North Western Electricity Board Area 1963/64–1974/75	I. Landgrebe Miss L. Rumbelow	February 1976
EF 71	An Analysis of Domestic Electricity Sales in the Southern Electricity Board Area 1963/64–1974/75	A. Anscomb S. King	February 1976
EF 72	UK Economic Prospects 1975/85	G. R. Martin S. Junankar	February 1976
EF 73	Breakdown of Domestic Electricity Consumption 1932/33–1974/75 (Supplement to EF 61)	D. J. Hatch S. Scott	April 1976
EF 74	Forecast of Major Domestic Appliance Sales 1976/77–1977/78	D. J. Hatch	May 1976
EF 75	METVAL—A system of unit weather correction	M. Bridge A. N. Bates	May 1976

APPENDICES 291

We wish to acknowledge permission granted to us by the Controller of Her Majesty's Stationary Office for the reproduction of this form.

Department of Energy
EcS
Thames House South
Millbank
London SW1P 4QJ

E. Ret. 6

1975
ELECTRICITY SUPPLY INDUSTRY: DISTRIBUTION

Annual Return
for the year ended 31 December 1975
under Section 8(5) of the Electricity Act, 1957

The completed Return should be sent to the Department of Energy
EcS not later than 27 February 1976

Name of Area Board covered by this return _____

Address _____

SECTION 1 – ELECTRICITY PURCHASED AND DISPOSED OF	Million kilowatt hours	Cost £ Thousand
Electricity purchased from:-		
1. Central Electricity Generating Board		
2. Other Electricity Boards		
3. All other sources:-		
(a) purchased		
(b) from own generation		–
4. Total (headings 1 to 3(b))		–
Electricity disposed of:-		Net Selling Value £ Thousand
5. Sold to other Electricity Boards		
6. All other sales		
7. Used in own offices		–
8. Conversion, transmission and distribution losses and units unaccounted for		–
9. Total (headings 5 to 8)	*	–

*To agree with the entry against heading 4.

DECLARATION

I hereby declare that the information contained in this return is complete and correct to the best of my knowledge and belief.

Signature _____

Status _____ Date _____ 1976

ELECTRICITY

SECTION 2 - ANALYSIS OF UNITS SOLD TO CONSUMERS

(a) Heading 1. "Domestic premises" means all premises used wholly or mainly for private residential purposes.

(b) Combined premises. Enter against heading 2 sales to all domestic/commercial premises except where supplied solely at a commercial tariff. In the latter case particulars should be included under headings 6 to 11 as appropriate.

(c) Public lighting authorities. Include under heading 4 only lighting controlled by a street lighting or highway authority. Exclude kiosks and other highway supplies which should be recorded under heading 11.

(d) Heading 5. Figures relating to supplies to traction undertakings for purposes other than traction (eg railway workshops), should, if available, be entered under the appropriate headings.

(e) HM Forces. Enter against heading 10 sales to the Army, Royal Navy and Royal Air Force, but exclude sales to Royal Navy Dockyards, Royal Ordnance Factories, etc., which should be included against heading 14.

(f) In calculating the number of consumers, one consumer should normally be counted for each account on the Board's books, irrespective of the number of meters involved in the supply. However, where one account is rendered in respect of (i) more than one set of premises of similar type (eg multiple shops, railways) or (ii) premises of more than one type (eg farm and milk processing factories), each premises should be counted as a consumer.

(g) The net selling values should be the amounts charged or chargeable to consumers, whether by meter or on contract, less trade discounts, etc.

Class of consumer	Number of Consumers	Million kilowatt hours	Net selling value (£ 000)
1. Domestic premises (excluding farms, etc.)			
2. Combined domestic/commercial premises (see note (b))			
3. Farms (including farmhouses and farm buildings) and horticultural premises			
4. Public lighting authorities (see note (c))			
5. Traction Undertakings (see note (d))			
Shops, commercial premises, etc :-			
6. Shops (including garages and licensed premises other than hotels and Electricity Board Showrooms)			
7. Offices (including banks and wholesale warehouses)			
8. Public buildings, schools, places of entertainment etc (including hospitals, public baths and public wash-houses)			
9. Hotels			
10. HM Forces (see note (e))			
11. Other premises			
12. Total (headings 6 to 11)			
13. Waterworks, gasworks and drainage and sewage pumping stations			
14. Factories, works, workshops and other industrial premises for manufacturing and processing			
15. Total sales to consumers (headings 1, 2, 3, 4, 5, 12, 13 and 14)		*	

*This should agree with the figures given against heading 6 in Section 1.

SUBJECT INDEX TO ELECTRICITY

Accuracy of meters, 4.2.5
Administration, cost of 5.3.1
Agricultural consumption, 4.5.1; 4.5.2; 4.5.3; 4.5.4; 4.5.5
Alderney, 4.5.1.1; 4.6.1.1
Alternating current, three-phase 3.2.1
Appliance shops, 6.2.1; 6.2.4
Appliances, hire purchase of 6.2.1
Appliances, sales of 4.7.4; 5.3.1
Area board balance sheets, 5.4.1
Area board expenditure, 5.3.1
Area board income, 5.3.1
Area consumption, 4.5.1.1; 4.6.1.1
Area electricity boards, 3.1; 3.2
Assets, 5.4.1
Assets, research 5.4.1; 8.3.1
Association of Manufacturers of Domestic Electrical Appliances, 6.2.4
Audits of Great Britain, 6.2.4
Average consumptions, 4.5.1

Balance of payments *see* Energy Review
Balance sheet, CEGB 5.4.1
Balance sheets, Area Board 5.4.1
Belfast Corporation, 3.5
Billed units, 4.2.6
Bills outstanding, 5.4.1
Board of Trade unit, 4.2.2
British Electrical Appliance Manufacturers' Association, 6.2.4
British Electricity Authority, 3.1
British Nuclear Fuels Ltd, 4.5.2
Bulk transmission of power, 3.2.1; 4.3.1.2

Cable, submarine 4.3.3.2
Cable, underground 4.3.1.2; 4.3.2.2; 4.3.3.2; 4.3.5.2
Cables, cost of lines and 4.3.2.1
Calorific value, 4.3.1.1
Calorific value *see* Energy Review
Capability, declared net 4.3.1.1
Capability, gross 4.3.1.1
Capacity charges, 4.7.1
Capacity, installed 4.3.1.1; 4.3.2.1; 4.3.3.1; 4.3.5.1
Capacity, maximum output 4.3.1.1; 4.3.2.1; 4.3.6
Capacity, transformer 4.3.1.2; 4.3.2.2; 4.3.3.2; 4.3.5.2
Capital, 5.4; 5.5
CEGB balance sheet, 5.4.1

CEGB bulk supply tariff, 4.7.1
CEGB expenditure, 5.3.1; 5.4.1
CEGB income, 5.3.1
Census of production, 2
Central Electricity Authority, 3.1
Central Electricity Board, 2; 3.2.1
Central Electricity Generating Board, 3.2
Central heating systems, 6.2.4
Channel Islands, 4.5.1.1; 4.6.1.1
Charges, capacity 4.7.1
Charges, running 4.7.1
Charges, service 4.7.1
Chemical industry consumption, 4.5.5
Circuit kilometre, 4.3.1.2; 4.6.2.2; 4.6.3.2; 4.6.5.2
Classification of customers, 4.5.1; 4.5.2; 4.5.4; 4.6
Clothing industry consumption, textile and 4.5.5
Coal and coke, price of domestic 4.7.4
Coal consumed, 4.3.1.1; 4.3.2.1; 4.5.1; 4.5.5
Coal equivalent, 4.3.1.1; 4.5.1; 4.5.5
Coal equivalent *see* Energy Review
Coal, sources of 4.3.1.1
Coefficient *see* Energy Review, Energy
Colliery consumption, 4.5.1; 4.5.5
Combined domestic commercial sales, 4.5.1; 4.5.5
Commercial sales, 4.5.1; 4.5.2; 4.5.3
Commercial sales, combined domestic 4.5.1; 4.5.5
Commissioners, Electricity 2
Comparability of fuels *see* Energy Review
Comparative cost of generation, 4.1
Comparison with other fuels, 4.5.5; 5.3.4
Compensation, Government 5.3.1; 5.5.5
Confederation of British Industry *see* Energy Review
Construction industry consumption, 4.5.5
Consumed, electricity 4.5
Consumers' expenditure on coal and coke, 4.7.4
Consumers' expenditure on electricity, 4.7.4
Consumers' expenditure on fuel and light, 4.7.4
Consumers' expenditure on gas, 4.7.4
Consumers' expenditure on oil, 4.7.4
Contracting work, 4.7.4; 5.3.1; 6
Conversion factors *see* Energy Review
Cookers, 6.2.1; 6.2.2; 6.2.3; 6.2.4
Cost of administration, 5.3.1
Cost of distribution 5.3.1; 5.3.2; 5.3.3
Cost of fuel, 5.3.1; 5.3.4
Cost of generation, 5.3.1; 5.3.2; 5.3.3
Cost of generation, comparative 4.1

294 ELECTRICITY

Cost of lines and cables, 4.3.2.1
Cost of rates, 5.3.1
Cost of repairs and maintenance, 5.3.1
Cost of research, 5.3.1; 8.3.1
Cost of safety, 5.3.1
Cost of salaries and superannuation, 5.3.1
Cost of training, 5.3.1
Cost of transmission, 5.3.1; 5.3.2; 5.3.3
Cost of welfare, 5.3.1
Cost, works 4.3.1.1; 4.3.6
Crisis see Energy Review, Oil
Current, direct 3.2.1
Current, three-phase alternating 3.2.1
Customer numbers, 4.6
Customers, classification of 4.5.1; 4.5.2; 4.5.4; 4.6

Declared net capability, 4.3.1.1
Demand, maximum 4.2.1; 4.2.2; 4.3.5.1; 4.4
Demand measurements, 4.4.1.1; 4.4.1.2
Demand, potential 4.4.1.1; 4.4.6
Demand, simultaneous maximum 2; 4.4; 4.4.1.1; 4.4.1.2
Department of Energy see Energy Review
Depreciation, 5.3.1; 5.3.2; 5.4.1
Development for fuel and power see Energy Review, Research and
Direct consumers, 3.2; 4.4.1.1; 4.7.1
Direct current, 3.2.1
Distribution, cost of 5.3.1; 5.3.2; 5.3.3
Distribution plant, 4.3.1.2; 4.3.2.2; 4.3.3.2; 4.3.5.2
Distribution plant, units used in generation and 4.2.6; 4.3.1.1; 4.3.3.1; 4.3.5.1; 4.5; 4.5.1; 4.5.4
District consumption, 4.5.1.1; 4.6.1.1
Domestic commercial sales, combined 4.5.1; 4.5.5
Domestic sales, 4.5.1; 4.5.2; 4.5.3; 4.5.4; 4.5.5
Drainage and pumping station consumption, 4.5.5
Drink industry consumption, food and 4.5.5

Earnings, 7.1; 7.2
Efficiency, operational 4.3.1.1; 4.3.5.1
Efficiency, thermal 2; 4.3.1.1; 4.3.2.1; 4.3.6; 4.4.6
Eire, electricity supplied to 4.5.4
Eire, purchases from 4.5.4
Electrical shops, 6.2.4
Electricity Act 1947, 2; 3.1
Electricity Act 1957, 3.2
Electricity Commissioners, 2
Electricity consumed, 4.5
Electricity Council, 3.2
Electricity Council Research Centre, 8.1
Electricity produced, 4.3.1.1; 4.3.2.1; 4.3.3.1; 4.3.5.1; 4.5
Electricity Reorganisation (Scotland) Act 1954, 3.1
Electricity supplied, 4.3.1.1; 4.3.2.1; 4.3.3.1; 4.3.5.1; 4.3.6; 4.5
Electricity supplied to Eire, 4.5.4
Electricity supplied to France, 4.4.1.1; 4.5.1; 4.5.2
Electricity supplied to SSEB, 4.4.1.1; 4.5.1; 4.5.2
Electricity Supply (Northern Ireland) Order 1972, 3.5

Electricity Supply Act 1919, 2
Electricity Supply Act 1926, 2; 3.2.1
Employee classifications, 7.1; 7.2
Employees, generation 4.3.1.1
Employees in coal industry, 7.4
Employees in gas industry, 7.4
Employees in oil industry, 7.4
Employment agreements, 7
Energy balances see Energy Review
Energy coefficient see Energy Review
Energy model group see Energy Review
Energy modelling see Energy Review
Energy papers see Energy Review
Energy sector see Energy Review
Engineering industry consumption, 4.5.5
Equipment, manufacture of 1
Estimate of unbilled units, 4.2.6; 5.4.1
European Economic Community, 4.5.8
European electricity production, 4.5.8
European energy data see Energy Review
Expenditure, Area Board 5.3.1
Expenditure, CEGB 5.3.1; 5.4.1
Expenditure on coal and coke, consumers' 4.7.4
Expenditure on electricity, consumers' 4.7.4
Expenditure on fuel and energy, see Energy Review
Expenditure on fuel and light, consumers' 4.7.4
Expenditure on gas, consumers' 4.7.4
Expenditure on oil, consumers' 4.7.4
Expenditure on research, 8.3

Farm sales, 4.5.1; 4.5.2; 4.5.3; 4.5.4
Financial objectives, 5.5.1
Food and drink industry consumption, 4.5.5
Forecasting, 8.1
Forecasts see Energy Review
France, electricity supplied to 4.4.1.1; 4.5.1; 4.5.2
France, purchases from 4.5.1; 4.5.2
Freezers, 6.2.3; 6.2.4
Frequency, 2
Fuel consumed, 2; 4.3.1.1; 4.3.2.1; 4.5.1; 4.5.5
Fuel conversion industry consumption, 4.5.5
Fuel, cost of 5.3.1; 5.3.4

Gas heaters, 6.2.4
Gas industry, employees in 7.4
Gas, price of domestic 4.7.4
Gas works consumption, 4.5.1; 4.5.5
Generating plant, 4.3.1.1; 4.3.2.1; 4.3.3.1; 4.3.5.1; 4.3.6
Generating stations—siting of, 3.2.1
Generation and distribution plant, units used in 4.2.6; 4.3.1.1; 4.3.3.1; 4.3.5.1; 4.5; 4.5.1; 4.5.4
Generation by South Western Board, 3.2; 4.4.1.2; 4.5.1; 5.4.1
Generation, cost of 5.3.1; 5.3.2; 5.3.3
Generation employees, 4.3.1.1
Generation stations, Magnox nuclear 4.1
Government compensation, 5.3.1; 5.5.5
Government fuel policy see Energy Review
Government intervention, 5.2.1
Government intervention see Energy Review

SUBJECT INDEX

Grid, 2; 3.1; 3.2; 3.2.1
Gross capability, 4.3.1.1
Gross domestic product *see* Energy Review
Gross head of water, 4.3.3.1
Gross output, 5.3.4
Guernsey, 4.5.1.1; 4.6.1.1

Heat supplied, 4.5.5
Heat supplied *see* Energy Review
Hire purchase business of area boards, 5.4.1
Hire purchase of appliances, 6.2.1
Historical data, 2
HM Forces, consumption, 4.5.5
Hotel consumption, 4.5.5
Hours worked, 7.1
Hydro-Electric Board, North of Scotland 3.1; 3.3
Hydro-Electric Development (Scotland) Act 1943, 3.1
Hydro-electric power *see* Energy Review

Illumination effect, 4.5.6
Impedance, 4.2.4
Income, Area Board 5.3.1
Income, CEGB 5.3.1
Indices, price 4.7.5
Indices, retail price 4.7.4
Industrial customer categories, 4.5.1; 4.5.2; 4.5.5
Industrial fuel, price of 4.7.4
Industrial producers, purchases from 4.5.5
Industrial sales, 4.5.1; 4.5.2; 4.5.3; 4.5.5
Inflation effect, 5.3.1
Input/output tables *see* Energy Review
Installed capacity, 4.3.1.1; 4.3.2.1; 4.3.3.1; 4.3.5.1
Invergordon smelter, 4.5.3
Investment in energy *see* Energy Review
Iron and steel industry consumption, 4.5.5
Isle of Man, 4.5.1.1; 4.6.1.1

Jersey, 4.5.1.1; 4.6.1.1
Joule, 4.2.2

Kilovolt-amperes, 4.2.1
Kilowatt-hour, 4.2.2
Kilowatts, 4.2.1

Labour productivity, 4.3.1.1
Liabilities, 5.4.1
Lighting sales, public 4.5.1; 4.5.2; 4.5.3; 4.5.4
Lines and cables, cost of 4.3.2.1
Lines, overhead 4.3.1.2; 4.3.2.2; 4.3.3.2; 4.3.5.2
Load curves, 4.4.1.1
Load factor, 2; 4.2.3; 4.3.2.1; 4.3.5.1; 4.3.6; 4.4.4.1; 4.4.6
Load factor, system 4.2.3
Load factor, utilisation 4.2.3; 4.3.1.1
Load, maximum 2
Londonderry Development Commission, 3.5
Loss, profit and 5.3.1
Losses in transmission, 4.5.1; 4.5.2; 4.5.3; 4.5.4
Losses, thermal 4.2.6
Lost energy, 4.2.6

Magnox nuclear generation stations, 4.1
Mains, 4.3.1.2
Manufacture of equipment, 1
Marginal costing, 5.2.1
Market research, 6.2.4
Marketing, 8.1
Maximum demand, 4.2.1; 4.2.2; 4.3.5.1; 4.4
Maximum demand, simultaneous 2; 4.4; 4.4.1.1; 4.4.1.2
Maximum load, 2
Maximum output capacity, 4.3.1.1; 4.3.2.1; 4.3.6
Meter reading, periodicity of 4.2.6
Meter rents, 4.7.4
Meters, 4.2.5
Meters, white 4.5.1
Mining and quarrying consumption, 4.5.5
Ministry of Fuel and Power, 2
Modelling *see* Energy Review, Energy

National energy research and development *see* Energy Review
Nationalisation, 3.1
Net capability, declared 4.3.1.1
Net output for all fuels, 5.3.4
North of Scotland Hydro-Electric Board, 3.1; 3.3
Northern Ireland Electricity Service, 3.5
Northern Ireland Joint Electricity Authority, 3.5
Nuclear generation stations, Magnox 4.1
Nuclear power, 4.1

OECD *see* Energy Review
Off-peak rates, 4.5.1; 4.5.2
Officers' consumption, 4.5.5
Oil consumed, 4.3.1.1; 4.3.2.1; 4.5.1; 4.5.5
Oil crisis *see* Energy Review
Oil equivalent, 4.5.5
Oil equivalent *see* Energy Review
Oil industry, employees in 7.4
Oil, price of domestic 4.7.4
Operational efficiency, 4.3.1.1; 4.3.5.1
Output capacity, maximum 4.3.1.1; 4.3.2.1; 4.3.6
Output for all fuels, net 5.3.4
Output, gross 5.3.4
Overhead lines, 4.3.1.2; 4.3.2.2; 4.3.3.2; 4.3.5.2

Paper and printing industry consumption, 4.5.5
Periodicity of meter reading, 4.2.6
Petroleum industry *see* Energy Review
Potential demand, 4.4.1.1; 4.4.6
Power, 4.2.1; 4.4
Power Engineering Research Steering Committee, 8.1
Pressure, 4.2.4
Price indices, 4.7.5
Price of domestic coal and coke, 4.7.4
Price of domestic gas, 4.7.4
Price of domestic oil, 4.7.4
Price of industrial fuel, 4.7.4
Prices, 4.7
Primary fuels *see* Energy Review
Primary voltages, 4.3.1.2

296 ELECTRICITY

Printing industry consumption, paper and 4.5.5
Private generation, 4.5.5; 4.5.7; 4.5.8
Productivity, labour 4.3.1.1
Profit and loss, 5.3.1
Public building consumption, 4.5.5
Public lighting sales, 4.5.1; 4.5.2; 4.5.3; 4.5.4
Public services' consumption, 4.5.5
Pumping station consumption, drainage and 4.5.5
Purchase Tax, 6.2.1
Purchases from Eire, 4.5.4
Purchases from France, 4.5.1; 4.5.2
Purchases from industrial producers, 4.5.5
Purchases from SSEB, 4.5.1; 4.5.2
Purchases of electricity from outside sources, 3.2; 4.4.1.2; 4.5.1; 4.5.5

Quantity, 4.2.2
Quarrying consumption, mining and 4.5.5

Radio and television rental, 6.2.4
Radio shops, 6.2.4
Railway consumption, 3.2; 4.4.1.1; 4.5.5; 4.7.1
Rainfall, 4.3.3.1
Rates, cost of 5.3.1
Refrigerators, 6.2.1; 6.2.2; 6.2.3; 6.2.4
Repairs and maintenance, cost of 5.3.1
Research, 8
Research and development for fuel and power see Energy Review
Research assets, 5.4.1; 8.3.1
Research, cost of 5.3.1; 8.3.1
Research, expenditure on 8.3
Retail price indices, 4.7.4
Revenue, 4.7; 5.3
Road transport consumption, 4.5.5
Route kilometre, 4.3.1.2; 4.3.2.2; 4.3.5.2
Running charges, 4.7.1

Safety, cost of 5.3.1
Salaries, 7.1; 7.2
Salaries and superannuation, cost of 5.3.1
Sales, 4.5
Sales of appliances, 4.7.4; 5.3.1
Sales of scrap, 4.7.4
Sales of steam, 4.7.4
Scotland Electricity Board, South of 3.1; 3.3
Scotland Hydro-Electric Board, North of 3.1; 3.3
Scrap, sales of 4.7.4
Secondary fuels see Energy Review
Secondary voltages, 4.3.1.2
Service charges, 4.7.1
Shops' consumption, 4.5.5
Showrooms, 6.2.4
SIC category sales, 4.5.1; 4.5.5
Simultaneous maximum demand, 2; 4.4; 4.4.1.1; 4.4.1.2
Sold units, 4.2.6
Sources of coal, 4.3.1.1
South of Scotland Electricity Board, 3.1; 3.3

South Western Board, generation by 3.2; 4.4.1.2; 4.5.1; 5.4.1
Spin dryers, 6.2.3
SSEB, purchases from 4.5.1; 4.5.2
Standby plant in industry, 4.3.7
Steam, sales of 4.7.4
Steel industry consumption, iron and 4.5.5
Storage radiators, 6.2.1; 6.2.2; 6.2.3; 6.2.4
Submarine cable, 4.3.3.2
Substitutability of fuels see Energy Review
Super-Grid, 3.2; 3.2.1
Superannuation, cost of salaries and 5.3.1
System load factor, 4.2.3

Tariff, CEGB bulk supply 4.7.1
Tariffs, 4.5.1; 4.7.5; 5.2.1
Television rental, radio and 6.2.4
Temperature effect, 4.5.6
Textile and clothing industry consumption, 4.5.5
Thermal content see Energy Review
Thermal efficiency, 2; 4.3.1.1; 4.3.2.1; 4.3.6; 4.4.6
Thermal losses, 4.2.6
Three-phase alternating current, 3.2.1
Tobacco industry consumption, 4.5.5
Traction sales, 4.5.1; 4.5.2
Training, cost of 5.3.1
Transformer capacity, 4.3.1.2; 4.3.2.2; 4.3.3.2; 4.3.5.2
Transformers, 4.3.1.2
Transmission, cost of 5.3.1; 5.3.2; 5.3.3
Transmission, losses in 4.5.1; 4.5.2; 4.5.3; 4.5.4
Transmission of power, bulk 3.2.1; 4.3.1.2
Transmission plant, 4.3.1.2; 4.3.2.2; 4.3.3.2; 4.3.5.2
Transmission voltages, 3.2.1; 4.3.1.2
Tumbler dryers, 6.2.3

Unbilled units, 4.2.6
Underground cable, 4.3.1.2; 4.3.2.2; 4.3.3.2; 4.3.5.2.
Unit, 4.2.2
United Kingdom Atomic Energy Authority, 4.5.3
Units, billed 4.2.6
Units of measurement, 4.2
Units of measurement see Energy Review
Units, sold 4.2.6
Units, unbilled 4.2.6
Units used in generation and distribution plant, 4.2.6; 4.3.1.1; 4.3.3.1; 4.3.5.1; 4.5; 4.5.1; 4.5.4
Useful energy see Energy Review
Utilisation load factor, 4.2.3; 4.3.1.1

Vacuum cleaners, 6.2.3
Value Added Tax, 6.2.1
Volt, 4.2.4
Voltages, transmission 3.2.1; 4.3.1.2

Wages, 7.1; 7.2
Washing machines, 6.2.1; 6.2.2; 6.2.3; 6.2.4
Water availability in Scotland, 4.3.3.1
Water, gross head of 4.3.3.1
Water heaters, 6.2.1; 6.2.2; 6.2.3; 6.2.4

SUBJECT INDEX

Water in store, 4.3.3.1
Water works' consumption, 4.5.1; 4.5.5
Weather effect, 4.5.6
Welfare, cost of 5.3.1

White meters, 4.5.1
White Paper 1961, 5.2.1
Wind cooling effect, 4.5.6
Works cost, 4.3.1.1; 4.3.6